Spelling
Workout

Phillip K. Trocki

Modern Curriculum Press
is an imprint of

SAVVAS
LEARNING COMPANY

COVER DESIGN: Pronk & Associates

ILLUSTRATIONS: Eric Larsen. 187: Jim Steck.

PHOTOGRAPHS: Cover: *l.* Maxim Petrichuk/Fotolia, *r.* Artbase Inc.
5: © BlooD2oo1/Fotolia.com. 8: © Jaak/Fotolia.com. 9: © Tomislav/Fotolia.com. 12: © Vladimir Popovic/Fotolia.com. 13: © Ryan Dunfee/Fotolia.com. 15: © hotshotsworldwide/Fotolia.com. 16: © Getty Images. 17: © Susan Stevenson/Fotolia.com. 20: © mkm3/Fotolia.com. 21: © gwimages/Fotolia.com. 24: © Comstock. 29: © Dmitry Knorre/Fotolia.com. 32: © Tyler Boyes/Fotolia.com. 33: NASA Ames Research Center. 36: © Madera/Fotolia.com. 37: © AbsentAnna/Fotolia.com. 40: © Maxim Petrichuk/Fotolia.com. 41: © Dreef/Fotolia.com. 44: © Monkey Business/Fotolia.com. 45: © Medioimages/PhotoDisc, Inc. 48: © ussatlantis/Fotolia.com. 53: © siloto/Fotolia.com. 56: © Dmytro Tkachuk/Fotolia.com. 57: © Anyka/Fotolia.com. 60: © Elenathewise/Fotolia.com. 61: © Wimbledon/Fotolia.com. 64: © Kurt De Bruyn/Fotolia.com. 65: Lindsley, H. B./Library of Congress Prints and Photographs Division Washington, D.C./LC-USZ62-7816. 68: © PhotoDisc, Inc. 69: © Ryan McVay/PhotoDisc, Inc. 72: Library of Congress Prints and Photographs Division. 77: © willtu/Fotolia.com. 80: © Arnie/Fotolia.com. 81: © Getty Images/Photos.com. 85: © blindfire/Fotolia.com. 88: © Thomas Perkins/Fotolia.com. 89: © Kenton/Fotolia.com. 92: © fuxart/Fotolia.com. 93: *t.* © Rob/Fotolia.com. *b.* © Andy Crawford/Dorling Kindersley. 96: © Rob/Fotolia.com. 101: © Darcy Finley/Fotolia.com. 104: © Thinkstock. 105: © Dorling Kindersley Ltd., Courtesy of St. Bride Printing. 108: © Igor Dutina/Fotolia.com. 112: © Hunta/Fotolia.com. 113: © Maria Teijeiro/Digital Vision. 117: © Thinkstock. 120: © Comstock. 125: Library Of Congress Prints and Photographs Division. 128: *t.* © Stockbyte. *b.* © klikk/Fotolia.com. 129: © Getty Images. 132: © Holger Mette/Fotolia.com. 133: © Getty Images. 136: © Jacek Chabraszewski/Fotolia.com. 137: © Getty Images/Hemera Technologies. 140: © JaM/Fotolia.com. 141: © Sean Prior/Fotolia.com.

Acknowledgments

ZB Font Method Copyright © 1996 Zaner-Bloser.

Some content in this product is based upon WEBSTER'S NEW WORLD DICTIONARY, 4/E. Copyright ©2013 by Houghton Mifflin Harcourt Publishing Company. Reprinted by permission of Houghton Mifflin Harcourt Publishing Company. All rights reserved.

The Tournament of Roses is a registered trademark of Pasadena Tournament of Roses Association, Inc. Use of this trademark implies no relationship, sponsorship, endorsement, sale, or promotion on the part of Modern Curriculum Press.

ISBN-13: 978-0-7652-2485-9
ISBN-10: 0-7652-2485-2
37 2024

Table of Contents

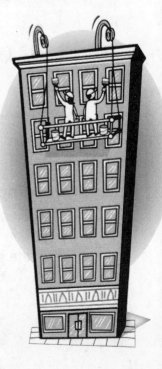

Learning to Spell a Word

1. Say the word.
   Look at the word and say the letters.

2. Print the word with your finger.

3. Close your eyes and think of the word.

4. Cover the word and print it on paper.

5. Check your spelling.

Keeping a Spelling Notebook

A spelling notebook will help you when you write.
Write the words you're having trouble with on a
separate sheet of paper or in the **Spelling Notebook**
at the back of the book.

Spelling Words in Action

What does it take to make a superstar?

Shaping a Superstar

You are the producer of a space adventure movie. Your script calls for a **unique** character. You must find an actor who will **qualify** for the part. Masks, make-up, and costumes can turn the actor into a truly **remarkable** character from space. Applying the make-up for an alien character is a highly **technical** job that can take hours. If you're working on a tight **schedule**, you may not have time. What do you do? You can build your own character!

First, artists make a great **quantity** of sketches. Then the sketches are brought to life in one of two ways. The design can be part of a computer program.

Then, the character exists only on the computer and on the film. Or, the character can be built as a model. This **technique** uses materials such as foam rubber, fiberglass, plastic, and **chrome**. Complex systems control the model's actions. Three or four people might be **required** to operate the controls.

Knowledge and technology have joined hands to shape superstars that can do almost anything but sign autographs!

Say each boldfaced word in the selection. Listen for the sounds of k̲, k̲w̲, and n̲. What do you notice about the spellings for each sound?

5

TIP

The **k** sound can be spelled several different ways:
k, as in keyboard;
ck, as in locksmith;
que, as in technique;
ch, as in chorus.
The **kw** sound is spelled **qu**, as in quantity and banquet. The **n** sound is sometimes spelled **kn**, as in knowledge and knelt.

Spelling Practice

LIST WORDS

1. echoes
2. chorus
3. chemistry
4. qualify
5. acknowledge
6. remarkable
7. locksmith
8. quantity
9. technical
10. banquet
11. knowledge
12. required
13. keyboard
14. chrome
15. antique
16. knelt
17. headache
18. unique
19. schedule
20. technique

Words with the Sound of k, kw, and n

Write the **list words** that contain the sound given. You will write two words twice.

k spells the sound of **k**, as in king

1. _____   2. _____

ch spells the sound of **k**, as in chord

3. _____   4. _____
5. _____   6. _____
7. _____   8. _____
9. _____   10. _____

ck spells the sound of **k**, as in deck

11. _____   12. _____

que spells the sound of **k**, as in boutique

13. _____   14. _____
15. _____

kn spells the sound of **n**, as in knife

16. _____   17. _____
18. _____

qu spells the sound of **kw**, as in quite

19. _____   20. _____
21. _____   22. _____

Missing Words

Write the **list word** that completes each sentence.

1. The cat tiptoed along the _____, making a little song.

2. We had to call a _____ after Sam lost the key.

3. I received this trophy at the awards _____ last night.

4. Are you singing in the school _____ this year?

5. Dad polished the _____ on his car until it was shiny.

6. Karen _____ to play with the little puppy.

7. The loud music gave me a _____.

8. By studying computer science, he gained _____ knowledge.

9. Before she became a scientist, she received her degree in _____.

10. Mom has a busy _____ at her new job.

Mixed-Up Words

Parts of these **list words** have become mixed up: <u>qualify</u>, <u>antique</u>, <u>required</u>, <u>unique</u>, <u>acknowledge</u>, <u>remarkable</u>, <u>quantity</u>, <u>technique</u>, <u>echoes</u>, <u>knowledge</u>. Put the word parts back where they belong and write the two correct words on the lines.

1. acknowlique   technedge   _____   _____

2. remarkoes   echable   _____   _____

3. qualired   requify   _____   _____

4. antity   quantique   _____   _____

5. unedge   knowlique   _____   _____

Spelling and Writing

Proofreading

This dialogue from the movie "My Friend Is a Robot" has ten mistakes. Use the proofreading marks to correct them. Then, write the misspelled **list words** correctly on the lines.

ROBOT (in a panicky voice): I'm having tecnicle difficulties. I'm losing all of my knowlege. Now I know what a headake feels like! you must skeduel time to make the requyred repairs

IRMA (rolling her eyes in amusement): Don't panic! All you need is to have your batteries recharged

ROBOT (more frantic): Hurry up and recharge them! I'm quickly becoming a useless pile of krome

Proofreading Marks

 spelling mistake

 capital letter

⊙ add period

1. _____ 2. _____ 3. _____

4. _____ 5. _____ 6. _____

Writing a Dialogue

Put yourself into a movie about a space adventure with a <u>remarkable</u> robot. Write the dialogue for the scene that takes place when you first meet this <u>unique</u> character. If you like, add descriptions that go with the actions. Use any **list words** that you can. Remember to proofread your dialogue and fix any mistakes.

_____

_____

_____

_____

_____

knothole

mechanic

plaque

quiz

kindling

Lesson 2

Spelling Words in Action

What can you do with a diamond?

Hard Rock

Have you ever heard the expression "Diamonds are forever"? Diamonds can last as long as they take to make. They are made of **carbon**. That's the same substance as the graphite in your pencil. Diamonds become **processed** over millions of years, far below the earth's surface. For a miner, finding a **genuine** diamond is cause for **celebration**.

A diamond is the hardest substance found on the earth. To turn a rough diamond into a gem, flat surfaces called *facets* are carefully carved out of the stone. To increase the sparkle, each facet is ground at a certain **angle**.

Ancient people thought this type of **crystal** had **magical** powers. They were thought to bring luck, power, good health, and long life. It has long been a custom for men to give diamond rings to women as **pledges** of their love when they become **engaged** to be married. They also have less romantic uses. The space program used diamonds in a window of a spacecraft that went to Venus. This window had a big **advantage**. The diamond surface was not destroyed by the heat and atmospheric pressure of the far-off planet.

Look back at the boldfaced words in the selection. What do you notice about the sounds made with the letters <u>c</u> and <u>g</u>?

9

TIP

The letter **g** makes a hard sound, as in <u>angle</u>, and a soft sound, as in <u>magical</u>. The letters **dge** often spell the soft **g** sound, as in <u>cartridge</u>. The letter **c** makes a hard sound, as in <u>carbon</u>, and a soft sound, as in <u>recipe</u>. Be careful when spelling words with **c** or **g**, because their sounds can easily be confused with **s** or **j**.

LIST WORDS

1. crystal
2. angle
3. engaged
4. advantage
5. pledges
6. carbon
7. processed
8. medicine
9. celebration
10. icicles
11. language
12. budget
13. guesses
14. refrigerator
15. conjugate
16. magical
17. intelligent
18. cartridge
19. genuine
20. recipe

Words with Hard and Soft <u>c</u> and <u>g</u> and <u>dge</u>

Write each **list word** under the correct heading. Some words are used more than once.

g, as in <u>giant</u> or <u>edge</u>   **c**, as in <u>card</u>

1. _____   16. _____
2. _____   17. _____
3. _____   18. _____
4. _____   19. _____
5. _____   20. _____
6. _____   21. _____
7. _____
8. _____
9. _____
10. _____

g, as in <u>gate</u>   **c**, as in <u>cinema</u>

11. _____   22. _____
12. _____   23. _____
13. _____   24. _____
14. _____   25. _____
15. _____   26. _____

Definitions

Write a **list word** to solve each definition clue.

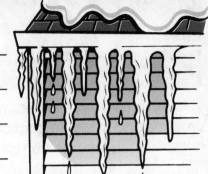

1. case for holding something   _____
2. directions for making food   _____
3. real or true   _____
4. figure formed by two lines   _____
5. helps make sick people well   _____
6. frozen spears of water   _____
7. supposes   _____
8. promises or agreements   _____
9. produced   _____
10. spending plan   _____
11. speech of a nation or group   _____
12. giving a feeling of enchantment   _____

Scrambled Words

What **list word** can be made from the letters in each of these phrases?
Write the word on the line.

1. at once jug   _____
2. salt cry   _____
3. nag edge   _____
4. van gad ate   _____
5. crab on   _____
6. rarer fog tire   _____
7. elect a robin   _____
8. get lint line   _____

advantage
carbon
celebration
conjugate
crystal
engaged
intelligent
refrigerator

Spelling and Writing

Proofreading

This advertisement has ten mistakes. Use the proofreading marks to correct them. Then, write the misspelled **list words** correctly on the lines.

Proofreading Marks

⬭ spelling mistake

≡ capital letter

˅ add apostrophe

Its time that you bought a jenuin diamond! visit the Sparkle Bright diamond store nearest you and take advantidge of our week-long sale selebrasson. We have prices that fit every budjit. Keep in mind that each Sparkle bright store pleges to give you the best. Remember our motto: Buy diamonds, youll be making an intellijant investment.

1. _____ 2. _____

3. _____ 4. _____

5. _____ 6. _____

Writing a Descriptive Paragraph

Think up a new use for diamonds. Write a paragraph that describes your idea. Try to use as many **list words** as you can. Remember to proofread your paragraph and fix any mistakes.

_____

_____

_____

_____

_____

_____

_____

BONUS WORDS

foliage

gallery

recently

capacity

fidget

Spelling Words in Action

How many flowers does it take to cover a Tournament of Roses Parade float?

Flower Power

Every year in Pasadena, California, a parade called The Tournament of Roses is held. It is one of the most **photographed** events in the world. The focus of this parade, held every January 1, is the **magnificent** floats, all made of flowers. Some of the floats are **laughable**. Others are beautiful, like a ship made of **fragrant** carnations and roses. All must have a **sufficient** number of flowers and other natural materials, such as leaves or fruit, to cover every inch of the float. It isn't easy to **afford** a float. The average float uses 100,000 flowers and costs around $250,000!

The **phrase** "The Tournament of Roses" was invented by the president of the first parade. It was held in 1890 to **emphasize** the beautiful weather in Pasadena. Horses and buggies were decorated with flowers. Today horses still march in the parade. So do lively bands with **saxophone** players, flutes, bass drums, and other instruments.

Some people camp out all night to get a spot along the parade route. Others **prefer** to join the hundreds of millions of viewers who watch the parade on TV!

Look back at the boldfaced words in the selection. How many different ways is the sound of f spelled?

TIP

The **f** sound can be spelled four different ways:
f, as in fifteen;
ff, as in coffee;
ph, as in photographed;
gh, as in laughable.

Spelling Practice

LIST WORDS

1. photographed
2. officer
3. triumphant
4. afford
5. toughen
6. fifteen
7. prefer
8. physician
9. fragrant
10. pamphlet
11. saxophone
12. effective
13. coffee
14. phrase
15. hyphenate
16. magnificent
17. sufficient
18. emphasize
19. hemisphere
20. laughable

Words with the Sound of f

Write each **list word** in the correct category to show how the **f** sound is spelled.

f as in final

1. _____
2. _____
3. _____
4. _____

ff as in sheriff

5. _____ 6. _____
7. _____ 8. _____
9. _____

ph as in photo

10. _____ 11. _____
12. _____ 13. _____
14. _____ 15. _____
16. _____ 17. _____
18. _____

gh as in enough

19. _____
20. _____

Complete the Paragraph

Write the **list word** that completes each blank in the paragraph.

Costa Rica, in Central America, is located in the Northern

_____. My parents saved money for a long time so

we could _____ our trip to Costa Rica. Much of the

_____ that people drink grows in this country. Its rair

forests, teeming with tropical trees, plants, and wildlife, were

absolutely _____! You can smell the _____ flowers as you walk

through the rain forests. Visitors from around the world have _____ the flora

and fauna found in rain forests in Costa Rica. If you don't bring _____ film, you

will not be able to capture all the great photos. Now my family can't _____

enough the importance of protecting the rain forests. We brought back a _____

with more information on how we can do our part. We think countries everywhere should

_____ their laws that help save the rain forests!

Move the Words

Each underlined **list word** in the sentences below must be moved to a different sentence to
make sense. Write the correct word in the blanks at the end of the sentence.

1. I have started taking <u>officer</u> lessons.   _____

2. If you don't feel well, you should see your <u>laughable</u>.   _____

3. Can you show me where to <u>effective</u> this two-syllable word?   _____

4. My favorite saying is the <u>prefer</u> "Never give up."   _____

5. My feeble attempt to play the clarinet was truly <u>saxophone</u>.   _____

6. <u>Physician</u>, where should I turn in this lost wallet?   _____

7. The winner made a <u>hyphenate</u> lap around the racecourse.   _____

8. I drink tomato juice, but I really <u>fifteen</u> orange juice.   _____

9. My big sister is <u>triumphant</u> years old.   _____

10. The new law has been very <u>phrase</u> in stopping speeding.   _____

Spelling and Writing

Proofreading

Mayor Green's speech, to be given at a parade, has ten mistakes. Use the proofreading marks to fix each mistake. Then, write the misspelled **list words** correctly on the lines.

Proofreading Marks

⬭ spelling mistake

≡ capital letter

∧ add something

good day to all of my fellow citizens! Have you ever seen such a magnificent parade I'm told that there are fiffteen more floats this year than at last year's parade. I can't enfasize enough how much this parade means to our town. That's why I'm surprised that my opponent thinks that we can't aforde a parade every year. what a lauphabel idea! I say that we can't afford not to hold a parade. our town needs to celebrate its triumfant history. Thank you.

1. _____   2. _____

3. _____   4. _____

5. _____   6. _____

Writing a News Story

Write a newspaper story about a parade. Were the floats <u>effective</u> or <u>laughable</u>? Describe the sights, smells, and sounds. Try to use as many **list words** as you can. Remember to proofread your story and fix any mistakes.

_____

_____

_____

_____

_____

_____

BONUS WORDS

affection

fender

phenomenon

roughen

orphanage

Spelling Words in Action

Would you enjoy being in a jazz band? Why or why not?

All That Jazz

Do you play one of the brass or percussion **instruments**? If you do, consider joining a jazz band! Most jazz bands include trumpets, saxophones, trombones, drums, and piano. Some jazz bands have a **position** for a guitar player. Others include flutes. The band might **resemble** a concert band. A jazz band, though, usually has a smaller number of instruments.

A jazz band's **purpose** is to play music in the jazz, swing, and rock styles. There is a great **treasury** of songs to play. Some are new and some are old. A jazz band can play a new jazzy **version** of an old classic, too.

Most school jazz bands are led by a music **instructor**. They play before a **casual** crowd in a **gymnasium** or for special events. Some even cut their own CDs. They practice before or after school. It takes dedication to make a 7:20 A.M. rehearsal once or twice a week, but members **usually** don't mind the early practice times. Whether they're practicing or performing, they have a good time!

Say the boldfaced words in the selection. Notice the sound that the letter s̲ makes in each word. How many different sounds for s̲ do you hear?

17

Spelling Practice

TIP

The letter **s** can stand for different sounds. For example, in the word purpose, the letter **s** spells the **s** sound. In the word resemble, the letter **s** spells the **z** sound. In the word usually, the letter **s** spells the **zh** sound.

LIST WORDS

1. purpose
2. composure
3. diseases
4. casual
5. seasonal
6. resemble
7. measuring
8. husband
9. position
10. visual
11. trousers
12. instruments
13. desirable
14. instructor
15. leisurely
16. deserving
17. gymnasium
18. version
19. treasury
20. usually

Words With the Sound of s, z, and zh

Write each **list word** under the sound that **s** stands for. One word will be written twice.

s spells the sound of s, as in secure

1. _____ 2. _____

3. _____ 4. _____

s spells the sound of z, as in music

5. _____ 6. _____

7. _____ 8. _____

9. _____ 10. _____

11. _____ 12. _____

13. _____

s spells the sound of zh, as in pleasure

14. _____ 15. _____

16. _____ 17. _____

18. _____ 19. _____

20. _____ 21. _____

Puzzle

Fill in the crossword puzzle by writing a **list word** to answer
each definition clue.

ACROSS

1. place or location
3. finding the length or width
4. not formal
7. pianos and drums
10. almost always
11. related to sight
12. at a certain time of year
13. pants

DOWN

1. goal or aim
2. room for athletics
5. without hurry
6. one who teaches
8. wife's spouse
9. copy, variant

Synonyms

Write a **list word** that means the same or almost the same as the word or phrase given.

1. reason _____
2. generally _____
3. worth wanting _____
4. teacher _____
5. once a season _____
6. unhurried _____
7. self-control _____
8. look like _____
9. weighing _____
10. place for treasures _____
11. illnesses _____
12. placement _____
13. worthy _____
14. married man _____
15. variation _____

Spelling and Writing

Proofreading

Proofreading Marks

⬭ spelling mistake

≡ capital letter

⌃ add something

This journal entry from a jazz band member has twelve mistakes. Use the proofreading marks to correct them. Then, write the misspelled **list words** correctly on the lines.

November 28

Jazz band was fun this morning. The entire trumpet section was there—that's Jordan Sam, Ari, Alex, and me. The music room, where we uzhally meet, is being painted, so we rehearsed in the gimnaseum. Our instruckter, Mr lesco, said we might enter the city's Jazz Festival next may. The perpos of the festival isto raise money for a new playground. only the most disurving bands get in, so we'd better practice our instrimints between now and May!

1. _____   2. _____   3. _____

4. _____   5. _____   6. _____

Writing a Speech

Write a brief speech praising the performance of your school band or orchestra. Explain why the members are deserving of praise. Try to use as many **list words** as you can. Remember to proofread your speech and fix any mistakes.

_____

_____

_____

_____

_____

_____

Bonus Words

releases

resolve

foreclosure

intrusion

diffuse

Spelling Words in Action

How have eyeglasses changed over the years?

Hocus Focus

No one is really sure who is responsible for the **invention** of eyeglasses. Using pieces of glass to make printed words look bigger goes back to ancient times. Written **information** about eyeglasses goes back to the year 1268 in England.

Eyeglasses were first put in frames made of leather. The wearer tied leather strips around his head to **insure** that the glasses stayed in place. Wearers did not **appreciate** having glasses so close to their eyes. The Chinese found a **partial** solution to **assure** comfort. They added weights to silk ribbon frames. Wearers draped the ribbons over their ears. This held the glasses comfortably—until the weights hit the wearer in the head!

The big breakthrough in frames came in London, England, in 1730. An optician attached the lenses to stiff side pieces. The glasses stayed on and there was less **facial** discomfort. Still, some people were **ashamed** to wear glasses in **social** situations. Then, new **machinery** produced lightweight, attractive frames and lenses. Now, glasses are a fashion statement!

Say the boldfaced words in the selection. How many ways do you find to spell the sound of sh?

TIP

The **sh** sound can be spelled in several ways:

sh, as in sh<u>oe</u>
su, as in in<u>su</u>re
ti, as in conven<u>ti</u>on and par<u>ti</u>al
ci, as in fa<u>ci</u>al
ch, as in ma<u>ch</u>inery

Spelling Practice

LIST WORDS

1. insure
2. information
3. exploration
4. ashamed
5. partial
6. nourish
7. social
8. brochure
9. invention
10. assure
11. facial
12. convention
13. official
14. machinery
15. parachute
16. negotiate
17. accomplish
18. potential
19. appreciate
20. quotient

Words with the sh Sound

Write each **list word** in the correct category to show how the sound of **sh** is spelled.

sh as in <u>sh</u>oe

1. _____
2. _____
3. _____

ch as in ma<u>ch</u>ine

4. _____
5. _____
6. _____

ci as in gla<u>ci</u>al

7. _____
8. _____
9. _____
10. _____

ti as in mo<u>ti</u>on

11. _____
12. _____
13. _____
14. _____
15. _____
16. _____
17. _____
18. _____

su as in <u>su</u>re

19. _____
20. _____

Comparing Words

Study the relationship between the first two underlined words. Then, write a **list word** that has the same relationship with the third underlined word.

1. <u>movie</u> is to <u>entertainment</u> as <u>newspaper</u> is to _____

2. <u>wrong</u> is to <u>incorrect</u> as <u>possible</u> is to _____

3. <u>dislike</u> is to <u>criticize</u> as <u>enjoy</u> is to _____

4. <u>find</u> is to <u>seek</u> as <u>discovery</u> is to _____

5. <u>happy</u> is to <u>cheerful</u> as <u>friendly</u> is to _____

6. <u>swimming</u> is to <u>life preserver</u> as <u>jumping</u> is to _____

7. <u>determine</u> is to <u>decide</u> as <u>bargain</u> is to _____

8. <u>water</u> is to <u>quench</u> as <u>food</u> is to _____

9. <u>whole</u> is to <u>half</u> as <u>completed</u> is to _____

10. <u>innocent</u> is to <u>guilty</u> as <u>proud</u> is to _____

Word Building

Add and subtract letters to form **list words**.

1. in + surely – ly = _____

2. broad – ad + chin – in + sure – s = _____

3. inventory – ory + lion – l = _____

4. has – h + surge – g = _____

5. fact – t + vial – v = _____

6. convene – e + action – ac = _____

7. of + fish – sh + special – spe = _____

8. stomach – sto + dine – d + ry = _____

9. accompany – any + list – t + h = _____

10. quota – a + patient – pat = _____

Spelling and Writing

Proofreading

This letter to Benjamin Franklin has ten mistakes. Use the proofreading marks to correct them. Then, write the misspelled **list words** correctly on the lines.

August 15, 1789

Dear benjamin,
*   I'm so grateful to you for inventing bifocal lenses.*
I apreshiate the the pair you sent to me. I can
ackomplis so much more work with your invenshon.
I'm ashshamd that I haven't written sooner, but I
have so many offishule duties. I ashure you that
George and I think of you often.
best, regards,

Martha Washington

1. _____   2. _____   3. _____

4. _____   5. _____   6. _____

Writing a Letter

You have a great idea for an invention. Write a letter to a friend naming and describing your invention and its benefits. Try to use as many **list words** as you can. Remember to proofread your letter and fix any mistakes.

_____

_____

_____

_____

_____

_____

BONUS WORDS

flourish

ensure

gracious

chagrin

regulation

Lessons 1–5 • Review

In lessons 1 through 5, you have learned how to spell words with different consonant sounds. Some sounds, like **k**, **f**, and **sh**, are spelled more than one way. The letters **g** and **c** have a hard and a soft sound. The letter **s** can stand for more than one sound.

Check Your Spelling Notebook

Look at the words in your spelling notebook. Which words for lessons 1 through 5 did you have the most trouble with? Write them here.

_____

_____

_____

Practice writing your troublesome words with a partner. Say the words and point out to your partner what part of the word is spelled differently than you expected.

Lesson 1

 Consonant sounds can be spelled in different ways. <u>Keyboard</u>, <u>acknowledge</u>, <u>echoes</u>, and <u>antique</u> all have the **k** sound. <u>Qualify</u> has the **kw** sound. <u>Knelt</u> has the **n** sound.

Write a **list word** that means the same or almost the same as the word given. Not all the words will be used.

List Words

chorus
schedule
echoes
keyboard
quantity
banquet
required
chrome
knowledge
antique
knelt
unique

1. piano _____
2. necessary _____
3. timetable _____
4. amount _____
5. singers _____
6. feast _____
7. old _____
8. unequaled _____
9. bowed _____
10. understanding _____

25

The letter **g** makes a hard sound, as in <u>guesses</u>, and a soft sound, as in <u>budget</u>. The letter **c** makes a hard sound, as in <u>magical</u>, and a soft sound, as in <u>celebration</u>.

List Words

crystal
engaged
processed
medicine
icicles
language
guesses
intelligent
budget
cartridge
genuine
recipe

Write a **list word** to complete each sentence. Not all the words will be used.

1. I like the way that _____ sounds when it is spoken.

2. Anna was _____ two years before she got married.

3. My doctor told me to take this _____.

4. The _____ requires two cups of flour.

5. So far, all your _____ have been wrong.

6. An _____ dog learns tricks easily.

7. Is that a _____ ruby or a fake?

8. Many fine drinking glasses are made from _____.

9. This _____ does not fit my tape player.

10. Every winter, long _____ form.

 The sound of **f** can be spelled with **f**, **ff**, **ph**, and **gh**, as in <u>prefer</u>, <u>afford</u>, <u>phrase</u>, and <u>toughen</u>.

List Words

officer
afford
toughen
magnificent
fifteen
prefer
physician
fragrant
hyphenate
pamphlet
phrase
hemisphere

Write the **list word** that belongs in each group. Not all the words will be used.

1. catalog, booklet, _____

2. five, ten, _____

3. sergeant, captain, _____

4. globe, planet, _____

5. word, sentence, _____

6. scented, perfumed, _____

7. save, spend, _____

8. like, favor, _____

9. strengthen, stiffen, _____

10. nurse, medic, _____

The letter **s** can spell the **s** sound, as in <u>instruments</u>; the **z** sound, as in <u>husband</u>; and the **zh** sound, as in <u>treasury</u>.

List Words

composure
diseases
visual
casual
seasonal
resemble
husband
instructor
desirable
leisurely
deserving
usually

Write a **list word** that is an **antonym** for the word given. Not all the words will be used.

1. differ _____

2. never _____

3. health _____

4. year-round _____

5. quick _____

6. unworthy _____

7. formal _____

8. wife _____

9. unwanted _____

10. nervousness _____

 The **sh** sound can be spelled with **sh**, as in <u>nourish</u>; **su**, as in <u>assure</u>; **ti**, as in <u>invention</u>; **ci**, as in <u>social</u>; and **ch**, as in <u>brochure</u>.

List Words

insure
ashamed
partial
nourish
quotient
brochure
invention
assure
social
facial
machinery
parachute

Write five **list words** that could be found listed between each set of dictionary guide words given. Write the words in alphabetical order. Not all the words will be used.

able/intact   interest/patio

1. _____   6. _____

2. _____   7. _____

3. _____   8. _____

4. _____   9. _____

5. _____   10. _____

Show What You Know

One word is misspelled in each set of **list words**. Fill in the circle next to the **list word** that is spelled incorrectly.

1. ○ remarkable   ○ genuine   ○ fragrant   ○ inventshon   ○ schedule

2. ○ deserving   ○ information   ○ echoes   ○ crystal   ○ efective

3. ○ facial   ○ pledges   ○ refridgerator   ○ measuring   ○ social

4. ○ triumfant   ○ qualify   ○ instructor   ○ fifteen   ○ laughable

5. ○ bankuet   ○ parachute   ○ angle   ○ carbon   ○ purpose

6. ○ usually   ○ appreciate   ○ hyphenate   ○ keyboard   ○ negochiate

7. ○ intellijint   ○ officer   ○ icicles   ○ medicine   ○ knelt

8. ○ krome   ○ quantity   ○ resemble   ○ assure   ○ casual

9. ○ insure   ○ dizeases   ○ guesses   ○ phrase   ○ recipe

10. ○ unique   ○ official   ○ techniqe   ○ husband   ○ exploration

11. ○ trowsers   ○ conjugate   ○ chorus   ○ saxophone   ○ magical

12. ○ acomplesh   ○ afford   ○ knowledge   ○ treasury   ○ headache

13. ○ photographed   ○ chemistry   ○ nourish   ○ qotient   ○ sufficient

14. ○ magnificent   ○ desirable   ○ potenchal   ○ engaged   ○ toughen

15. ○ gymnasium   ○ ashamed   ○ processed   ○ aknowledge   ○ version

16. ○ partial   ○ emphasize   ○ compochure   ○ prefer   ○ brochure

17. ○ celebration   ○ locksmith   ○ position   ○ convencian   ○ machinery

18. ○ physician   ○ tecknical   ○ cartridge   ○ leisurely   ○ coffee

19. ○ antique   ○ budget   ○ visual   ○ seasanol   ○ pamphlet

20. ○ langwij   ○ instruments   ○ hemisphere   ○ required   ○ advantage

Spelling Words in Action

How are fisher spiders like and unlike other spiders?

Something Fishy

What would you call a creature that **scampered** over the surface of a stream before **descending** upon a fish twice its own size? A fisher spider! These **fascinating** spiders live on the land and water and fish for their prey. Fisher spiders can be found near ponds, streams, and lakes. Besides eating insects, they can actually catch tadpoles and **miscellaneous** types of tiny fish. If you disturb a fisher spider as it sits by the water's edge, it will probably **escape** into the water to hide.

The **scientific** name for fisher spiders is the family Pisauridae. They have large bodies and long legs. While they can hunt on land, they are best known for their ability to walk over water. They can also dive below the water to catch their prey. It takes **discipline** to sit quietly waiting for a meal to swim by.

Fisher spiders include the raft spider and the nursery-web spider. The nursery-web spider is named for the web it weaves to hold its egg sac. Most of the time it stays with the eggs until all have hatched and the **adolescent** spiders have **scattered**. Once in a while it may venture out across the water for a **luscious** seafood supper!

Say the boldfaced words in the selection. How many different sounds can you find made by the letters sc?

TIP

The letters **sc** can make three different sounds:
the **sk** sound, as in escape
the **s** sound, as in scissors
the **sh** sound, as in conscience

LIST WORDS

1. scented
2. adolescent
3. scattered
4. scissors
5. scientific
6. screaming
7. muscles
8. scalding
9. scenery
10. crescent
11. descending
12. sculpture
13. escape
14. scampered
15. scenic
16. miscellaneous
17. fascinating
18. luscious
19. discipline
20. conscience

Words with sc

Write each **list word** under the sound **sc** makes.

sc spells the **s** sound, as in scene

1. _____
2. _____
3. _____
4. _____
5. _____
6. _____
7. _____
8. _____
9. _____
10. _____
11. _____
12. _____

sc spells the **sk** sound, as in scoop

13. _____ 14. _____
15. _____ 16. _____
17. _____ 18. _____

sc spells the **sh** sound, as in unconscious

19. _____ 20. _____

Complete the Paragraph

Use **list words** to fill in the blanks in the paragraph. Write the words on the lines.

My friend Andrew Smith was sitting on a dock near the lake last week, enjoying the

_____ , when he noticed a large spider next to him. He jumped up,

_____ , and ran back home as fast as his _____ would carry

him. He told his father about his narrow _____ . "Let's go back and look at

the spider," Mr. Smith suggested. "It sounds _____ !" When they reached the

dock, the spider was nowhere to be found. Then Mr. Smith pointed to the water, where the

spider _____ rapidly over the surface. "It's a fisher spider," he said. "They are

very interesting from a _____ point of view

because they can walk on water. I bet this one is

looking for a _____ tadpole!"

Solve the Riddles

Use the **list words** to solve the riddles.

1. I can describe soap, a candle, or bath oil. _____

2. You could say that I'm all over the place. _____

3. I'm quite a cut-up, especially when I'm around paper. _____

4. I'm not a child, yet I'm not a grown-up. _____

5. I'm too hot to handle! _____

6. The moon sometimes appears to take my shape. _____

7. When you listen to me, you remember the right thing to do. _____

8. I'm a synonym for hard work or self-control. _____

9. I'm going down, not up. _____

10. I'm lovely to look at, especially when you're outdoors. _____

11. I'm a work of art that has been carved or modeled. _____

12. I don't fit in anywhere. _____

Spelling and Writing

Proofreading

These nature poems have ten mistakes. Use the proofreading marks to correct them. Then, write the misspelled **list words** correctly on the lines.

The Fassenating Spider

She uses thread, but doesnt need sizzers;
She is making a skulpcher withno tools but her legs;
And though the lines she forms are thin,
Theyre so strong that a fly can't eskape them!

1. _____   2. _____

3. _____   4. _____

Hungry Night

Crecint Moon, the night
Has taken abite from you.
What a lussious meal!

5. _____   6. _____

Proofreading Marks

- ⬭ spelling mistake
- ⌄ add apostrophe
- ⌃ add something

Writing a Poem

Write a nature poem. You might write about a fascinating creature, your favorite season, or a scenic place. Use any **list words** that you can. Remember to proofread your poem and fix any mistakes.

_____

_____

_____

_____

_____

_____

BONUS WORDS

scrimp

ascend

scour

conscious

scheme

Spelling Words in Action

How is the story of the *Hindenburg* disaster like other famous disasters?

The Last Voyage of the Hindenburg

On May 6, 1937, people at the landing field at Lakehurst, New Jersey, waited for the *Hindenburg* to arrive. Over 800 feet long, the great airship **reigned** over the Atlantic Ocean travel route. The luxurious craft had everything from a **kitchen** to a baby grand piano.

The flight was one of the routine **stretches** crossing the Atlantic Ocean. It had dropped off an airbag over Cologne, Germany, the city that gave perfumed **cologne** its name. Then it headed across the Atlantic. As the airship swung low over the landing field in Lakehurst, something went **awry**. The *Hindenburg* burst into flames and fell to the ground. Within a minute, nothing was left but **gnarled**, melted **wreckage**. Thirty-five of the 97 people on board lost their lives.

Some people blamed the **wrath** of nature. They believed that a spark of lightning had ignited the *Hindenburg*'s hydrogen gas. People **resigned** themselves to the end of airship travel. Later investigations suggested the airship's **designer** was at fault. The aircraft's fabric cover might have burst into flame. Whatever is to blame, the accident was one of the great disasters of the 20th century.

Look back at the boldfaced words in the selection. Say the words. Listen for the sounds of n, r, and ch. What do you notice about how these sounds are spelled?

TIP

Sometimes you don't hear every letter in a word. The letters **gn** can spell the **n** sound, as in designer, but the **g** is silent. The letters **wr** can spell the **r** sound, as in wrath, but the **w** is silent. The letters **tch** can spell the **ch** sound, as in scratched, but the **t** is silent.

Spelling Practice

LIST WORDS

1. stretches
2. designer
3. wristwatch
4. fetched
5. kitchen
6. wreckage
7. wrestling
8. crutches
9. hatchet
10. wrath
11. unmatched
12. cologne
13. scratched
14. resigned
15. sketching
16. foreigner
17. campaign
18. awry
19. gnarled
20. reigned

Words with gn, wr, and tch

Write each **list word** under the correct heading. One word will be written twice.

gn spells the n sound

1. _____
2. _____
3. _____
4. _____
5. _____
6. _____
7. _____

wr spells the r sound

8. _____ 9. _____
10. _____ 11. _____
12. _____

tch spells the ch sound

13. _____ 14. _____
15. _____ 16. _____
17. _____ 18. _____
19. _____ 20. _____
21. _____

Word Clues

Fill in each mini-puzzle with a **list word**. Use the word or words already filled in as a clue.

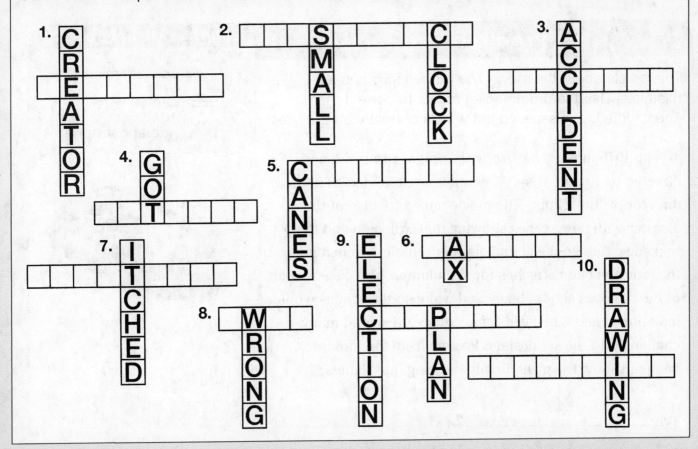

Dictionary

Write the **list words** from the box that would appear on a dictionary page that has the guide words below. Put the words in alphabetical order.

gnarled	
foreigner	
resigned	
cologne	
unmatched	
wrath	
wrestling	
kitchen	
stretches	
reigned	

collision/rein

1. _____
2. _____
3. _____
4. _____
5. _____

residue/wretch

6. _____
7. _____
8. _____
9. _____
10. _____

Spelling and Writing

Proofreading

This article about the movie *The Hindenburg* has ten mistakes. Use the proofreading marks to correct them. Then, write the misspelled **list words** correctly on the lines.

Proofreading Marks

 spelling mistake

 capital letter

 add apostrophe

The 1975 movie *The Hindenburg* was produced and directed by Robert Wise. At the time, wise reined as a top director of "big" films. The movie mixed footage of the disaster with new scenes showing the explosion and the reckedge. though the actual disaster took less than a minute, the movie version streches for six minutes. The disaster part of the film was shot in black and white so the scenes wouldnt look unmached. The need for accuracy presented many challenges to the set desiner. Posters from the movies kampain show the giant airship bursting into flames.

1. _____   2. _____

3. _____   4. _____

5. _____   6. _____

Writing a Review

Imagine that you just saw a movie about the *Hindenburg* disaster. Write a review of the movie. Were the special effects exciting? Did the movie stick to the facts or make up new scenes? Use any **list words** that you can. Remember to proofread your review and fix any mistakes.

_____

_____

_____

_____

_____

BONUS WORDS

gnomes

wring

wrench

twitch

stitched

Spelling Words in Action

What would your coat of arms say about you?

Coat of Arms

Does your school or city have a coat of arms? If so, they're in **debt** to the knights of the Middle Ages. When knights defended their kings' **castles**, uniforms had not been invented. Nobody's **eyesight** was keen enough to tell one knight dressed in full armor from another. So, each knight would **fasten** a "coat of arms" to his armor. This coat showed a design identified with the knight's family. The design could also be displayed on a shield or flag. When a **column** of knights approached another in battle, there was no **doubt** about who was fighting.

Coats of arms are still in use today. Imagine how you would design a coat of arms for your own family. If there was a **plumber** in your family, you might include a wrench. If you were a fast runner, you might put in a **lightning** bolt. Your coat could be **solemn** or silly, showing anything from a flag waving proudly to a **whistling** cat!

Say the boldfaced words in the selection. Do you hear all of the consonants in each word? What do you notice about some of the consonants?

Spelling Practice

TIP

Use the following rules to help you spell words with silent consonants:

- Silent **t** often comes before **en** or **le**, as in fasten and castles.
- Silent **b** often comes before **t**, as in debt, or after **m**, as in crumbs.
- Silent **n** often follows **m**, as in hymns.
- Silent **k** often comes before **n**, as in knickers.
- Silent **gh** often follows **i**, as in eyesight.

LIST WORDS

1. doubt
2. knickers
3. tombstone
4. lightning
5. debt
6. softener
7. almighty
8. solemn
9. fasten
10. whistling
11. castles
12. column
13. hymns
14. eyesight
15. listening
16. plumber
17. playwright
18. condemn
19. moisten
20. crumbs

Words with Silent Consonants

Write each **list word** in the category that tells what silent consonant or consonants it contains.

silent **b**, as in thumb

1. _____
2. _____
3. _____
4. _____
5. _____

silent **n**, as in autumn

6. _____
7. _____
8. _____
9. _____

silent **k**, as in knife

10. _____

silent **t**, as in glisten

11. _____
12. _____
13. _____
14. _____
15. _____
16. _____

silent **gh**, as in flight

17. _____
18. _____
19. _____
20. _____

38   Lesson 9 • Silent Consonants

Comparing Words

Study the relationship between the first two underlined words. Then, write a **list word** that has the same relationship with the third underlined word.

1. poem is to poet as play is to _____

2. birds are to nests as kings are to _____

3. vegetables are to peas as songs are to _____

4. shoe is to tie as seatbelt is to _____

5. big is to huge as powerful is to _____

6. music is to hearing as colors are to _____

7. water is to drops as bread is to _____

8. shoes are to sandals as pants are to _____

9. keep is to promise as pay is to _____

10. television is to watching as radio is to _____

Solve the Code

Use the code to complete the sentences.

A B C D E F G H I J K L M N O P Q R S T U V W

1. She won the _ _ _ _ _ _ _ _ _ contest when her opponent stopped

   to _ _ _ _ _ _ _ his lips.

2. A row of straight-faced people can be called a _ _ _ _ _ _

   _ _ _ _ _ _ .

3. _ _ _ _ _ _ _ _ _ illuminated the message on the hermit's

   _ _ _ _ _ _ _ _ _ : "Go away."

4. There is no _ _ _ _ _ : If you don't clean your room, the board of health

   will _ _ _ _ _ _ _ it.

5. Oh, no—the _ _ _ _ _ _ _ mixed up the water

   _ _ _ _ _ _ _ with the fabric _ _ _ _ _ _ _ _ _ !

Spelling and Writing

Proofreading

The following book review has eight mistakes. Use the proofreading marks to correct them. Then, write the misspelled **list words** correctly on the lines.

There are so many drawings in *The True Book of knights and Cassels* that you can spend hours looking at just one page. This book will take you to thirteenth-century europe You'll see a solum knighthood ceremony You'll spot an unlucky knight who is in det after losing a joust and you'll learn how knights used to fassin their armor.

1. _____   2. _____

3. _____   4. _____

Proofreading Marks

⬭ spelling mistake

≡ capital letter

⊙ add period

Writing a Mini-Mystery

Write a mini-mystery story, solved in one paragraph, titled "The Case of the Missing Coat of Arms." Try to use as many **list words** as you can. Remember to proofread your story and fix any mistakes.

_____

_____

_____

_____

_____

_____

_____

_____

BONUS WORDS

knuckles

thistle

numb

throughout

corps

Spelling Words in Action

How does luge racing differ from sledding?

Super Sledding

Imagine whizzing down an ice-covered course on a sled traveling 90 miles an hour, **earning** cheers from admiring onlookers! That's what the sport of luge racing is all about. A luge is a fast, lightweight sled that holds one person. It can be **compared** to a bobsled in some ways, but a luger lies on his or her back on the sled.

A luger can reach incredible speeds for a vehicle with no motor or **gears**. To steer the sled down the course's twists and turns, the rider **carefully** moves his or her legs and shoulders. These movements are **barely** noticeable to others.

The riders wear helmets with face shields and form-fitting rubber suits. The idea is to reduce air friction. Racers **despair** when they lose even a few hundredths of a second off their finish times.

Though Europeans had been luging for centuries, Americans were **unaware** of the sport until modern times. Luge racing first **appeared** in the Winter Olympics in 1964. Coaches and athletes searched for new talent. The best athletes got to train on ice courses as a **rehearsal** for competitions. These Olympic hopefuls practiced in **earnest** for the chance to compete with the world's best lugers.

Look back at the boldfaced words in the selection. Say the words. Compare the sound made by the letters <u>ear</u>, <u>are</u>, and <u>air</u>.

41

TIP

Sometimes the letters **ear** make the /ir/ sound, as in <u>years</u> and <u>appeared</u>. The letters **ear** can also make the /ur/ sound, as in earnest and earning. Sometimes the /er/ sound can be spelled **are**, as in <u>barely</u>, or **air**, as in <u>stairway</u>.

Spelling Practice

LIST WORDS

1. searching
2. appeared
3. millionaire
4. silverware
5. compared
6. stairway
7. earthenware
8. carefully
9. barely
10. squares
11. gears
12. earning
13. unfairly
14. unaware
15. earrings
16. earnest
17. research
18. despair
19. questionnaire
20. rehearsal

Words with ear, are, and air

Write the **list words** that contain the sound given. You will write one word twice.

ear spells the /ur/ sound, as in earth

1. _____ 2. _____
3. _____ 4. _____
5. _____ 6. _____

air spells the /er/ sound, as in chair

7. _____ 8. _____
9. _____ 10. _____
11. _____

are spells the /er/ sound, as in care

12. _____
13. _____
14. _____
15. _____
16. _____
17. _____
18. _____

ear spells the /ir/ sound, as in clear

19. _____ 20. _____
21. _____

Missing Words

Write the **list word** that completes each sentence.

1. A rescue team is _____ for the lost boy.

2. Mountain bikes are equipped with several _____.

3. She is saving part of the money she is _____ every month.

4. Although the _____ pot was very old, it had no cracks.

5. The younger brother didn't appreciate being _____ to his older brother.

6. The sun was shining while it was showering, and a rainbow _____.

7. I was so sick I could _____ get out of bed.

8. Since she had no idea about the surprise party, it caught her _____.

9. The angry defendant felt that he had been treated _____ by the judge.

10. He gave an _____ and moving speech about his fight with the disease.

11. Members will fill out a _____ to participate in the survey.

12. When the economy is strong, it's easier to become a _____.

Riddles

Choose the **list word** that answers each riddle. Write it on the line. The words in bold are contained in the answers.

1. A **search** for information can be called this. _____

2. How to handle a box **full** of dynamite. _____

3. What to call **silver** knives, forks, and spoons. _____

4. How to describe the attitude of a gloomy **pair** of friends. _____

5. If you **are** shapes with four equal sides, you are these. _____

6. If **he** needs more practice, this is where he should go. _____

7. It's the **way** up to the second floor. _____

8. What jewelry for your **ear** can be called. _____

Spelling and Writing

Proofreading

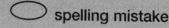

Proofreading Marks

- ⬭ spelling mistake
- ⊙ add period
- ℓ take out something

These how-to directions for a Trivia Olympics have eleven mistakes. Use the proofreading marks to correct them. Then, write the misspelled **list words** correctly on the lines.

1. You will need two teams and a a judge.
2. Each team has to reserch five questions for the other team to answer. Start by surching through reference books List the books where the information appaired. Work cairfully
3. Each correctly answered question is worth 50 points
4. Each incorrectly answered question results in the opposite team team erning a 25-point bonus.
5. At the end of the game, the scores are compard. The team with the most points wins.

1. _____   2. _____

3. _____   4. _____

5. _____   6. _____

Writing a Questionnaire

Think of a sport that you feel should be in the Olympics. Write a questionnaire about the sport. The questionnaire could follow a question-and-answer format or multiple choice. Use any **list words** that you can. Remember to proofread your questionnaire and fix any mistakes.

_____

_____

_____

_____

_____

_____

BONUS WORDS

concessionaire

smeared

yearn

impair

welfare

Spelling Words in Action

Who are the competitors in the Special Olympics?

OLYMPIC GOLD

There are some very special athletes who know they have **succeeded** every time they compete. They are part of the Special Olympics. Each **athlete** in the competition is mentally challenged, yet all have developed the skills and the **esteem** it takes to make them winners.

The Special Olympics began in 1968. Eunice Kennedy Shriver **revealed** the need for a contest for athletes with mental retardation. She believed the benefits for the athletes, including physical fitness and self-confidence, would be **extreme**. Today, about a million athletes compete in over 140 countries. There are more than 20 events.

Every two years, either the World Winter Games or the World Summer Games are **repeated**. Thousands of athletes take part. The games begin with a parade. Friends, parents, **nieces** or nephews, and other fans watch the athletes enter proudly. Then they are ready to **proceed**. After every event, the top three athletes are presented with gold, silver, or bronze medals. Everyone's **achievement** is recognized. All contestants are awarded a well-deserved ribbon.

Most athletes only have to compete against one another. Athletes in the Special Olympics go one step further. They compete against themselves. Their efforts **guarantee** that they will win.

Say the boldfaced words in the selection. What vowel sound do you hear in each of these words? How many ways can you find to spell that sound?

Spelling Practice

LIST WORDS

1. athlete
2. proceed
3. delete
4. extreme
5. repeated
6. esteem
7. reasonable
8. revealed
9. complete
10. greasy
11. achievement
12. squeezed
13. delivery
14. trolley
15. ecology
16. nieces
17. concealed
18. guarantee
19. believable
20. succeeded

Words with the Sound of Long e

Write each **list word** under the spelling of its long **e** sound. Some **list words** are used more than once.

ee, as in <u>succeed</u>   **e**, as in <u>equal</u>

1. _____   15. _____
2. _____   16. _____
3. _____   17. _____
4. _____   18. _____
5. _____   19. _____

ea, as in <u>speak</u>   **ie**, as in <u>piece</u>

6. _____   20. _____
7. _____   21. _____
8. _____   22. _____

9. _____   **e_e**, as in <u>scheme</u>

10. _____   23. _____

y, as in <u>apology</u>   24. _____

11. _____   25. _____
12. _____   26. _____
13. _____

ey, as in <u>volleyball</u>

14. _____

Classification

Write the **list word** that belongs in each group.

1. omit, erase, _____
2. pressed, kneaded, _____
3. respect, admiration, _____
4. farthest, utmost, _____
5. total, whole, _____
6. train, bus, _____
7. sisters, aunts, _____
8. feat, accomplishment, _____
9. uncovered, unveiled, _____
10. did again, persisted, _____

11. warranty, promise, _____
12. fair, sensible, _____
13. true, likely, _____
14. oily, slick, _____
15. advance, move ahead, _____
16. hid, obscured, _____

Solve the Code

Use the code to complete the jokes.

A	B	C	D	E	F	G	H	I	J	K	L	M	N	O	P	Q	R	S	T	U	V	W	X	Y	Z
✗	✳	♣	◆	◇	★	◎	✶	✧	＋	☭	✿	✱	❖	✲	✴	☆	✦	✓	✺	✸	∞	••	☆

1. I ___ ___ ___ ___ ___ ___ ___ ___ ___ in crossing a parrot and a centipede . . . now
   ☆ ✓ ♣ ♣ ◇ ◇ ◆ ◇ ◆
   I have a walkie talkie!

2. Q: What ___ ___ ___ ___ ___ ___ ___ can jump higher than a stop sign?
   ✗ ★ ☆ ✱ ◇ ★ ◇
   A: All of them—stop signs can't jump!

3. Teacher: Class, today we'll study the ___ ___ ___ ___ ___ ___ ___ of the rain forest.
   ◇ ♣ ✺ ✱ ✱ ◎ ••
   Who knows what tree frogs like to eat?

   Student: Lollihops!

4. Patient: Doctor, Doctor, I can't decide if I'm a comedian or a mailman!

   Doctor: Well, keep working on your ___ ___ ___ ___ ___ ___ ___ ___!
   ◆ ◇ ✱ ★ ✱ ◇ ✱ ••

Spelling and Writing

Proofreading

This speech presenting an award to an athlete has twelve mistakes. Use the proofreading marks to correct them. Then, write the misspelled **list words** correctly on the lines.

Proofreading Marks

⬭ spelling mistake

☰ capital letter

℮ take out something

Most Improved Athleet of the Year

P. S. 321 recognizes Russell lee for his acheivment in track. although Russ did not win any races, he suceded in winning our admiration. At at first, Russ could not even compleet a 100-yard dash. instead of quitting or giving up, Russ ran each day, even under the most extream weather conditions. At Field Day, Russ came in third in the the 3-mile race. He has truly earned our our highest esteam.

1. _____ 2. _____

3. _____ 4. _____

5. _____ 6. _____

Writing a Report

Write a report about your favorite sports hero. Describe the way in which your hero has succeeded. Try to use as many **list words** as you can. Remember to proofread your report and fix any mistakes.

_____

_____

_____

_____

_____

_____

BONUS WORDS

precede

eastward

bleak

folly

siege

Lessons 7–11 • Review

In lessons 7 through 11, you learned that some words are spelled differently than you expect. The letters **sc** and **ear** can stand for more than one sound. In addition, one sound, like **er, n, r, ch,** or long **e,** may be spelled in many different ways. Some words contain silent consonants.

Check Your Spelling Notebook

Look at the words in your spelling notebook. Which words for lessons 7 through 11 did you have the most trouble with? Write them here.

_____

_____

Practice writing your troublesome words with a partner. Erase certain letters from the words, trade papers with your partner, and fill in the missing letters.

Lesson 7

 The letters **sc** can stand for three different sounds: the **sk** sound, as in <u>scalding</u>; the **s** sound, as in <u>muscles</u>; and the **sh** sound, as in <u>luscious</u>.

List Words

- scented
- scattered
- discipline
- scissors
- screaming
- muscles
- scalding
- scenic
- crescent
- descending
- escape
- luscious

Study the relationship between the first two underlined words. Then, write a **list word** that has the same relationship with the third underlined word or phrase. Not all the words will be used.

1. <u>catch</u> is to <u>throw</u> as <u>capture</u> is to _____

2. <u>draw</u> is to <u>sketch</u> as <u>tasty</u> is to _____

3. <u>sew</u> is to <u>needle</u> as <u>cut</u> is to _____

4. <u>reading</u> is to your <u>mind</u> as <u>exercise</u> is to your _____

5. <u>cool</u> is to <u>chilly</u> as <u>hot</u> is to _____

6. <u>up</u> is to <u>down</u> as <u>climbing</u> is to _____

7. <u>whispering</u> is to <u>murmuring</u> as <u>yelling</u> is to _____

8. <u>whole</u> is to <u>part</u> as <u>full moon</u> is to _____ moon

9. <u>food</u> is to <u>flavored</u> as <u>flower</u> is to _____

10. <u>gathered</u> is to <u>spread</u> as <u>collected</u> is to _____

The **n** sound can be spelled with **gn** but the **g** is silent, as in <u>gnarled</u>. The **r** sound can be spelled with **wr** but the **w** is silent, as in <u>awry</u>. The **ch** sound can be spelled with **tch** but the **t** is silent, as in <u>kitchen</u>.

List Words

stretches
fetched
wrath
cologne
wristwatch
gnarled
resigned
sketching
kitchen
foreigner
awry
wreckage

Find the **list words** that mean the same as the underlined words in the sentences. Write the words on the lines. Not all the words will be used.

1. By my <u>small clock</u>, it's almost twelve o'clock. _____
2. The apology ended my <u>fury</u>. _____
3. Tim <u>reaches</u> for the box on the top shelf. _____
4. That tree is so <u>twisted</u>! _____
5. Eileen <u>quit</u> after a week. _____
6. He is a <u>stranger</u> to our land. _____
7. Kirk <u>brought</u> the book I had left behind. _____
8. The storm left <u>damage</u> everywhere. _____
9. Dad is <u>drawing</u> a boat. _____
10. Our plans for the trip went <u>wrong</u>. _____

Some words contain silent letters, such as the **t** in <u>softener</u>, the **b** in <u>plumber</u>, the **n** in <u>column</u>, the **k** in <u>knickers</u>, and the **gh** in <u>almighty</u>.

List Words

doubt
knickers
softener
lightning
debt
solemn
column
fasten
hymns
condemn
moisten
crumbs

Write the **list word** to match each clue. Not all the words will be used.

1. short pants _____
2. declare unfit for use _____
3. make damp _____
4. comes with thunder _____
5. something owed _____
6. be uncertain about _____
7. songs of praise _____
8. not laughing _____
9. bits of bread _____
10. attach or join _____

The letters **ear** make the /ir/ sound, as in <u>earrings</u>, and the /ʉr/ sound, as in <u>research</u>. The /er/ sound is sometimes spelled **are**, as in <u>unaware</u>, or **air**, as in <u>unfairly</u>.

Each word below is hidden in a **list word**. Write the **list words** on the lines. Not all the words will be used.

List Words

searching
appeared
stairway
millionaire
carefully
earthenware
earrings
earning
unfairly
questionnaire
despair
rehearsal

1. mill _____
2. fully _____
3. earn _____
4. fair _____
5. hear _____

6. pair _____
7. rings _____
8. arch _____
9. pear _____
10. then _____

 The long **e** sound can be spelled several ways: **e,** as in <u>ecology</u>; **ee,** as in <u>esteem</u>; **ea,** as in <u>revealed</u>; **ie,** as in <u>believable</u>; **e_e,** as in <u>delete</u>; **y,** as in <u>delivery</u>; and **ey,** as <u>trolley</u>.

Write a **list word** to complete each sentence. Not all the words will be used.

List Words

trolley
delivery
delete
greasy
reasonable
revealed
concealed
squeezed
nieces
succeeded
repeated
achievement

1. These dirty dishes are _____.
2. What an _____ it was to win first prize!
3. We can ride on the _____.
4. My baby sister finally _____ in walking.
5. No one heard, so I _____ the question.
6. Send it by special _____.
7. Just _____ the extra names.
8. Ty _____ the winner's name to us.
9. Jon _____ the sponge dry.
10. The actor's face was _____ by a beard.

Show What You Know

One word is misspelled in each set of **list words**. Fill in the circle next to the **list word** that is spelled incorrectly.

1. ○ wrestling ○ searching ○ whistling ○ screaming ○ silverwair

2. ○ fascinating ○ unfairly ○ softener ○ resined ○ scenic

3. ○ listening ○ scenery ○ delivery ○ skratched ○ condemn

4. ○ descending ○ ristwatch ○ achievement ○ nieces ○ reasonable

5. ○ earthenware ○ crumbs ○ misellaneous ○ earnest ○ awry

6. ○ playwrite ○ trolley ○ hymns ○ sketching ○ sculpture

7. ○ research ○ scattered ○ garanty ○ muscles ○ solemn

8. ○ doubt ○ appeared ○ earrings ○ revealed ○ deziner

9. ○ succeeded ○ luscious ○ kichen ○ moisten ○ extreme

10. ○ adolesent ○ tombstone ○ questionnaire ○ conscience ○ proceed

11. ○ cairfully ○ wrath ○ scissors ○ castles ○ squares

12. ○ listening ○ esteem ○ escape ○ gnarled ○ greesy

13. ○ crutches ○ gears ○ foreigner ○ dispair ○ athlete

14. ○ debt ○ cologne ○ cressent ○ scientific ○ earning

15. ○ compared ○ compleate ○ millionaire ○ believable ○ plumber

16. ○ wreckage ○ scalding ○ unaware ○ ecologey ○ scented

17. ○ campane ○ fetched ○ almighty ○ barely ○ eyesight

18. ○ stairway ○ delete ○ reigned ○ hatchet ○ rehersal

19. ○ concealed ○ scampered ○ repeated ○ discipline ○ fascen

20. ○ column ○ squeezed ○ streches ○ knickers ○ unmatched

Words with the Sound of Long o

Spelling Words in Action

Why might prehistoric artists have made paintings of animals?

Cave of Wonders

Imagine making one of the greatest archaeological discoveries of all time. You may shrug your **shoulders** at the idea, but that really happened to four French teenagers in 1940. While exploring the woods of Lascaux (Lah-SKO), France, the boys slid past **boulders** into an underground cave. As they **tiptoed** farther into the cave, they were **thoroughly** surprised by what they found. The walls had beautiful paintings of enormous mammoths, reindeer, horses, bulls, and other animals. Later, they learned that

prehistoric artists drew these 17,000 years ago! The prehistoric artists had made paint by mixing animal fat with red and **yellow** earth.

The cave had lain **fallow** for years, but now it was opened to the public. Hundreds of thousands of people entered it to marvel at the realistic paintings. **Although** nobody meant to damage the cave, the **approaches** of so many people harmed the paintings. In 1963, the cave was closed. Plans were made to build a copy of the cave nearby. The **growth** of the cave continued for several years, and finally, "Lascaux II" was opened in 1983. Any modern artist who visits the site must consider himself a **borrower** of techniques dating back thousands of years.

Say the boldfaced words in the selection. What vowel sound do you hear in each word? How many ways can you find to spell that vowel sound?

53

TIP

The long **o** sound can be spelled many ways:

oa, as in <u>rowboat</u>
oe, as in <u>oboe</u>
ou, as in <u>doughnut</u>
ow, as in <u>growth</u>

Spelling Practice

LIST WORDS

1. borrower
2. doughnut
3. although
4. poultry
5. bowling
6. fallow
7. mistletoe
8. yellow
9. growth
10. approaches
11. boulders
12. stowaway
13. thoroughly
14. cocoa
15. oboe
16. bungalow
17. tiptoed
18. rowboat
19. cantaloupe
20. shoulders

Words with the Long o Sound

Write each **list word** under the spelling of its long **o** sound. One word will be used twice.

ow spells long **o**, as in <u>throw</u>

1. _____
2. _____
3. _____
4. _____
5. _____
6. _____
7. _____
8. _____

oa spells long **o**, as in <u>boat</u>

9. _____
10. _____
11. _____

ou spells long **o**, as in <u>dough</u>

12. _____
13. _____
14. _____
15. _____
16. _____
17. _____
18. _____

oe spells long **o**, as in <u>toe</u>

19. _____
20. _____
21. _____

Find the Words

The underlined word in each sentence does not make sense. Replace the word with a **list word** that does make sense. Write the **list word** on the line.

1. Would you like a steaming cup of <u>boulders</u>? _____

2. In the story, the boy was a secret <u>rowboat</u> aboard the ship. _____

3. The <u>tiptoed</u> is a melon with light orange flesh. _____

4. The farmer made a wall out of <u>cocoa</u>. _____

5. <u>Bungalow</u> is a sport the whole family enjoys. _____

6. Stand back when the train <u>shoulders</u> the station. _____

7. <u>Thoroughly</u> I tried, I couldn't lift the rock. _____

8. The <u>doughnut</u> paid back the money I loaned her. _____

9. He <u>oboe</u> softly down the hall. _____

Classification

Write the **list word** that belongs in each group.

1. red, blue, _____

2. increase, development, _____

3. barren, unplanted, _____

4. ranch, townhouse, _____

5. hen, rooster, _____

6. completely, totally, _____

7. holly, cactus, _____

8. elbows, knees, _____

9. pancake, waffle, _____

10. flute, clarinet, _____

11. canoe, sailboat, _____

Spelling and Writing

Proofreading

This journal entry about making an archaeological discovery has ten mistakes. Use the proofreading marks to correct them. Then, write the misspelled **list words** correctly on the lines.

Proofreading Marks

⬭ spelling mistake

≡ capital letter

⌃ add something

July 30

As I was climbing around the boalders, my yelloe camera strap became wedged between two rocks. I was trying to pull itout when I noticed the opening to a passage. Thorohly intrigued, I called to my parents. althow the boulder was large, we were able to move it together. the hole was just wide enough formy showelders to pass through. It led to a small cave, and when I tiptoad farther inside I saw the jars that held the ancient scrolls.

1. _____   2. _____

3. _____   4. _____

5. _____   6. _____

Writing a Descriptive Paragraph

Imagine a painting that shows objects found in the **list words**, such as a boulder, a rowboat, or a stowaway. Write a paragraph describing the painting. Try to use as many **list words** as you can. Remember to proofread your paragraph and fix any mistakes.

_____

_____

_____

_____

_____

_____

BONUS WORDS

overgrown

woeful

approach

borough

mellow

Spelling Words in Action

Why might people enjoy bonsai trees?

Tiny Trees

Growing bonsai trees is an **ancient** art that comes from Asia. The word "bonsai" means "tray planting." Gardeners train their plants to look like miniature and very beautifully shaped trees.

The art of bonsai began in China over a thousand years ago. It spread to Japan about 800 years ago. More and more people have **seized** this beautiful and unusual form of gardening.

A picture of a bonsai tree on a plain background might be **perceived** to be as large as a giant oak. It is perfectly formed. Yet, a bonsai tree is usually no more than a few feet in **height**. A bonsai maple tree, for example, might reach three feet tall and **yields** very small leaves.

The life span of these tiny trees is **unbelievable**. One tree can live in a small pot for 200 years or more. Some are handed down in families from parent to child. Each generation takes its turn bending and pruning the branches to keep the tree from growing larger. It isn't surprising that growers are **fiercely** proud of their art.

If you're looking for a hobby to pursue **briefly**, growing these tiny trees is not for you. Keeping a bonsai plant looking its best takes time and energy. If you are interested in this long-term pastime, you'll be **relieved** to know that classes are available. You can **retrieve** information from the Internet or at your local library.

Look back at the boldfaced words. Notice the vowel sounds made by the letters ei and ie. How many different sounds do you hear?

The vowels **ie** and **ei** can be vowel pairs as well as vowel digraphs. Vowel pair **ei** can spell the long e sound (<u>conceit</u>). Vowel digraph **ie** can also spell the long **e** sound (<u>diesel</u>). Vowel digraph **ei** can spell the long a sound (<u>veil</u>). Here's a helpful rule:
I before **E** except after **C** or when sounded like **A** as in <u>neighborly</u> or <u>sleigh</u>. There are exceptions to this rule, as in <u>weird</u> and <u>height</u>.

LIST WORDS

1. conceit
2. sleigh
3. height
4. veil
5. seized
6. yields
7. weird
8. mischief
9. neighborly
10. reindeer
11. fiercely
12. unbelievable
13. briefly
14. pierced
15. diesel
16. perceived
17. relieved
18. protein
19. ancient
20. retrieve

Words with ei and ie

Write each **list word** under the correct heading.

ie as in thief

1. _____
2. _____
3. _____
4. _____
5. _____
6. _____
7. _____
8. _____

ei after c

9. _____
10. _____

ei as in weigh

11. _____
12. _____
13. _____
14. _____

ie or ei—no rule

15. _____
16. _____
17. _____
18. _____
19. _____
20. _____

Comparing Words

Study the relationship between the first two underlined words or phrases. Then, write a **list word** that has the same relationship with the third underlined word or phrase.

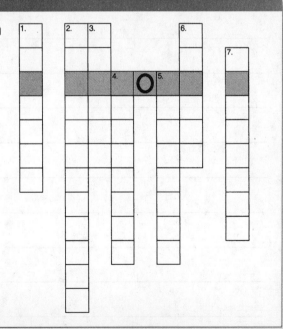

1. orange is to vitamin C as cheese is to _____

2. gave is to provided as took is to _____

3. water is to rowboat as snow is to _____

4. heavy is to weight as tall is to _____

5. new is to young as old is to _____

6. friend is to neighbor as friendly is to _____

7. knife is to sliced as arrow is to _____

8. generosity is to stinginess as modesty is to _____

9. happy is to content as strange is to _____

10. causing problems is to trouble as playing pranks is to _____

11. tusk is to elephant as antler is to _____

12. hear is to heard as perceive is to _____

13. furniture is to chair as covering is to _____

Puzzle

Fill in the puzzle by writing a **list word** to answer each definition clue. Then, read across the shaded boxes to find out how these **list words** are spelled.

1. for a short time

2. incredible

3. type of engine

4. wildly

5. fetch

6. gives way to

7. eased

Spelling and Writing

Proofreading

Proofreading Marks

⬭ spelling mistake

🔽 🔽 add quotation marks

¶ indent paragraph

This myth has eleven mistakes. Use the proofreading marks to correct them. Then, write the misspelled **list words** correctly on the lines.

"Your pointy leaves are wierd," said Oak Tree.

"That's not very naighborley," said Pine Tree.

Mine are ever so much more beautiful, said Oak Tree. I'd be relived if you found another forest to live in. North Wind did not like Oak Tree's conseit. She blew feersely, causing all of Oak Tree's leaves to fall. Oak Tree tried desperately to retreave his leaves, but he couldn't. That is why oak trees lose their leaves every autumn.

1. _____

2. _____

3. _____

4. _____

5. _____

6. _____

Writing a Letter

You and your neighbors have received a notice that a very old and beautiful tree in your neighborhood is about to be cut down. Write a letter to the City Council to protest the action. Use any **list words** that you can. Remember to proofread your letter and fix any mistakes.

_____

_____

_____

_____

_____

_____

_____

_____

_____

BONUS WORDS

mischievous

receipt

freight

debrief

masterpiece

Spelling Words in Action

How is windsurfing like both sailing and surfing?

NEW WAVE

Although windsurfing was **launched** only a few decades ago, the sport has become very popular. Depending on where you live, the sailing season might begin in the spring and run into **autumn**, or it might be year-round.

Windsurfing, also called boardsailing, uses a craft called a sailboard. It looks like a surfboard with a sail. It's not necessary to be big or **brawny** to guide the sailboard! This exciting sport has its hazards. There are **precautions** to take, such as **automatically** checking the wind and weather forecast. If it's too windy or stormy, it's best not to go windsurfing.

You can be **taught** to windsurf in the water, but this method has a **drawback**. Beginners can be quickly **exhausted** by constantly having to pull the sail out of the water. You might prefer to start out on land. Special equipment can almost recreate the **authentic** feeling of being on the waves. Once on the water, you will feel the **awesome** power of the wind and waves. You might even hear some **applause**!

Look back at the boldfaced words in the selection. What vowel sound do you hear in each word?

61

TIP

The vowel digraphs **au** and **aw** sound alike. They both spell the **aw** sound you hear in <u>paused</u> and <u>awesome</u>.

Spelling Practice

LIST WORDS

1. brawny
2. laundry
3. taught
4. paused
5. autumn
6. awning
7. awesome
8. launched
9. astronauts
10. squawking
11. drawback
12. exhausted
13. saucepan
14. automatically
15. dinosaur
16. authentic
17. withdrawal
18. thesaurus
19. precautions
20. applause

Words with au and aw

Write the **list words** in the correct category.

vowel digraph **au**	vowel digraph **aw**
1. _____	15. _____
2. _____	16. _____
3. _____	17. _____
4. _____	18. _____
5. _____	19. _____
6. _____	20. _____
7. _____	
8. _____	
9. _____	
10. _____	
11. _____	
12. _____	
13. _____	
14. _____	

Synonyms and Antonyms

Write a **list word** to match the synonyms and antonyms given.

1. **synonyms**: instinctively, self-powered
   antonyms: consciously, by hand

   _____

2. **synonyms**: real, genuine, true
   antonyms: fake, unreal

   _____

3. **synonyms**: took off, began, started
   antonyms: halted, stopped

   _____

4. **synonyms**: muscular, sturdy, strong
   antonyms: weak, delicate, frail

   _____

5. **synonyms**: tired, worn out, depleted
   antonyms: energetic, lively

   _____

6. **synonyms**: amazing, overwhelming
   antonyms: ordinary, unexceptional

   _____

7. **synonyms**: disadvantage, shortcoming
   antonyms: advantage, blessing

   _____

Puzzle

Fill in the crossword puzzle by writing a **list word** to answer each definition clue.

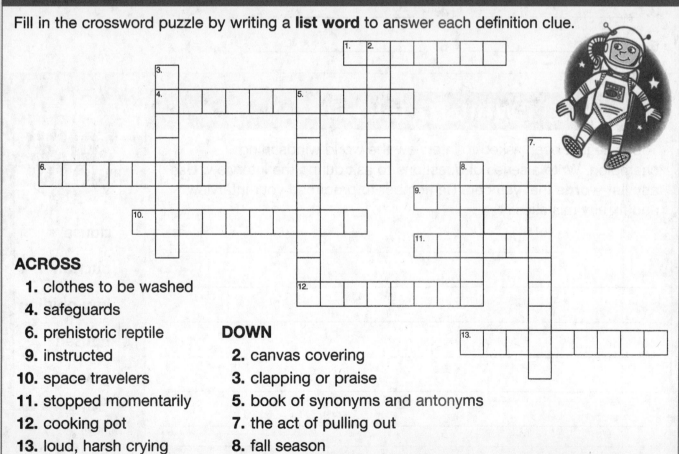

ACROSS

1. clothes to be washed
4. safeguards
6. prehistoric reptile
9. instructed
10. space travelers
11. stopped momentarily
12. cooking pot
13. loud, harsh crying

DOWN

2. canvas covering
3. clapping or praise
5. book of synonyms and antonyms
7. the act of pulling out
8. fall season

Spelling and Writing

Proofreading

The course description that follows has nine mistakes. Use the proofreading marks to correct them. Then, write the misspelled **list words** correctly on the lines.

Semester at Sea—Take classes aboard a sailboat Sail from Massachusetts to the Bahamas aboard an awthentick 19th century sailing vessel. Students are tougt navigation, maritime history literature of the sea, and marine biology. You'll come back exshawsted but filled with stories about an awsume experience If you pass, you are outomaticaly enrolled in the advanced marine biology class. This course is available both awtum and spring terms. *15 credits*

Proofreading Marks

⬭ spelling mistake

⊙ add period

⌃ add something

1. _____   2. _____

3. _____   4. _____

5. _____   6. _____

Writing a Interview

You have just been asked to interview the world windsurfing champion. Write a series of questions to ask during the interview. Use any **list words** that you can. Remember to proofread your interview and fix any mistakes.

_____

_____

_____

_____

_____

_____

BONUS WORDS

clause

auction

law-abiding

nausea

gawk

Spelling Words in Action

Was the name "Underground Railroad" a good one? Why or why not?

Passage to Freedom

In the years before slavery was illegal, the Underground Railroad helped escaping slaves to find freedom in the north. Everyone who took part in the Underground Railroad was **guilty** of breaking the law, but their efforts were **fruitful**. An estimated 40,000 to 100,000 escaped slaves reached freedom this way.

On the plantations, slaves readied themselves in many ways. They listened to stories or songs about escape routes. Other clues might have come in **quilted** form. It is possible that quilt patterns showed the slaves how to prepare for the journey.

The success of the "railroad" depended on its "conductors." Some helped the runaways by **building** hiding places for them. The houses along the Underground Railroad were known as "stations." **Bruised** and hungry runaways would reach a station and stay in a **suitable** hiding spot. Then they would be sent on their way with a **biscuit** or a **juicy** apple to eat. Some "conductors," like the famous Harriet Tubman, personally accompanied the runaways. When prospects looked **gloomy**, Tubman would use clever disguises to throw off slave catchers who **pursued** them. She is one of the Underground Railroad's many heroes.

Say the boldfaced words in the selection. Which words have the sound you hear in poodle? Which words have the sound you hear in build?

TIP

The sound of **yoo**, as in <u>curfew</u>, can be spelled **ew**.

The **oo** sound, as in <u>smoother</u>, can be spelled in the following ways:

ew, as in <u>mildew</u>
ue, as in <u>pursued</u>
oo, as in <u>gloomy</u>
ui, as in <u>fruitful</u>

The letters **ui** also can spell the short **i** sound you hear in <u>biscuit</u>.

Spelling Practice

LIST WORDS

1. mildew
2. guitar
3. gloomy
4. cruise
5. guilty
6. curfew
7. pewter
8. juicy
9. smoother
10. bruised
11. quilted
12. building
13. fruitful
14. shampoo
15. soothing
16. suitable
17. pursued
18. biscuit
19. circuit
20. nuisance

Words with oo, ew, ue, and ui

Write each **list word** under the correct heading.

ew spells the sound of oo or yoo

1. _____
2. _____
3. _____

ui spells the sound of oo

4. _____ 5. _____
6. _____ 7. _____
8. _____ 9. _____

ue spells the sound of oo

10. _____

oo spells the sound of oo

11. _____ 12. _____
13. _____ 14. _____

ui spells the short i sound

15. _____
16. _____
17. _____
18. _____
19. _____
20. _____

Complete the Paragraph

Use the **list words** below to fill in the blanks in the paragraphs. Write the words on the lines.

In my family, we have an old mug made of _____ that has a very special

story. It once played a part in helping people to escape on the Underground Railroad! My

ancestors had been _____ a small room behind a wall to hide the fleeing slaves.

Though they tried to conceal the door, it was _____ than the rest of the wall.

The first time people were hidden in the room, they were followed by an official who had

_____ them for miles. When he came to the house, he became suspicious about

the wall. My great-great-great-grandmother Anne distracted the man by offering him a

_____ piece of apple pie and a hot _____ on her best plate, with a

cool drink of cider in the mug. He said the refreshments were _____ for a king,

and he apologized for being a _____ before he left the house. The runaways

were safe, thanks to Anne's quick thinking and _____ ways!

Word Building

Add and subtract letters to form **list words**.

1. mild + few – f = _____

2. gust – st + silt – s + y = _____

3. quill – l + wanted – wan = _____

4. go – o + suit – s + art – t = _____

5. brush – ush + disguised – disg = _____

6. curtain – tain + f + new – n = _____

7. shame – e + pool – l = _____

8. circus – s + item – em = _____

9. g + look – k + enemy – ene = _____

10. crust – st + bruise – bru = _____

11. fry – y + quit – q + fully – ly = _____

Spelling and Writing

Proofreading

This scene from a TV show about the Underground Railroad has nine mistakes. Use the proofreading marks to fix the mistakes. Then, write the misspelled **list words** correctly on the lines.

MAMA: "This way, George! Move quickly, now, because I think we are are being persooed!"

GEORGE: "I'm running as fast as I can, Mama. I brewsed my my foot, and I'm so hungry. I'd do anything for a biskit or a joocy piece of fruit."

MAMA (in a suithing tone): "We'll eat after we meet up with our conductor. Where could she be? At the the last station, they said we'd find her holding a lantern and waiting by a big oak tree!"

GEORGE: "Mama, look! That's her her, right over there!"

Proofreading Marks

⬭ spelling mistake

⟲ take out something

1. _____

2. _____

3. _____

4. _____

5. _____

Writing a Journal Entry

Write a journal entry from the point of view of a young person helping his or her family to participate in the Underground Railroad. Use any **list words** that you can. Remember to proofread your paragraph and fix any mistakes.

_____

_____

_____

_____

_____

_____

BONUS WORDS

steward

typhoon

undue

recruit

monsoon

Spelling Words in Action

What other kinds of animals lay eggs besides birds?

The World's Best Container

The world's most **praised** and well-designed **container** is not a gift-wrapped box. It's an eggshell. An eggshell may seem fragile, but it's able to withstand a lot of pressure. Try holding an egg in the palm of your hand and squeezing it tightly. It usually won't break. Don't drop the egg, though, unless you want **disappointment**—and a big mess!

Hens lay most of the eggs that we eat, though people also eat eggs from ducks, geese, and other birds. Raising poultry to produce eggs requires a great deal of **maintenance**. The birds need proper nutrition, and the temperature and lighting of their cages must be controlled. Under the right conditions, hens are **faithful** layers. One chicken can produce about 300 eggs a year. Of the billions of eggs produced in America each year, two-thirds are sold whole and the **remainder** are used in various food products.

People eat eggs many ways. Entire **essays** have been written about how to make scrambled eggs! Eggs can also be **boiled** or fried. They are used to make everything from cake to **mayonnaise**. Eating eggs that are raw or undercooked should be **avoided** because they might be contaminated with bacteria. To enjoy your eggs, cook them thoroughly!

Say the boldfaced words in the selection. What vowel sound do you hear in each word? How are the vowel sounds alike? How are they different?

TIP

The letters **ay** and **ai** make the long **a** sound you hear in <u>crayons</u> and <u>praised</u>.

The letters **oy** and **oi** make the **oi** sound you hear in <u>oysters</u> and <u>rejoicing</u>.

Spelling Practice

LIST WORDS

1. essays
2. boiled
3. oysters
4. maintenance
5. employment
6. embroidery
7. crayons
8. exploit
9. turmoil
10. ointment
11. strainer
12. praised
13. disappointment
14. container
15. remainder
16. faithful
17. avoided
18. rejoicing
19. mayonnaise
20. acquaintance

Words with ai, ay, oi, and oy

Write each **list word** under the spelling of its long **a** or **oi** sound. One word is used twice.

ai spells the long a sound, as in <u>train</u>

1. _____
2. _____
3. _____
4. _____
5. _____
6. _____
7. _____
8. _____

oi spells the oi sound, as in <u>oil</u>

12. _____
13. _____
14. _____
15. _____
16. _____
17. _____
18. _____
19. _____

ay spells the long a sound, as in <u>play</u>

9. _____
10. _____
11. _____

oy spells the oi sound, as in <u>toy</u>

20. _____
21. _____

70   Lesson 17 • Words with **ai, ay, oi,** and **oy**

Classification

Write the **list word** that belongs in each group.

1. sewing, knitting, _____

2. repairs, improvements, _____

3. friend, neighbor, _____

4. enjoying, celebrating, _____

5. baked, fried, _____

6. cream, lotion, _____

7. stories, poems, _____

8. paints, pencils, _____

9. clams, mussels, _____

10. unwavering, devoted, _____

11. complimented, applauded, _____

12. uproar, disturbance, _____

Scrambled Words

Unscramble the words below to make these **list words**: avoided, container, disappointment, employment, exploit, mayonnaise, remainder, strainer.

1. art rinse _____

2. video ad _____

3. ear remind _____

4. it ran once _____

5. elm met pony _____

6. aim any nose _____

7. exit lop _____

8. met pond pianist _____

Spelling and Writing

Proofreading

This menu for Edna's Diner has ten mistakes. Use the proofreading marks to correct them. Then, write the misspelled **list words** correctly on the lines.

All Lunch Specials Only $2.99

Our low, low prices are good for the remayndor of the week.

egg Salad—Its made with crunchy celery and maiyonayse.

Boiled Beef—Our most fathfull customers always enjoy this. order some and find out why.

Oyster Stew—Each bowl is made with a half-pint contaynor of milk. It's so thick with oisters, it wont go through a straynor!

Proofreading Marks

 spelling mistake

 capital letter

⌄ add apostrophe

1. _____

2. _____

3. _____

4. _____

5. _____

6. _____

Writing a Recipe

Write a recipe for a dish that contains eggs. The recipe can be real or made-up. Be sure to number your steps or use clue words such as *first*, *next*, *then*, *after*, and *finally*. Use any **list words** that you can. Remember to proofread your recipe and fix any mistakes.

_____

_____

_____

_____

_____

_____

_____

_____

Bonus Words

bail

attain

overjoyed

void

mainstay

Lessons 13–17 · Review

In lessons 13 through 17, you learned that vowel sounds can be spelled many different ways.

Check Your Spelling Notebook

Look at the words in your spelling notebook. Which words for lessons 13 through 17 did you have the most trouble with? Write them here.

_____

_____

Practice writing your troublesome words with a partner. Write the words on slips of paper and put them in a container. Take turns drawing a word, illustrating it, and having the other person guess the word.

Lesson 13

 The long **o** sound can be spelled in more than one way: **oa**, as in cocoa; **oe**, as in mistletoe; **ou**, as in boulders; and **ow**, as in bowling.

Write a **list word** to complete each sentence. Not all the words will be used.

List Words

- bowling
- yellow
- growth
- approaches
- boulders
- although
- thoroughly
- cocoa
- oboe
- borrower
- rowboat
- shoulders

1. School buses are often _____.
2. That jacket is tight across your _____.
3. If a strange dog _____ you, you should never scream or run.
4. Wear a life jacket in the _____.
5. An _____ is a woodwind instrument.
6. These _____ are blocking the hiking trail.
7. Make sure the _____ is not too hot.
8. I'm getting better at _____ with our team.
9. Plant _____ depends upon light and water.
10. Mix the batter _____ to make it smooth.

73

Use the spelling rule you learned when spelling words with **ie** or **ei**. It will help you spell words such as <u>pierce</u>, <u>ceiling</u>, and <u>weigh</u>. Remember that some words, such as <u>ancient</u>, are exceptions.

List Words

ancient
seized
conceit
veil
height
relieved
fiercely
briefly
perceived
sleigh
neighborly
weird

Write a **list word** that means the opposite of the word given. Not all the words will be used.

1. normal _____

2. aggravated _____

3. width _____

4. lengthily _____

5. new _____

6. sweetly _____

7. unfriendly _____

8. modesty _____

9. overlooked _____

10. released _____

 The **aw** sound can be spelled with **au**, as in <u>dinosaur</u>, and **aw**, as in <u>drawback</u>.

List Words

brawny
paused
autumn
awesome
laundry
exhausted
squawking
drawback
saucepan
authentic
withdrawal
applause

Write a **list word** that means the same or almost the same as the word given. Not all the words will be used.

1. fatigued _____

2. waited _____

3. clapping _____

4. muscular _____

5. clucking _____

6. genuine _____

7. fall _____

8. removal _____

9. wonderful _____

10. shortcoming _____

The **yoo** sound can be spelled **ew**, as in <u>pewter</u>. The **oo** sound can be spelled in several ways: **ew**, as in <u>mildew</u>; **ue**, as in <u>pursued</u>; **oo**, as in <u>smoother</u>; **ui**, as in <u>juicy</u>. The short **i** sound can also be spelled with **ui**, as in <u>circuit</u>.

Write the **list word** that belongs in each group. Not all the words will be used.

List Words

mildew
guitar
pewter
quilted
cruise
shampoo
bruised
biscuit
pursued
nuisance
guilty
soothing

1. bother, annoyance, _____
2. copper, bronze, _____
3. mold, fungus, _____
4. soap, detergent, _____
5. sewed, stitched, _____
6. chased, followed, _____
7. banjo, mandolin, _____
8. muffin, toast, _____
9. calming, quieting, _____
10. voyage, trip, _____

 The long **a** sound can be spelled with **ay**, as in <u>crayons</u>, and **ai**, as in <u>strainer</u>. The **oi** sound can be spelled with **oy**, as in <u>employment</u>, and **oi**, as in <u>exploit</u>.

Write the two **list words** that fit each description.

List Words

essays
boiled
oysters
maintenance
employment
ointment
praised
container
faithful
avoided

1. What people did who turned down every job:

_____ _____

2. What the teacher who liked my writing did:

_____ my _____

3. What you could call a jar for a creamy medicine:

an _____ _____

4. One kind of cooked shellfish:

_____ _____

5. What you could call regular care of a building:

_____ _____

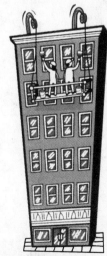

Show What You Know

One word is misspelled in each set of **list words**. Fill in the circle next to the **list word** that is spelled incorrectly.

1. ○ faithful ○ suitable ○ unbeleivable ○ bungalow ○ disappointment
2. ○ sqawking ○ growth ○ smoother ○ pursued ○ awning
3. ○ perceived ○ mayonnase ○ conceit ○ cantaloupe ○ cruise
4. ○ applause ○ crayons ○ gilty ○ ancient ○ veil
5. ○ borrower ○ dinosaur ○ deisel ○ essays ○ cocoa
6. ○ nuesance ○ saucepan ○ oysters ○ boulders ○ strainer
7. ○ building ○ brauny ○ seized ○ mischief ○ withdrawal
8. ○ fallow ○ taught ○ biskit ○ turmoil ○ launched
9. ○ raindeer ○ mistletoe ○ pewter ○ rejoicing ○ employment
10. ○ shampoo ○ doughnut ○ peirced ○ drawback ○ acquaintance
11. ○ remaneder ○ yields ○ stowaway ○ guitar ○ poultry
12. ○ thesaurus ○ proteen ○ tiptoed ○ quilted ○ paused
13. ○ sleigh ○ boiled ○ oboe ○ precawtions ○ yellow
14. ○ mildoo ○ weird ○ avoided ○ laundry ○ bowling
15. ○ praised ○ neighborly ○ relieved ○ circuit ○ oyntment
16. ○ rowboat ○ automatically ○ authentic ○ gluemy ○ bruised
17. ○ shoalders ○ astronauts ○ exploit ○ juicy ○ approaches
18. ○ maintenance ○ soothing ○ awtumn ○ awesome ○ container
19. ○ feircely ○ although ○ briefly ○ fruitful ○ embroidery
20. ○ curfew ○ retreive ○ exhausted ○ height ○ thoroughly

Spelling Words in Action

Why is the great white shark considered the sea's most ferocious animal?

Great White Shark

Ask everyone in your **household** to name the most feared animal in the ocean. You may get a **resounding** vote for the great white shark. Anyone who ran into one would probably feel like a **coward**. It is the sea's most ferocious animal.

Nature did not **endow** the white shark with good eyesight. Rather, its hearing and sense of smell are excellent. It can smell its prey in the **surrounding** area from as far as a quarter-mile away. It strikes from below, and few creatures can escape its steel-trap jaws. Its **mouthful** of 3,000 teeth are razor-sharp. If you've heard an **account** of a white shark eating a human, however, you should **discount** it. Great white sharks attack a few humans each year but do not eat them.

Sharks are elasmobranchs (**pronounced** i-LAZ-ma-branks). Unlike true fish, they have skeleton made of cartilage rather than bones. A white shark can grow to over 20 feet in length. One great white shark was found that weighed an **outrageous** amount—about 7,000 pounds!

Look back at the boldfaced words in the selection. Say the words. Compare the sounds made by the letters <u>ou</u> and <u>ow</u>.

TIP

The diphthongs **ou** and **ow** spell the **ow** sound you hear in <u>bough</u> and <u>coward</u>.

Listen for the **ow** sound in the **list words**. Notice the letters that spell the sound in each word.

Spelling Practice

LIST WORDS

1. coward
2. drowsily
3. bough
4. endow
5. mouthful
6. compound
7. pronoun
8. household
9. downstream
10. discount
11. surrounding
12. pronounced
13. foundation
14. resounding
15. lounge
16. announce
17. account
18. counterpart
19. outrageous
20. drought

Words with <u>ou</u> and <u>ow</u>

Write the **list words** in the correct category to show how the **ow** sound is spelled.

ou spells the sound of ow

1. _____   2. _____

3. _____   4. _____

5. _____   6. _____

7. _____   8. _____

9. _____   10. _____

11. _____   12. _____

13. _____   14. _____

15. _____   16. _____

ow spells the sound of ow

17. _____   18. _____

19. _____   20. _____

Puzzle

Fill in the crossword puzzle by writing a **list word** to answer each definition clue.

ACROSS

1. made up of two parts
4. amount the mouth can hold
8. word that replaces a noun
10. loud and echoing
11. person or thing that closely resembles another
12. one who lacks courage
13. declare publicly
14. relax or be lazy
15. reduced price

DOWN

2. shocking
3. the direction of a stream's current
5. the base of a building
6. to donate; to provide with
7. going around all sides
9. spoke the sounds of a word
13. bank record

Missing Letters

Fill in the missing letters to form **list words**. Then, write the **list words** on the lines.

1. d __ __ __ sily _____

2. c __ __ __ rd _____

3. b __ __ __ h _____

4. pro __ __ __ n _____

5. dr __ __ __ ht _____

6. h __ __ __ ehold _____

Spelling and Writing

Proofreading

This flyer for an aquarium has ten mistakes. Use the proofreading marks to correct them. Then, write the misspelled **list words** correctly on the lines.

Where can you have your picture taken with a white shark a penguin, or a seal Where can everyone in your howshold have outrajous fun watching a dolphin do tricks? Where can you follow a river donstreem in a glass-bottomed boat Where can you lownge around and enjoy the ocean view? The answer is at the Marine Life Aquarium. We are pleased to announse that we now give a discownt to students senior citizens, and aquarium members.

1. _____   2. _____

3. _____   4. _____

5. _____   6. _____

Writing a Tall Tale

Write a brief tall tale that features a shark. Make yourself the hero. The more outrageous your exaggerations, the better your tale will be. Try to use as many **list words** as you can. Remember to proofread your tall tale and fix any mistakes.

_____

_____

_____

_____

_____

_____

Bonus Words

profound

counsel

founder

cauliflower

scowl

Prefixes ir, in, il, and im

Spelling Words in Action

Why do we make New Year's resolutions?

About Face

To the ancient Romans, Janus was an **immortal** god who represented new beginnings. Janus was portrayed as a figure with two faces. One face looked west—toward the setting sun. The other face looked east—toward the new day. The face that looked at the past, toward the setting sun, was old. The one facing the dawn was that of an **immature** youth.

The idea of a two-faced figure seems **incredible** today. However, the god Janus still has an **indirect** influence on customs that people observe in modern times. January, the first month of the year, is named in honor of Janus. On January 1, people continue to review the past and look forward to the new year with hope.

Though it may be **illogical**, people make New Year's resolutions every January 1. On this day, people become **intolerant** of their imperfections. They may vow never to be **irresponsible** again. They may decide to stop being **impatient** or to stop gobbling down **irregular** snacks. Deciding to be perfect is an **impractical** goal, however. No one, not even Janus, can do a complete about-face!

Look back at the boldfaced words in the selection. These words have prefixes at the beginning of each word. How many prefixes can you find?

TIP

The prefixes **ir, in, il,** and **im** usually mean <u>not</u>, as in <u>ir</u>regular, <u>in</u>capable, <u>il</u>legal, and <u>im</u>mature.
The prefix **im** can also mean <u>to</u> or <u>into</u>, as in <u>im</u>migrant.
Here are some helpful spelling rules.

Words that follow:	begin with:
The prefix **im**	**m, p,** or **b**
The prefix **il**	**l**
The prefix **ir**	**r**
The prefix **in**	different letters

Spelling Practice

Words with <u>ir</u>, <u>in</u>, <u>il</u>, and <u>im</u>

Add a prefix to each of these words. Then, write each **list word** under the correct heading.

1. legible

2. mature

3. capable

4. logical

5. properly

6. responsible

7. direct

8. practical

9. tolerant

10. politely

11. patient

12. credible

13. rational

14. migrant

15. material

16. legal

17. literate

18. definite

19. mortal

20. regular

LIST WORDS

1. incredible
2. immortal
3. intolerant
4. immigrant
5. illogical
6. immature
7. illegal
8. improperly
9. incapable
10. irregular
11. impatient
12. impolitely
13. indirect
14. indefinite
15. immaterial
16. illiterate
17. impractical
18. irresponsible
19. irrational
20. illegible

82   Lesson 20 • Prefixes **ir, in, il,** and **im**

Missing Words

Write a **list word** to complete each sentence. Prefix clues are provided.

1. A person who acts childishly is _____. **(im)**

2. A person who has little patience is _____. **(im)**

3. An _____ person cannot read and write. **(il)**

4. Something that is _____ is against the law. **(il)**

5. A person who moves to a new country is an _____. **(im)**

6. Something that will never die is called _____. **(im)**

7. A piece of writing that is impossible to read is _____. **(il)**

8. A poor plan is _____ or _____. **(im, ir)**

9. Something that really doesn't matter is _____. **(im)**

10. Someone who doesn't tolerate new ideas is _____. **(in)**

11. A badly paved road was done _____ and may look _____. **(im, ir)**

12. Someone who can't be trusted is _____. **(ir)**

Word Clues

Fill in each mini-puzzle with a **list word**. Use the word or words already filled in as a clue.

13.
14. ABSURD
15.
16. UNCERTAIN
17.
18. ROUNDABOUT

UNBELIEVABLE

RUDELY

HELPLESS

Spelling and Writing

January

Sunday	Monday	Tuesday	Wednesday	Thursday	Friday	Saturday
		1	2	3	4	5
6	7	8	9	10	11	12
13	14	15	16	17	18	19
20	21	22	23	24	25	26
27	28	29	30	31		

Proofreading

This magazine article has eight mistakes. Use the proofreading marks to correct them. Then, write the misspelled **list words** correctly on the lines.

Are winter blues making you inpatiant for spring Don't just lie around and moan. Remember, january is a good month to do some new or different things.

- Tutor someone who is illiterite.
- Spend the day in bed reading an imcreditable adventure story
- Clean out a closet and give away those inpractical gadgets that gather dust.
- Try to master something that you assumed you were ircapible of learning.

Proofreading Marks

⬭ spelling mistake

≡ capital letter

⌄ add something

⊙ add period

1. _____

2. _____

3. _____

4. _____

5. _____

Writing Resolutions

A resolution is something that you resolve or decide to do. Write one or more resolutions that you feel everyone should try to keep. Write an explanation for why you feel these resolutions are important. Use any **list words** that you can. Remember to proofread your resolutions and fix any mistakes.

_____

_____

_____

_____

_____

_____

Bonus Words

inability

irrelevant

illuminate

imperfect

imprint

Spelling Words in Action

How is modern fencing different from duels fought long ago?

Touché

Imagine that you're in a duel. There is no way your opponent's next move can be **predicted**. If you make a wrong move, you could be jabbed with a foil, a flexible blade sometimes used in fencing.

Fencing is somewhat of a **misunderstood** sport. Those who **dedicate** their time to the sport do not want their fans to be **confused**. Some fans **presume** that the **competitors** get hurt. That is not the case today.

Fencing competitors used to engage in a duel to settle an argument. Only the winner survived. Modern fencing, however, does not involve danger. Injuries are **prevented** in several ways. Fencers wear protective clothing, and the points of the swords are covered. Another sign of **progress** in the sport is the use of electrical judging. Swords are wired to help judges determine how many touches, or hits, have been made. When the electrified sword touches the other fencer's vest or mask, a light appears on the scoring machine in **confirmation** of the hit.

One **complaint** from spectators new to the sport is that fencing is hard to follow. A good way to watch a fencing bout is to concentrate on just one fencer's actions. If you follow the sport long enough, you will learn to appreciate its fast pace!

Say the boldfaced words in the selection. These words have prefixes at the beginning of each word. How many prefixes can you find?

85

Spelling Practice

TIP

The prefixes **pre** and **pro** usually mean before. **Pro** can also mean forward, as in progress.
The prefix **de** means down, not, or reverse. **De** can also mean apart or aside, as in dedicate.
The prefixes **con** and **com** mean with or together.
The prefix **mis** usually means bad or badly or wrong or wrongly.

LIST WORDS

1. propelling
2. competitors
3. provision
4. conference
5. previous
6. dedicate
7. deposited
8. complaint
9. depended
10. decreased
11. predicted
12. progress
13. misunderstood
14. confused
15. presume
16. prescription
17. mispronounced
18. prevented
19. compelled
20. confirmation

Words with de, pre, pro, con, com, and mis

Write the **list words** under the correct category.

Words with the prefix **pre** or **pro**

1. _____
2. _____
3. _____
4. _____
5. _____
6. _____
7. _____
8. _____

Words with the prefix **con** or **com**

15. _____
16. _____
17. _____
18. _____
19. _____
20. _____

Words with the prefix **de**

9. _____
10. _____
11. _____
12. _____

Words with the prefix **mis**

13. _____
14. _____

Move the Words

The underlined word in each sentence does not make sense. Replace the word with a **list word** that does make sense. Write that word on the line.

1. James <u>predicted</u> the soda can in the recycling bin. _____

2. Who are the <u>deposited</u> in this Olympic event? _____

3. They will <u>compelled</u> the statue of the library's founder today. _____

4. The book was so good, I was <u>misunderstood</u> to write to the author. _____

5. I have no <u>competitors</u> about the way that was handled. _____

6. The protesters <u>dedicate</u> the issue by bringing in other opinions. _____

7. Luis <u>confused</u> the way the story would end. _____

8. Amy's request was <u>complaint</u> by everyone in the room. _____

Word Parts

Write a **list word** that contains the same root as the word given.

1. increase _____

2. refuse _____

3. invented _____

4. devious _____

5. compelling _____

6. inference _____

7. indicate _____

8. division _____

9. inscription _____

10. announce _____

11. assume _____

12. suspended _____

13. affirmation _____

14. digress _____

Spelling and Writing

Proofreading

This letter has eleven mistakes. Use the proofreading marks to correct them. Then, write the misspelled **list words** correctly on the lines.

Proofreading Marks

	spelling mistake
	capital letter
∧	add something

Dear consuelo

　　My friend and I will both be conpetiters ina fencing tournament. She believes that if we are matched against each other, that I should feel compaled to lose because she talked me into entering. During pervious tournaments I always dapended on my friend to be fair and she was. I never would have perdicted that I would be writing to you, but I'm very confuzed.

Signed,

A Friend in Need

1. _____

2. _____

3. _____

4. _____

5. _____

6. _____

Writing a Letter

Write a letter that answers the letter to Consuelo in the proofreading activity. Try to use as many **list words** as you can. Remember to proofread your letter and fix any mistakes.

_____

_____

_____

_____

_____

_____

BONUS WORDS

miscalculate

commotion

provoke

prelude

decline

Spelling Words in Action

How would you stop a flood of sticky molasses?

The Molasses Flood

It was a January day in Boston. The year was 1919, shortly after the end of World War I. A story that people would tell and **embellish** for years to come was about to unfold.

At around noontime, without any **forewarning**, a 52-foot-tall storage tank holding over 2 million gallons of molasses began to split apart. As chunks of metal flew in every direction, **postwar** veterans must have thought they were back in battle. Molasses began to **overflow** onto the street. An enormous gooey wave nearly 15 feet high swept down the streets. It began to **endanger** everything in its path. It destroyed houses and even hit one of the supports for the elevated train. Luckily, the engineer glimpsed the disaster ahead and stopped the train in time. His **foreknowledge** saved many lives.

The cleanup effort lasted for weeks. Workers hired to fight the sticky substance were knee-deep in molasses. Wishing they had had the **foresight** to do it earlier, city officials finally brought in nearby fireboats. The **enlistment** of the fireboats, which hosed down the area with saltwater, finally helped to clean the streets.

As a **postscript**, the company that owned the molasses tank was fined $1 million. An inspection on the tank had been long **overdue**.

Say the boldfaced words in the selection. Each boldfaced word has a prefix. How many prefixes can you find? How do the prefixes change the meanings of the base words?

Spelling Practice

TIP

The prefixes **em** and **en** can mean <u>in</u> or <u>into</u>, as in end<u>anger</u>. They can also mean <u>cause to be</u>, as in embitter, or <u>to make</u>, as in en<u>grave</u>. The prefix **fore** means <u>front</u> or <u>before</u>, as in fore<u>sight</u>. The prefix **post** means <u>after</u>, as in postwar. The prefix **over** usually means <u>too much</u> or <u>above</u>, as in <u>overdue</u>.

LIST WORDS

1. forewarning
2. postscript
3. postwar
4. encourage
5. overweight
6. overflow
7. foresight
8. embellish
9. emblazon
10. engrave
11. endanger
12. foreground
13. embitter
14. overdue
15. foreknowledge
16. overprotect
17. embankment
18. embattle
19. enlistment
20. enlighten

Words with em, en, fore, post, and over

Write each **list word** under the correct category.

Words with the prefix **em** or **en**

1. _____
2. _____
3. _____
4. _____
5. _____
6. _____
7. _____
8. _____
9. _____
10. _____

Words with the prefix **fore**

11. _____
12. _____
13. _____
14. _____

Words with the prefix **over**

15. _____
16. _____
17. _____
18. _____

Words with the prefix **post**

19. _____
20. _____

Comparing Words

Study the relationship between the first two underlined words. Then, write a **list word** that has the same relationship with the third underlined word.

1. road is to curb as river is to _____

2. hinder is to discourage as help is to _____

3. lake is to flood as bathtub is to _____

4. careful is to careless as protect is to _____

5. wood is to carve as metal is to _____

6. Mr. is to Mister as p.s. is to _____

7. far is to near as background is to _____

8. prompt is to timely as late is to _____

9. advice is to caution as hint is to _____

10. yesterday is to tomorrow as prewar is to _____

Mixed-Up Words

The prefixes in these **list words** have become mixed up: embattle, emblazon, embellish, embitter, enlighten, enlistment, foreknowledge, foresight, overprotect, overweight. Put the prefixes back where they belong and write the two correct words on the lines.

1. emweight   overbellish   _____ _____

2. enbitter   emlighten   _____ _____

3. enknowledge   forelistment   _____ _____

4. forebattle   emsight   _____ _____

5. overblazon   emprotect   _____ _____

Spelling and Writing

Proofreading

This pamphlet on storm safety tips has ten mistakes. Use the proofreading marks to correct them. Then, write the misspelled **list words** correctly on the lines.

Proofreading Marks

 spelling mistake

 capital letter

 add something

 add apostrophe

When a storm is coming, you cant overpertect yourself. With forsite and planning you can remain safe. If you don't have a portable radio, you're overdew to get one. Follow any forworning about flooding if you live in a low-lying area. Keep batteries bottled water, and candles on hand. During the storm, encaurage everyone to keep away from windows electrical appliances, and telephones. after the storm, don't emdanger yourself by going near downed wires.

1. _____   2. _____   3. _____

4. _____   5. _____   6. _____

Writing Quotations

What do you think people who were on the train that nearly plunged into the molasses flood might have said? Write quotations for several different people who may have experienced this train ride. Use any **list words** that you can. Remember to proofread your quotations and fix any mistakes.

_____

_____

_____

_____

_____

_____

Bonus Words

empower

encompass

foremost

oversensitive

overemotional

Spelling Words in Action

How closely are people connected from all around the world?

It's a Small World

Did you ever hear of the "small world" theory, sometimes called "six degrees of separation"? Here's how it works. Say you read a letter from a girl in Ohio, Jill Romero, in a magazine to which you have a **subscription**. Jill wrote the letter as an **antidote** to **counteract** the idea that nothing exciting ever happens in her town. Her letter tells how her brother Will scored the winning basket in his **semifinal** basketball playoffs when he was put in for a **substitution**.

How many "people connections," or *degrees of separation*, would it take to get from you to Jill? The small world theory says that on the average, it would take no more than six.

You start by asking your mom whom she knows in Ohio. Mom is the *first* person connecting you to Jill. She offers to ask her friend Josie (the 2nd person). Josie is the gas station attendant who put **antifreeze** in Mom's car. She lived in Ohio before her husband was **transferred** to your city's **submarine** base.

Josie doesn't know the Romeros, so she calls her friend Mary in Ohio. Mary (the 3rd person) helps to **supervise** her son Frank's basketball team. Frank (the 4th person) turns out to have a **superficial** acquaintance with Jill's brother, Will (the 5th person). Will, of course, knows Jill, for the sixth and last connection. There you have it—six "people connections," or degrees of separation, between you and Jill Romero. It's a small world after all!

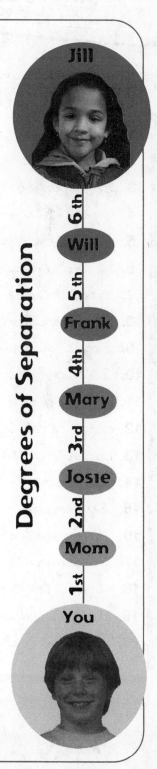

Degrees of Separation

Jill
6th — Will
5th — Frank
4th — Mary
3rd — Josie
2nd — Mom
1st — You

Look back at the boldfaced words in the selection. Each word has a prefix at the beginning of the word. How many different prefixes can you find?

93

anti = against; opposite
ultra = beyond; very
sub = under; below; not quite
semi = half; partly
counter = against; opposite
super = over; very;
 greater than others
trans = across; over; beyond

Spelling Practice

LIST WORDS

1. antifreeze
2. supervise
3. semifinal
4. antiseptic
5. transparent
6. substitution
7. antidote
8. submarine
9. superficial
10. subscription
11. semicircle
12. counteract
13. counterattack
14. semicolon
15. supersonic
16. transistor
17. ultraviolet
18. transferred
19. counterfeit
20. antibodies

Words with Prefixes

Write each **list word** under the correct heading.

Words with the prefixes
anti and **counter**

1. _____
2. _____
3. _____
4. _____
5. _____
6. _____
7. _____

Words with the prefix **super**

8. _____
9. _____
10. _____

Words with the prefix **ultra**

11. _____

Words with the prefix **sub**

12. _____
13. _____
14. _____

Words with the prefix
trans

15. _____
16. _____
17. _____

Words with the prefix
semi

18. _____
19. _____
20. _____

Definitions

Write a **list word** to match each definition.

1. something that works against a poison _____

2. takes place before a final match or round _____

3. limited to the surface area _____

4. device that controls the flow of electric current _____

5. attack that is a response to a fight _____

6. to oversee or direct work _____

7. moved from one person, place, or thing to another _____

8. the act of putting one thing in place of another _____

9. see-through _____

10. beyond the speed of sound _____

11. half of a round shape _____

12. something that acts against germs _____

13. to act directly against _____

Solve the Riddles

Use the **list words** to solve the riddles. Write the words on the lines.

1. This helps keep your car running in the winter. _____

2. It can describe a sandwich or an underwater boat. _____

3. You might use this to get newspapers, tickets, or magazines. _____

4. Without this, you wouldn't pause as long when you read certain sentences. _____

5. You don't want to get a dollar bill that is one of these. _____

6. The rays this describes cannot be seen. _____

7. They help your body to fight colds. _____

Spelling and Writing

Proofreading

The following paragraph has eleven mistakes. Use the proofreading marks to fix each mistake. Then, write the misspelled **list words** correctly on the lines.

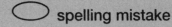

Proofreading Marks

⬭	spelling mistake
ℓ	take out something
⌃	add something
⌄	add apostrophe

When my parents volunteered to to suporvise their high school reunion, they couldnt locate two classmates. "What should we do" they wondered. They advertised the reunion in the local newspaper, but it seemed that neither of the the missing classmates had a subscrition. One had been transfered to a Naval submereen base, so Dad wrote to a friend in the in Navy. Another one had a superfishal role in a Broadway play, so Mom wrote to a relative who was an actor. Their efforts paid off when the two classmates addresses were found.

1. _____   2. _____   3. _____

4. _____   5. _____

Writing an Advertisement

Imagine that it's 20 years in the future, and you are writing a newspaper advertisement to help find students from your class for a reunion. What would you say? Create an ad that would encourage your classmates to contact you. Use any **list words** that you can. Remember to proofread your advertisement and fix any mistakes.

_____

_____

_____

_____

_____

BONUS WORDS

antisocial

counterbalance

subcontract

transaction

semiprecious

96   Lesson 23 • Prefixes **anti**, **counter**, **super**, **sub**, **ultra**, **trans**, and **semi**

Lessons 19–23 · Review

In lessons 19 through 23, you learned more about the spelling of vowel sounds in words. You also learned about words with prefixes added to the base word. Look at those words again and think about what the prefixes mean.

Check Your Spelling Notebook

Look at the words in your spelling notebook. Which words for lessons 19 through 23 did you have the most trouble with? Write them here.

_____

_____

_____

Practice writing your troublesome words with a partner. Say a sentence for each word and spell the word aloud for your partner.

Lesson 19

 The **ow** sound can be spelled two ways: **ou**, as in <u>surrounding</u>, and **ow**, as in <u>drowsily</u>.

Write a **list word** to match each clue. Not all the words will be used.

List Words

coward
bough
mouthful
compound
downstream
pronoun
discount
foundation
lounge
endow
announce
outrageous

1. tree part _____

2. a room to relax in _____

3. a bargain price _____

4. base of a house _____

5. shocking; excessive _____

6. proclaim, make known _____

7. don't talk with this _____

8. he, she, they, or it _____

9. mixture made of two or more parts _____

10. person who lacks courage _____

The prefixes **ir**, **in**, **il**, and **im** usually mean <u>not</u>, as in <u>irresponsible</u>, <u>indirect</u>, <u>illogical</u>, and <u>immaterial</u>. The prefix **im** can also mean <u>to</u> or <u>into</u>, as in <u>immigrant</u>.

Write the **list word** that has the same base word or root as the word given. Not all the words will be used.

List Words

immortal
irregular
intolerant
indirect
illegal
immature
illegible
immigrant
incapable
irrational
impatient
indefinite

1. definitely _____
2. migrate _____
3. capability _____
4. mortality _____
5. legalize _____
6. tolerate _____
7. patience _____
8. regulate _____
9. direction _____
10. legibility _____

 pre, pro = <u>before</u>
pro = <u>forward</u>

con, com = <u>with</u> or <u>together</u>
mis = <u>bad</u> or <u>badly</u>, or <u>wrong</u> or <u>wrongly</u>
de = <u>down</u>, <u>not</u>, <u>reverse</u>, <u>apart</u>, <u>aside</u>

Write five **list words** that could be found listed between each set of dictionary guide words given. Write the words in alphabetical order. Not all the words will be used.

List Words

prevented
depended
compelled
confused
predicted
complaint
provision
conference
prescription
decreased
progress
misunderstood

compile/deposit

1. _____
2. _____
3. _____
4. _____
5. _____

mistake/protect

6. _____
7. _____
8. _____
9. _____
10. _____

em, en = in, into, cause to be, to make   **post** = after
over = too much or above   **fore** = front or before

Make **list words** by choosing a prefix from the chart above to add to each base word. Write the words on the lines. Not all the words will be used.

List Words

postscript
foresight
overweight
overdue
postwar
embattle
engrave
embitter
foreknowledge
encourage
embankment
overflow

1. sight _____ 2. bitter _____

3. script _____ 4. war _____

5. weight _____ 6. flow _____

7. courage _____ 8. battle _____

9. knowledge _____ 10. due _____

anti = against or opposite   **counter** = against or opposite
ultra = beyond or very   **semi** = half or partly
sub = under, below, or not quite   **trans** = across, over, or beyond
super = over, very, or greater than others

Write a **list word** to complete each sentence. Not all the words will be used.

List Words

antiseptic
supersonic
antifreeze
ultraviolet
semifinal
semicolon
semicircle
submarine
transparent
subscription
counterfeit
counterattack

1. Our team will play in the _____ match.

2. The bill was fake; it was _____.

3. We put _____ in the car in the winter.

4. After we ate half the pie, a _____ shape was left.

5. A _____ travels underwater.

6. Use a _____ to separate those clauses.

7. The nurse uses an _____ to kill germs.

8. Our _____ to that magazine is for one year.

9. That window is _____; you can see through it.

10. A _____ aircraft exceeds the speed of sound.

Show What You Know

One word is misspelled in each set of **list words**. Fill in the circle next to the **list word** that is spelled incorrectly.

1. ○ drought ○ immortal ○ antifreeze ○ semicolon ○ confrence
2. ○ depended ○ illegul ○ downstream ○ progress ○ foreground
3. ○ propelling ○ impractical ○ risounding ○ antibodies ○ overdue
4. ○ lounge ○ impolitely ○ previous ○ indefinate ○ semifinal
5. ○ substitution ○ coward ○ poastwar ○ misunderstood ○ transistor
6. ○ forknowledge ○ embattle ○ competitors ○ bough ○ indirect
7. ○ pronoun ○ counterract ○ foresight ○ superficial ○ prevented
8. ○ incapable ○ supervise ○ counterfit ○ enlistment ○ incredible
9. ○ intolerant ○ overwait ○ pronounced ○ irrational ○ engrave
10. ○ forewarning ○ immaterial ○ illogical ○ confurmation ○ account
11. ○ confused ○ mouthful ○ compelled ○ drousily ○ enlighten
12. ○ counterpart ○ provision ○ antidote ○ overprotect ○ impashunt
13. ○ illiterate ○ enblazon ○ transparent ○ compound ○ complaint
14. ○ antiseptic ○ overflow ○ illegible ○ perscription ○ discount
15. ○ predicted ○ ultraviolet ○ semcircle ○ outrageous ○ dedicate
16. ○ immature ○ embellish ○ submareen ○ embitter ○ presume
17. ○ supersonic ○ diposited ○ improperly ○ foundation ○ decreased
18. ○ encourage ○ household ○ endanger ○ transferred ○ annownce
19. ○ counterattack ○ imigrant ○ surrounding ○ irregular ○ postscript
20. ○ endough ○ subscription ○ embankment ○ irresponsible ○ mispronounced

Spelling Words in Action

How did barnstorming get its name?

BARNSTORMING

Picture yourself on a **midsummer** afternoon in the 1920s. You've just heard that some of those new flying machines would be landing at Farmer Jones's field in your **midwestern** town. You hop in your Model-T and drive off.

There they are—half a dozen biplanes sitting on the field. You pick out faces in the growing crowd, including the president of the local **university**. The audience has **tripled** by the time you hear an announcer's **monotonous** voice droning over the loudspeaker.

The **biplane** speeds down the grassy "runway." It lifts off, carrying a pilot and one passenger. Then you see the passenger step out onto the wing. You're glad you brought your **binoculars** to get a close-up look. Everyone gasps in **unison** as the passenger, a stuntwoman, hangs from a ladder below the plane.

Another plane takes off, and then another. These planes don't carry stuntmen. Instead, they fly in a **triangular** pattern, zigzagging through the clouds. Then the engine of one of the planes starts to make a sputtering sound. It's falling in a spiral down toward the earth. The pilot leaps out and safely floats to the ground in his parachute. The plane, however, crashes through the farmer's barn and neatly **bisects** the roof. At that moment, it's perfectly clear to you why this type of flying is called "barnstorming."

Look back at the boldfaced words in the selection. Find the different prefixes in the words. Try coming up with the meaning for each prefix.

101

TIP

The prefixes **uni** and **mono** mean one or single.
The prefix **bi** means two or twice.
The prefix **tri** means three or three times.
The prefix **mid** means in the middle of.

Spelling Practice

LIST WORDS

1. tricolor
2. midwestern
3. tripled
4. university
5. midsummer
6. biweekly
7. unicycle
8. monorail
9. uniform
10. bisects
11. biplane
12. triangular
13. binoculars
14. unison
15. trilogy
16. monotonous
17. monosyllable
18. universal
19. triplicate
20. biannual

Words with uni, mono, bi, tri, and mid

Write each **list word** in the correct category to show the prefix it contains.

uni

1. _____
2. _____
3. _____
4. _____
5. _____

bi

11. _____
12. _____
13. _____
14. _____
15. _____

mono

6. _____
7. _____
8. _____

tri

16. _____
17. _____
18. _____
19. _____
20. _____

mid

9. _____
10. _____

102   Lesson 25 • Prefixes **uni**, **mono**, **bi**, **tri**, and **mid**

Definitions

Write a **list word** to solve each definition clue.

1. once every two weeks _____

2. multiplied by three _____

3. plane with one wing above the other _____

4. twice a year _____

5. having three sides _____

6. train with one track _____

7. something made of three colors _____

8. boring and repetitive _____

9. one-wheeled vehicle _____

10. three copies _____

11. divides into two parts _____

12. the middle of the summer _____

Scrambled Words

What **list word** can be made from the letters in each of these phrases?
Write the word on the line.

1. survey in it _____

2. end sew trim _____

3. in forum _____

4. is noun _____

5. glory it _____

6. mall by lone so _____

7. lunar vise _____

8. boa curls in _____

binoculars
midwestern
monosyllable
trilogy
uniform
unison
universal
university

Spelling and Writing

Proofreading Marks

- ⬭ spelling mistake
- ⌃ add something
- ℮ take out something
- / make small letter

This biography has ten mistakes. Use the proofreading marks to correct them. Then, write the misspelled **list words** correctly on the lines.

Bessie Coleman was the first African American woman to become a pilot. Tired of monotenus work, Coleman wanted to fly a a byplane. Prejudice nearly stopped her, but she earned a license in Europe. Her first exhibition was in a middwesdern city in 1922. Her stunts won her unaversil acclaim. Can you imagine Coleman in her her Pilot's unaforme standing before a cheering crowd If only we had a pair of magic binockulars that would enable us to see her soar across the sky.

1. _____   2. _____

3. _____   4. _____

5. _____   6. _____

Writing a Comparison

Write a paragraph comparing and contrasting two of the following means of transportation: a biplane, a monorail, and a unicycle. Be sure to include the advantages and disadvantages of each of these. Try to use as many **list words** as you can. Remember to proofread your paragraph and fix any mistakes.

_____

_____

_____

_____

_____

BONUS WORDS

- unilateral
- monogram
- bifocals
- trilingual
- midpoint

Lesson 26

Spelling Words in Action

How has the computer changed the way people get information?

Ancient Machines

Imagine that you want to find out how information reached people in the days before modern **technology**. You decide to visit a history museum. After riding an **escalator**, you reach a room full of ancient machines.

A guide points to a tall black machine. "The printing press was a great **transformer** of information," he says. "The earliest presses printed books and pamphlets. Eventually, presses were used to print newspapers. A **journalist** would write about important events. Then a **machinist** would set the letters for the story on a metal sheet. The process took a day, so a **consumer** bought a newspaper to read yesterday's news." His words almost sound like **mythology** as you think of what it's like to get news today. Although a journalist is still an **investigator**, he or she is also the **typist** who writes the story on a computer.

Next the man points to a machine with two wheels. "That's a film **projector**," he says. "It was invented by Thomas A. Edison. Pretty different from watching movies on a VCR, isn't it? But one thing hasn't changed. People still love to read the news and watch movies!"

Look back at the boldfaced words in the selection. These words have word parts, called suffixes, at the end of each word. How many suffixes can you find?

Spelling Practice

LIST WORDS

1. juror
2. consumer
3. biology
4. jeweler
5. aviator
6. spectator
7. insulator
8. typist
9. transformer
10. projector
11. machinist
12. geologist
13. florist
14. divisor
15. journalist
16. technology
17. mythology
18. escalator
19. manufacturer
20. investigator

Words with or, er, ist, logy, and ology

Write a **list word** that has the same root as the word given.

1. mythical
_____

2. biosphere
_____

3. consume
_____

4. machine
_____

5. geology
_____

6. investigate
_____

7. escalate
_____

8. type
_____

9. inspect
_____

10. jewel
_____

11. aviation
_____

12. flower
_____

13. journal
_____

14. jury
_____

15. technique
_____

16. divide
_____

17. factory
_____

18. form
_____

19. project
_____

20. insulate
_____

Describing Words

Write a **list word** to name the person whose work involves the items given.

1. rocks and minerals _____

2. bracelets and rings _____

3. flowers _____

4. machines and wrenches _____

5. clues and fingerprints _____

6. keyboards _____

7. news stories _____

8. airplanes _____

9. trials and juries _____

10. any sort of manufactured goods _____

Rhyming Words

Fill in the blanks with a word that rhymes with the underlined word or words.

1. I heard a <u>rumor</u> that you are a careful _____.

2. She showed us how hummingbirds drink <u>nectar</u> on the overhead _____.

3. I feel much <u>wiser</u>, now that I know which number is the _____.

4. The study of animals, <u>zoology</u>, is a branch of the science called _____.

5. When you went to see the <u>skater</u>, were you in the crowd as a _____?

6. Who was the <u>informer</u> who reported the broken _____?

7. What is the <u>chronology</u> of the growth of computer _____?

8. From the field of <u>archaeology</u> we've learned much about Greek and

    Roman _____.

9. Please stand <u>straighter</u> when you ride on the _____.

10. The heat in the apartment was <u>greater</u> because of the new _____.

Spelling and Writing

Proofreading

Proofreading Marks

⬭ spelling mistake

︿ add something

This article has ten mistakes. Use the proofreading marks to fix each mistake. Then, write the misspelled **list words** correctly on the lines.

There is a story in the school newspaper about a local spice manufackturer called Spicy's. The company makesmany different spices to flavor food. Thesespices include cinnamon garlic, and pepper. They are used to flavor vinegar mustard different sauces, and pickles. In the article, the jurnalist said that Spicy's also produces some artificial flavorings. Using modern technolojy and current knowledge in biahlogy, they can make flavors that a consumor cannot tell from natural spices.

1. _____   2. _____   3. _____

4. _____   5. _____

Writing a News Story

Write the lead paragraph of a news story about an interesting event in your school or your community. Try to tell the *who, what, where, when,* and *why* of the story. Use any **list words** that you can. Remember to proofread your paragraph and fix any mistakes.

_____

_____

_____

_____

_____

_____

BONUS WORDS

counselor

zoology

lecturer

hypnotist

theology

Spelling Words in Action

If you were a storyteller, what stories would you tell?

Weaving Stories

Storytelling is an art, but even people who tell the **simplest** stories can be storytellers. A good story touches an audience with humor, drama, wisdom, or all these things. A story can bring listeners **happiness** or even a healthier outlook on life.

You can sharpen your own storytelling skills. First, you should find a story you would enjoy telling. The library is a good place to start. Myths, tall tales, and folktales can all be fun to tell aloud. You might choose a folktale about the **noisiest** animal in the forest, or the **cruelest** or **strictest** king, or the **brightest** young woman in a land. Other stories tell about a character who is **tinier** than other people, like Thumbelina or Tom Thumb. Often, these tiny characters solve their problems through **cleverness**.

Learning a story doesn't have to be hard. Reading it over and over and picturing each of the events will help you to remember the story. It's not necessary to memorize it. In fact, telling a story in your own words helps you avoid **stiffness** in your speech. You might also want to shorten parts of a story, making it **tighter** to keep the plot moving along. Remember that small groups or large ones can be great audiences. With a story and an audience, a storyteller is always ready to perform.

Say the boldfaced words in the selection. These words have suffixes. See if you notice any spelling changes in the base words when the suffixes are added.

Spelling Practice

...ding in y,
... tiny-tinier.
...xes to words ending in e,
...p the e: simple-simplest.

LIST WORDS

1. happiness
2. muddiest
3. tighter
4. cruelest
5. noisiest
6. crazier
7. stiffness
8. dampness
9. sharpness
10. strictest
11. brightest
12. thickest
13. emptiness
14. tinier
15. firmest
16. cleverness
17. healthier
18. simplest
19. cleanliness
20. promptness

Words with er, est and ness

Write a **list word** under the correct heading.

Words with the suffix er

1. _____
2. _____
3. _____
4. _____

Words with the suffix est

5. _____
6. _____
7. _____
8. _____
9. _____
10. _____
11. _____
12. _____

Words that were changed from adjectives to nouns with the suffix ness

13. _____
14. _____
15. _____
16. _____
17. _____
18. _____
19. _____
20. _____

Synonyms

On the spaces at the right, write a **list word** that means the same as the word g[...]
Then, read the letters in the shaded box to solve the riddle.

1. shiniest   __ __ __ __ __ __ __ __
2. heartier   __ __ __ __ __ __ __ __
3. easiest   __ __ __ __ __ __ __ __
4. moistness   __ __ __ __ __ __ __ __
5. loudest   __ __ __ __ __ __ __ __
6. smaller   __ __ __ __ __ __
7. meanest   __ __ __ __ __ __ __
8. dirtiest   __ __ __ __ __ __ __ __
9. hardest   __ __ __ __ __ __ __

Riddle: What is extremely precious, can't be bought, but can be found?

Answer: _____

Word Parts

Add a suffix to each base word to form a **list word**. Write the word on the line.

1. tight   _____
2. empty   _____
3. thick   _____
4. clean   _____
5. sharp   _____
6. clever   _____
7. tiny   _____

8. muddy   _____
9. stiff   _____
10. noisy   _____
11. bright   _____
12. strict   _____
13. prompt   _____
14. crazy   _____

and Writing

...ading

...ok has nine mistakes. Use
... ...h mistake. Then, write the
... ...e lines.

...htbe listening to a story at the National
... Festival in Jonesborough tennessee. This
... the first such festival in the country and it is still the
best-known. What can you do there You can see the brietest
storytellers turn the simmplest stories into the most
fascinating tales you've ever heard. You will be amazed by
their clevarness.

Proofreading Marks

◯ spelling mistake

∧ add something

≡ captial letter

1. _____   2. _____

3. _____   4. _____

Writing a Summary

Stories can take you anywhere, anytime—even to places that do not
exist. Do you have a favorite story? Perhaps you have an idea for a
story. Write a paragraph that summarizes what your story is about.
Try to use as many **list words** as you can. Remember to proofread
your story summary and fix any mistakes.

_____

_____

_____

_____

_____

_____

_____

BONUS WORDS

bitterness

coarsest

filthier

gentler

painfulness

Spelling Words in Action

How does diabetes affect a person's life?

KIDS Managing Diabetes

What is diabetes? It's a disease in which a person's body does not produce enough of a hormone called *insulin*. Insulin helps the body to use sugar for energy. There is no cure for diabetes, and the disease is not **reversible**. It can be controlled, however. Eating proper foods regularly, taking insulin, and exercising are all part of the treatment for diabetes.

Diabetes can start in **adulthood** or childhood. The disease offers **unavoidable** challenges to young people. Usually, kids with diabetes soon become **successful** at testing their blood sugar level. They also learn what kinds of food and exercise are healthy for them. The tricky part for diabetics is balancing all those things to keep their blood sugar levels within the right range. These levels are **changeable**, so it takes some **adjustment** for diabetic kids to stay on track with their illness. For instance, they can show great **sportsmanship**, but they may need to eat something before exercising. They may need to catch up on an **assignment** they missed in order to make a doctor's **appointment**. Friends can help by offering support. Friends should never put up an **argument** when diabetics say they need to take a blood test or get a snack.

For diabetic kids, education and knowledge about managing their disease puts them in control so they can be kids first and diabetics second.

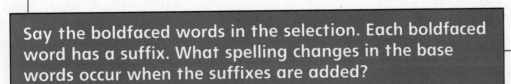

Say the boldfaced words in the selection. Each boldfaced word has a suffix. What spelling changes in the base words occur when the suffixes are added?

113

TIP

The suffixes **able** and **ible** usually mean can or able to be. The suffix **ful** means full of or having a tendency to be. The suffix **hood** usually means the state or condition of being. The suffix **ship** means having the qualities of. The suffix **ment** means act of or state of. Before adding the suffix to some words that end in **e** or **y**, drop the **e** or change **y** to **i**, as in like + **able** = likable, and fancy + **ful** = fanciful.

Spelling Practice

LIST WORDS

1. likable
2. appointment
3. parenthood
4. sportsmanship
5. changeable
6. adulthood
7. breakable
8. enrollment
9. fanciful
10. noticeable
11. successful
12. manageable
13. assignment
14. adjustment
15. argument
16. unavoidable
17. reversible
18. convertible
19. bountiful
20. scholarship

Adding Suffixes

Write each **list word** in the correct category to show the suffix it contains.

able

1. _____
2. _____
3. _____
4. _____
5. _____
6. _____

ible

7. _____
8. _____

hood

9. _____
10. _____

ment

11. _____
12. _____
13. _____
14. _____
15. _____

ful

16. _____
17. _____
18. _____

ship

19. _____
20. _____

Classification

Write the **list word** that belongs in each group.

1. inescapable, unmistakable, _____

2. fairness, generosity, _____

3. visible, remarkable, _____

4. friendly, kind, _____

5. homework, book report, _____

6. date, meeting, _____

7. victorious, excellent, _____

8. unreliable, shifting, _____

9. sedan, station wagon, _____

10. abundant, rich, _____

11. quarrel, feud, _____

12. fragile, delicate, _____

Mixed-up Words

The suffixes in these **list words** have become mixed up: <u>adjustment</u>, <u>adulthood</u>, <u>enrollment</u>, <u>fanciful</u>, <u>manageable</u>, <u>parenthood</u>, <u>reversible</u>, <u>scholarship</u>. Put the suffixes back where they belong and write the two correct words on the line.

1. fanciment   enrollful   _____

2. adultible   revershood   _____

3. parentable   managehood   _____

4. adjustship   scholarment   _____

Spelling and Writing

Proofreading

This biographical sketch has nine mistakes. Use the proofreading marks to fix each mistake. Then, write the misspelled **list words** correctly on the lines.

The actress Mary Tyler Moore was famous for the likeble roles she played on two long-running TV shows, "The Dick Van Dyke Show" and "The Mary Tyler Moore Show" Her fans thought this successfull woman was possessed with bountifel good health, like the energetic characters she played In fact, Moores health was a challenge to her because she had been diagnosed with diabetes in adulthode. She decided to do something for children with diabetes As the Juvenile Diabetes Foundations international chairperson, she has helped to raise millions of dollars toward researching a cure for the disease.

Proofreading Marks

 spelling mistake

 add period

add apostrophe

1. _____

2. _____

3. _____

4. _____

Writing a Descriptive Paragraph

How do you meet challenges in your own life? Write a paragraph that describes something you found difficult or challenging, and what you did to overcome that challenge. Use any **list words** that you can. Remember to proofread your paragraph and fix any mistakes.

_____

_____

_____

_____

_____

BONUS WORDS

digestible

inflatable

livelihood

fellowship

ailment

Spelling Words in Action

What made the Tri-State Tornado the worst ever to hit the U.S.?

TWISTER!

The United States has more **experience** with tornado **activity** than any other country. Many experts believe that the most **destructive** tornado ever to hit the U.S. was the 1925 Tri-State Tornado. In just hours, it roared through three states: Missouri, Illinois, and Indiana. Experts still aren't sure if the Tri-State Tornado was one twister or a group of twisters, because it is so hard to tell the **difference**. Still, this tornado qualifies as the worst in the U.S. for a **combination** of reasons. It was on the ground continuously for three and a half hours, the longest time ever recorded. In **addition**, it had the longest track of any tornado—219 miles. Tragically, the Tri-State Tornado claimed nearly 700 lives, more than any other U.S. tornado.

One **explanation** for the massive destruction caused by the Tri-State Tornado is that people had very little warning that the twister was coming their way. For much of its path, it looked like rolling clouds—not the funnel shape that people associate with a twister. Fortunately, with the **excellence** of modern weather prediction and the **existence** of mass **communication** systems, another tornado disaster of this magnitude should never occur again.

Look back at the boldfaced words in the selection. What are the base words? What spelling changes in the base words occur when the suffixes are added?

TIP

ion, ation, and ition = the act of or the condition of being, as in conversation and composition

ance, ence, and ity = quality or fact of being, as in resistance, experience, and activity

ive = likely to or having to do with, as in destructive and creative

Spelling Practice

LIST WORDS

1. difference
2. composition
3. electricity
4. abundance
5. conversation
6. existence
7. activity
8. communication
9. excellence
10. addition
11. combination
12. creative
13. explanation
14. passive
15. quotation
16. circulation
17. destructive
18. disturbance
19. experience
20. resistance

Adding Suffixes

Write the **list words** that contain the suffixes given.

ence

1. _____ 2. _____

3. _____ 4. _____

ation

5. _____ 6. _____

7. _____ 8. _____

ance

9. _____ 10. _____

11. _____

ion

12. _____

13. _____

ive

14. _____ 15. _____

16. _____

ition

17. _____ 18. _____

ity

19. _____ 20. _____

118   Lesson 29 • Suffixes **ion**, **ation**, **ition**, **ance**, **ence**, **ive**, and **ity**

Missing Words

Write the **list word** that belongs in each sentence.

1. Soccer is a recreational _____.

2. The _____ storm caused heavy damage.

3. Tom's _____ as a tutor will help him to be a teacher.

4. The heart controls the _____ of blood.

5. The title of his _____ was "Sources of Energy."

6. The telephone is a _____ tool.

7. Winnie received an award for _____ in science.

8. The _____ of computer technology has greatly helped weather prediction.

9. I memorized the _____ to the lock for my locker.

10. Our long-distance phone _____ lasted an hour!

11. We needed a more detailed _____ to fully understand how the machine worked.

12. That group was asked to leave because they were causing a _____.

13. We take _____ for granted until the power goes out.

14. I'm going to cite this famous _____ by Albert Einstein in my report.

Puzzle

This is a crossword puzzle without clues. Use the length and spacing of six **list words** to complete the puzzle.

Spelling and Writing

Proofreading

The news report below has ten mistakes. Use the proofreading marks to fix each mistake. Then, write the misspelled **list words** correctly on the lines.

The tornado that swooped through the area last night was quite a destruktive storm As one resident described it, I heard a roar like a huge freight train, and then it hit."
A conversashion with another witness resulted in this quoetasion: "My daughter Anna and I ran for the cellar as the electrisity flickered, and the tornado tore off the roof.

   It was a very frightening experience for many residents. Camunication systems were knocked out for several hours until the disturbence passed.

1. _____   2. _____

3. _____   4. _____

5. _____   6. _____

Proofreading Marks

⬯	spelling mistake
∧	add something
⟨⟨ ⟩⟩	add quotation marks
¶	insert paragraph

Writing Advice

What do you think people should do to prepare for a big storm? Write a paragraph stating your advice for someone who experiences a tornado, hurricane, blizzard, or flood. Use complete sentences and use any **list words** that you can. Remember to proofread your paragraph and fix any mistakes.

_____

_____

_____

_____

_____

BONUS WORDS

legislation

inspection

correspondence

radiance

originality

Lessons 25–29 · Review

In lessons 25 through 29, you learned about words with prefixes and suffixes. Look at those words again, and think about how the prefixes and suffixes can change the meanings and the spelling of some base words.

Check Your Spelling Notebook

Look at the words in your spelling notebook. Which words for lessons 25 through 29 did you have the most trouble with? Write them here.

_____

_____

Practice writing your troublesome words with a partner. Write a sentence for each word. Trade papers, circle the prefixes or suffixes, and tell the meaning of each prefix or suffix.

Lesson 25

 uni, mono = one, single   **bi = two, twice**
tri = three, three times   **mid = in the middle of**

List Words

unicycle
bisects
biplane
tricolor
triangular
binoculars
monotonous
midsummer
triplicate
monosyllable
universal
trilogy

Write a **list word** to match each clue. Not all the words will be used.

1. Wednesday is to midweek as July is to _____

2. unites is to joins as divides is to _____

3. round is to circular as three-sided is to _____

4. tricycle is to bicycle as bicycle is to _____

5. three artists are to trio as three books are to _____

6. double is to triple as duplicate is to _____

7. computer is to typewriter as jet is to _____

8. astronomers are to telescopes as bird watchers are to

   _____

9. illegal is to unlawful as global is to _____

10. interesting is to captivating as boring is to

   _____

or, er = <u>one who</u> or <u>something that</u>
ist = <u>one who</u>   logy, ology = <u>the study of</u>

Write a **list word** that means the same or almost the same as the word or phrase given. Not all the words will be used.

List Words

consumer
biology
jeweler
juror
aviator
spectator
typist
florist
journalist
technology
manufacturer
investigator

1. maker _____

2. jury member _____

3. detective _____

4. reporter _____

5. pilot _____

6. onlooker _____

7. technical knowledge _____

8. buyer or user _____

9. keyboarder _____

10. life science _____

---

 er = <u>more</u>, as in <u>healthier</u>   est = <u>most</u>, as in <u>simplest</u>
<u>ness</u> changes an adjective into a <u>noun</u>

Write the **list word** that belongs in each group. Not all the words will be used.

List Words

tighter
noisiest
dampness
brightest
thickest
emptiness
tinier
cleverness
crazier
simplest
muddiest
cleanliness

1. small, little, _____

2. loud, ear-splitting, _____

3. broad, wide, _____

4. easy, plain, _____

5. firm, snug, _____

6. bareness, blankness, _____

7. wet, moist, _____

8. intelligence, wit, _____

9. spotless, sanitary, _____

10. brilliant, shining, _____

able, ible = can, able to be   **ful** = full of, tending to be
ship = having the qualities of   **ment** = act of, state of
hood = state or condition of being

List Words

scholarship
likable
changeable
adulthood
fanciful
enrollment
successful
assignment
argument
reversible
convertible
bountiful

Write the **list word** that has the same root as the word given. Not all the words will be used.

1. exchange _____
2. arguing _____
3. bounteous _____
4. irreversibly _____
5. unlikely _____
6. scholarly _____
7. succeeding _____
8. reassign _____
9. enrolled _____
10. converter _____

 ion, ation, ition = the act of or the condition of being
ance, ence, ity = quality, fact of being
ive = likely to or having to do with

List Words

composition
passive
destructive
conversation
circulation
communication
explanation
abundance
activity
excellence
addition
creative

Write a **list word** to match each clue. Not all the words will be used.

1. could describe an artist _____
2. involves action _____
3. something you might write _____
4. describes a fire or storm _____
5. a phone call or a letter _____
6. tells why something happened _____
7. more than enough _____
8. 2 plus 2 _____
9. talking between people _____
10. the highest level of success _____

Show What You Know

One word is misspelled in each set of **list words**. Fill in the circle next to the **list word** that is spelled incorrectly.

1. ○ investigator ○ argument ○ bisects ○ adjustmint ○ electricity

2. ○ consumer ○ conversation ○ emptiness ○ kreativ ○ triangular

3. ○ university ○ communication ○ adulthood ○ uneforum ○ happiness

4. ○ dampness ○ escalator ○ convertible ○ addition ○ parenthod

5. ○ florist ○ crazyer ○ passive ○ triplicate ○ strictest

6. ○ diffirince ○ manageable ○ tighter ○ unicycle ○ simplest

7. ○ transformer ○ likable ○ machinest ○ divisor ○ monosyllable

8. ○ reversible ○ clevernus ○ activity ○ juror ○ unison

9. ○ tinier ○ aveeator ○ circulation ○ scholarship ○ muddiest

10. ○ biology ○ sportsmanship ○ trycolor ○ firmest ○ spectator

11. ○ cruelest ○ midwestern ○ explanation ○ thickest ○ tipist

12. ○ geologist ○ bountiful ○ biweekly ○ cleanliness ○ tecknologee

13. ○ trylogy ○ existence ○ noisiest ○ breakable ○ biplane

14. ○ universal ○ experiance ○ excellence ○ projector ○ appointment

15. ○ promptniss ○ tripled ○ manufacturer ○ enrollment ○ resistance

16. ○ composition ○ unavoidable ○ changeable ○ notissible ○ stiffness

17. ○ jeweler ○ monorail ○ britest ○ mythology ○ combination

18. ○ healthier ○ binoculars ○ sharpness ○ abundance ○ biennuel

19. ○ journalist ○ disturbance ○ fancyfull ○ midsummer ○ successful

20. ○ distructiv ○ assignment ○ insulator ○ monotonous ○ quotation

Lesson 31

Spelling Words in Action

Have you ever been to a museum like the National Civil Rights Museum?

The National Civil Rights Museum

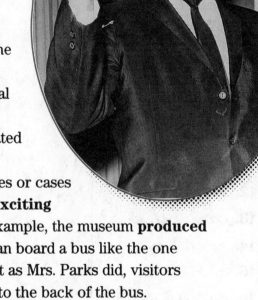

On April 4, 1968, a terrible tragedy **occurred** at the Lorraine Motel in Memphis, Tennessee. This is the place where Dr. Martin Luther King, Jr., was assassinated. On that spot now stands a moving tribute to Dr. King and all who fought for African Americans' equal rights.

When the Lorraine was going to be sold in 1982, a group of dedicated people **approved** a decision to buy the motel. They wanted to help preserve Dr. King's memory. In 1991, the National Civil Rights Museum opened there. It was the first museum in the country to show the history of the civil rights movement through exhibits. By **organizing** key legal challenges, marches, and other protests, the movement's leaders helped to change laws that treated African Americans unfairly.

In this museum, visitors don't just look at pictures or cases **crammed** with objects. It is **equipped** with many **exciting** interactive exhibits. To tell about Rosa Parks, for example, the museum **produced** an exhibit **combining** sights and sounds. Visitors can board a bus like the one Mrs. Parks once rode in Montgomery, Alabama. Just as Mrs. Parks did, visitors hear the voice of a bus driver telling them to move to the back of the bus. While many of the museum's visitors have **memorized** facts about the civil rights movement, this place brings those facts to life. It has truly **realized** the dream of its founders.

Look back at the boldfaced words in the selection. Find the base word in each word. What happened to the spelling of the base word when the suffixes were added?

125

TIP

When a short-vowel word or syllable ends in a single consonant, usually double the consonant before adding a suffix or ending that begins with a vowel, as in <u>equip</u> + **ed** = <u>equipped</u>.

When you add a suffix or ending that begins with a vowel to a word that ends with **e**, usually drop the **e** before adding the suffix or ending, as in <u>unpave</u> + **ed** = <u>unpaved</u> and <u>combine</u> + **ing** = <u>combining</u>.

LIST WORDS

1. evaporated
2. combining
3. graduated
4. unpaved
5. approved
6. referred
7. advertising
8. crammed
9. produced
10. equipped
11. occurred
12. memorized
13. controlled
14. exciting
15. abbreviated
16. calculation
17. hesitation
18. organizing
19. disguised
20. realized

Spelling Practice

Adding Suffixes and Endings

Write the **list words** in which the final consonant was doubled before the suffix or ending was added.

1. _____
2. _____
3. _____
4. _____
5. _____

Write the **list words** in which the final **e** was dropped before the suffix or ending was added.

6. _____ 14. _____
7. _____ 15. _____
8. _____ 16. _____
9. _____ 17. _____
10. _____ 18. _____
11. _____ 19. _____
12. _____ 20. _____
13. _____

Missing Words

Write a **list word** to complete each sentence.

1. The word "pound" is _____ as "lb."

2. She _____ us to an excellent dentist.

3. Tony _____ the poem so he would not need notes.

4. The chef is _____ all the ingredients in a large bowl.

5. Without any _____, the firefighter rushed into the burning building.

6. What could have _____ in the meeting to change everyone's mind?

7. Dad made a quick _____ to figure out how much grocery money we would need.

8. Aunt Betsy _____ herself as my cousin's favorite book character for the birthday party.

9. Consuelo will be _____ a new file system for the office files.

10. A giant billboard was _____ the company's new fruit drink.

11. I was so proud of my brother when he _____ at the top of his class.

12. The water in our science experiment _____ overnight.

Rhyming Words

Write the **list word** that rhymes with each word or phrase.

1. cup moved _____

2. deduced _____

3. we shipped _____

4. one rolled _____

5. Rex biting _____

6. meal sized _____

7. slammed _____

8. one waved _____

Spelling and Writing

Proofreading

The following article has ten mistakes. Use the proofreading marks to fix each mistake. Then, write the misspelled **list words** on the lines.

Proofreading Marks

⬭ spelling mistake

／ make small letter

⌃ add something

⌄ add apostrophe

One of the worlds Longest borders along which conflict has rarely ockured is in North America. The lasting peace between Canada and the United States has prodused a beautiful place that is refared to as the International Peace Garden. The garden sits on the border between the two countries in the Turtle Mountains. Aprouved in 1931, the garden is a symbol of peace, combineing beauty with a message. What kinds of things will you see there For one thing, youll see an exciteing clock made of flowers that keeps the park's official time.

1. _____ 2. _____ 3. _____

4. _____ 5. _____ 6. _____

Writing a Persuasive Paragraph

Write a paragraph telling what you think should be done about prejudice and intolerance and why your ideas would work. Use any **list words** that you can. Remember to proofread your paragraph and fix any mistakes.

_____

_____

_____

_____

_____

_____

BONUS WORDS

challenged

relating

patrolling

tolerated

admitted

Lesson
32

Spelling Words in Action

How are cranberries grown?

A "Berry" Interesting Fruit

Native Americans were the first people in
North America to discover the many uses of
the cranberry. They used the berries to make
food, dye, and even **remedies** to treat
wounds. It was the Pilgrims who **identified**
the berries as "crane-berries." They thought
the cranberries' pink flowers looked like the
heads of cranes.

Anyone who ate a cranberry right after it
had been picked would probably be **dismayed**
by the waxy coating and sour taste. The taste is
modified greatly when cranberries are used in recipes
and food products.

Various **companies** produce about 5 million barrels of cranberries each year.
Cranberry growing is one of the most important **industries** in Massachusetts.
The berries are also grown in other parts of the U.S. and Canada.

Cranberries grow in sandy marshes known as bogs. During the growing season,
growers are **occupied** by the need to protect the vines from frost. In very cold
weather, water runs **steadily** over the plants to keep them from freezing.
Harvesting begins in the fall, when the bogs are flooded with water. Stirring the
water causes the berries to float to the surface, where they are gathered.
Refrigeration keeps them from **decaying**. Some berries are sold as fresh fruit, while
others are made into cranberry juice, jams, **jellies**, and other delicious foods.

Look back at the boldfaced words in the selection. Each
of these words ends in a suffix. What happens to the
root words that end in y when the suffixes are added?

Spelling Practice

TIP

If a word ends in:
- a **vowel** and **y**, add **ed** or **s** without changing the base word, as in disobeyed.
- a **consonant** and **y**, change the **y** to **i** before adding **ed**, **es**, or **ly**, as in occupied, remedies, or sloppily.
- **y**, add **ing** without changing the base word, as in decaying.

LIST WORDS

1. companies
2. jellies
3. sloppily
4. surveying
5. theories
6. steadily
7. waterways
8. identified
9. occupied
10. disobeyed
11. remedies
12. thirstily
13. decaying
14. modified
15. galaxies
16. industries
17. attorneys
18. dismayed
19. magnified
20. portrayed

Adding Suffixes and Endings

Add a suffix or ending to each word to form a **list word**. Write the **list word** on the line.

1. attorney _____
2. modify _____
3. company _____
4. magnify _____
5. waterway _____
6. identify _____
7. industry _____
8. occupy _____
9. survey _____
10. galaxy _____
11. steady _____
12. theory _____
13. portray _____
14. dismay _____
15. jelly _____
16. decay _____
17. thirsty _____
18. sloppy _____
19. remedy _____
20. disobey _____

Synonyms and Antonyms

Write the **list word** that is the synonym or antonym of the word or phrase given.

1. antonym for <u>neatly</u> _____

2. synonym for <u>adjusted</u> _____

3. antonym for <u>periodically</u> _____

4. synonym for <u>lawyers</u> _____

5. antonym for <u>without thirst</u> _____

6. synonym for <u>enlarged</u> _____

7. antonym for <u>empty, vacant</u> _____

8. synonym for <u>alarmed, surprised</u> _____

9. antonym for <u>behaved</u> _____

10. synonym for <u>named</u> _____

Move the Words

The underlined word in each sentence does not make sense. Replace the word with a **list word** that does make sense. Write that word on the line.

1. Refrigeration is used to keep food from <u>portrayed</u>. _____

2. This garden contains many of the plants that the early settlers used for <u>companies</u> when they were ill. _____

3. Many <u>galaxies</u> offer summer internships for college students. _____

4. Not everyone knows that cranberry production is one of Wisconsin's <u>jellies</u>. _____

5. He is <u>decaying</u> the property where the new house will be built. _____

6. I like the way the actress <u>industries</u> the main character in that movie. _____

7. The St. Lawrence Seaway is one of our most important <u>theories</u>. _____

8. There are many <u>surveying</u> about the best growing methods. _____

9. In the science-fiction story, astronauts carried cranberries to distant <u>remedies</u>. _____

10. My aunt is famous for the jams and <u>waterways</u> she makes from cranberries. _____

Spelling and Writing

Proofreading

Proofreading Marks

◯ spelling mistake

／ make small letter

︿ add something

℮ take something out

This article has eleven mistakes. Use the proofreading marks to fix the mistakes. Then, write the misspelled **list words** correctly on the lines.

Along the watewayes of the Great Lakes region, a special harvest takes place in the summer. The Ojibway people begin survaying the Wild rice beds to plan their their harvest. Two people ride ride in each canoe, and one steedily pushes it through the water with a long pole. The Ojibway have occupyed thisarea and gathered wild rice for about 400 years. Their methods have not been modifyed very much over the years. They pull the stalks over, knock the tops, and send the grains into the bottom of the canoe. Nothing isdone slaupily.

1. _____   2. _____

3. _____   4. _____

5. _____   6. _____

Writing a Menu

Write a menu for a meal that features three different ways to serve cranberries. You might include a beverage, bread, side dish, main course, or dessert. Describe each item on your menu, using as many **list words** as you can. Remember to proofread your menu and fix any mistakes.

_____

_____

_____

_____

BONUS WORDS

jockeys

dictionaries

conveyed

glorified

greedily

Spelling Words in Action

What can be bought on the Internet?

Open for Business

Buying products on the Internet is very popular, and for good reason. Online stores are open 24 hours a day, and items are delivered right to the buyer's doorstep.

What are people buying online? High-tech items such as **stereos** and computers are very popular. Some buyers also like to order food over the Internet. Internet grocery stores offer everything from fresh pears and **avocados** to ordinary boxes of **spaghetti**. Toys are also popular with online consumers, from **dominoes** to stuffed **kangaroos**.

Online auction services do a lively business selling collectibles such as sports **mementos**. The motto here is "Let the buyer beware," as there are Internet **thieves**! One person stole over $37,000 from customers on an Internet auction site.

Specialty clothing can be found easily on the Internet, from **tuxedos** for a wedding to **ponchos** for camping. No item is overlooked, from fine linen **handkerchiefs** to designer suspenders.

Of course, the Internet isn't the solution to every shopping need. When people need a quart of milk, they still head to the nearest grocery store!

Look back at the boldfaced words in the selection. Say the singular form of each plural word. What do you notice about the spelling of some plural forms of words?

Spelling Practice

TIP

Some words remain the same in singular and plural form, as in species. For most words ending in **f** or **fe**, change the **f** or **fe** to **v** and add **es** to form the plural, as in thieves or knives. For some exceptions, form the plural by adding **s**, as in beliefs or tariffs. For most words ending in **o**, add **s** to form the plural, as in tuxedos. Some exceptions add **es**, as in mosquitoes or dominoes.

LIST WORDS

1. rodeos
2. kangaroos
3. tuxedos
4. patios
5. stereos
6. avocados
7. beliefs
8. thieves
9. tariffs
10. species
11. ponchos
12. dominoes
13. mementos
14. embargoes
15. broccoli
16. spaghetti
17. jackknives
18. handkerchiefs
19. Eskimos
20. mosquitoes

Plural Words

Write the **list words** under the correct headings.

Words that do not change to form the plural

1. _____
2. _____
3. _____

Words that change **f** or **fe** to **v** and add **es** to form the plural

4. _____
5. _____

Words that end in **o** and add **es** to form the plural

6. _____
7. _____
8. _____

Words that end in **f**, **ff**, or **o** and just add **s** to form the plural

9. _____
10. _____
11. _____
12. _____
13. _____
14. _____
15. _____
16. _____
17. _____
18. _____
19. _____
20. _____

Definitions

Write a **list word** to match each definition clue.

1. suits worn by bridegrooms _____

2. cloths used by people with colds _____

3. areas where barbecues may be held _____

4. contests showing riding skills _____

5. bugs that leave an itchy welt after biting _____

6. long strands of pasta _____

7. strongly held ideas _____

Puzzle

Fill in the crossword puzzle by writing a **list word** that is the plural form of the word given.

ACROSS
  1. jackknife
  4. broccoli
  5. kangaroo
  9. stereo
  10. memento
  13. Eskimo
  14. species

DOWN
  2. avocado
  3. embargo
  6. rodeo
  7. thief
  8. domino
  11. tariff
  12. poncho

Spelling and Writing

Proofreading

The journal entry below has ten mistakes. Use the proofreading marks to fix each mistake. Then, write the misspelled **list words** on the lines.

May 7

 Today William and I took our first cooking class. We made a pasta dish with Spagetti, broccolli, and other vegetables. We also learned a new way to serve avocadoes. Each of us received a chefs hat to wear, and we got to keep them as mementose of the Class. Afterward, we walked over to Williams house. It was raining, so we wore ponchoes. We had fun playing a game of dominows.

1. _____   2. _____

3. _____   4. _____

5. _____   6. _____

Proofreading Marks

⬭ spelling mistake

╱ make small letter

⌄ add apostrophe

Writing a Story

Write a short story that uses as many **list words** as possible. For instance, you might write about <u>kangaroos</u> wearing <u>tuxedos</u> while dining on <u>spaghetti</u>. Remember to proofread your story and fix any mistakes.

_____

_____

_____

_____

_____

_____

BONUS WORDS

heroes

confetti

videos

sheaves

soprano

Homonyms and Challenging Words

Spelling Words in Action

Why is fast, accurate fingerprint matching important?

One of a Kind Imprints

No two fingerprints are exactly alike. Every fingerprint has its own pattern of loops and swirls. Because fingerprints don't change as people age, they are truly a **personal** form of identification.

In the past, fingerprints were rarely used by police, **except** in really serious crimes. Law enforcement **personnel** had to **wait** a long time for the results of fingerprint searches. It took a great deal of **patience** to compare one set of fingerprints to another. Now, police use digital fingerprinting technology to help solve crimes.

In digital fingerprinting, prints are first scanned. Every place where the **course** of a ridge line ends is noted electronically. The digitized prints are then sent to a database. Thanks to the Internet, one suspect's fingerprints can be compared to those of millions of others to see **whether** or not a match can be found. Humans still look at the prints before they **accept** a final match, but the technology greatly shortens the process of sorting **through** records. In fact, the FBI's search engine is so powerful, it can take into account a suspect's age and physical features, including appearance and **weight**.

Maybe someday fingerprints will be used to unlock a door or operate a bank's ATM. The know-how is already at our fingertips.

Say the boldfaced words in the selection. Can you think of another word that sounds the same, but is spelled differently and has a different meaning?

137

Spelling Practice

LIST WORDS

1. through
2. threw
3. wait
4. weight
5. principle
6. principal
7. ceiling
8. sealing
9. weather
10. whether
11. coarse
12. course
13. patients
14. patience
15. except
16. accept
17. dessert
18. desert
19. personal
20. personnel

Homonyms and Challenging Words

Write a **list word** to match each clue. Then, write another **list word** that is the word's homonym or has a similar spelling.

1. rough _____ _____

2. rule _____ _____

3. calmness _____ _____

4. private _____ _____

5. pitched _____ _____

6. rain _____ _____

7. scale _____ _____

8. roof _____ _____

9. receive _____ _____

10. sand _____ _____

Missing Words

Write a **list word** that is a homonym for or sounds similar to the underlined word.

1. We are _____ the cracks in the <u>ceiling</u>.

2. I had to <u>wait</u> for the nurse to check my _____.

3. The doctor showed _____ with his young <u>patients</u>.

4. _____ or not we go will depend on the <u>weather</u> forecast.

5. The boy <u>threw</u> the ball _____ the open window.

6. <u>Except</u> for two people, they all arrived to _____ their awards.

7. He thought the <u>personnel</u> manager asked him some very _____ questions.

8. What do you think they eat for <u>dessert</u> in the _____?

9. She went <u>through</u> some practice motions before she _____ out the opening pitch.

10. "The _____ reason for this rule is the students' safety," the <u>principal</u> said.

11. Did you check the _____ outside before you decided <u>whether</u> or not to wear a raincoat?

Definitions

On the spaces at the right, write a **list word** to solve each definition clue. Then, use the letters in the shaded boxes to solve the riddle.

1. served at the end of a meal

2. a school subject

3. not fine or delicate; harsh

4. head of a school

5. remain until something happens

6. top part of a room

7. people who need a doctor's care

8. employed persons

9. other than; but

Riddle: What's the best way to communicate with a fish?

Answer: _____ ___ ___

Spelling and Writing

Proofreading

The book review below has twelve mistakes. Use the proofreading marks to fix each mistake. Then, write the **list words** correctly on the lines.

Proofreading Marks

⬭   spelling mistake

˅˅ ˅˅   add quotation marks

˄   add something

The Case of the Missing Fingerprints is such an exciting book There is nonstop action in this personnel story by a clever detective who had the patients to weight for the criminal tomake a mistake. One reviewer said, I read threw just the first ten pages, and I knew it was a book of principal." The author said, Of coarse, weather or not readers like it remainsto be seen."

1. _____

2. _____

3. _____

4. _____

5. _____

6. _____

7. _____

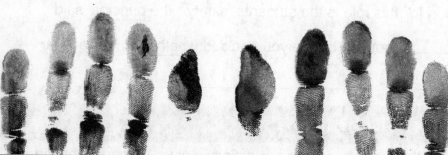

Writing a Letter

Write a letter to a company in which you describe a security device that you have invented for use in the future. Use any **list words** that you can. Remember to proofread your letter and fix any mistakes.

_____

_____

_____

_____

_____

_____

_____

BONUS WORDS

capitol

chute

stationary

reign

martial

Abbreviations

Spelling Words in Action

Can you figure out Joe Quick's message to Mrs. X?

Short and Sweet

Here's the letter that Mrs. X received from Joe Quick.

Speedy Co., Inc., 1001 Fast Blvd. Velocity, NY 00240

Dear Mrs. X,

As **Pres.** of Speedy **Co., Inc.**, I have read your **biog.** along with those of a **no.** of other applicants. I am pleased that you have applied for a position with us **vs.** one with the **govt.**; however, I believe that an **oz.** of experience is worth more than a pound of ability. Because the **vol.** of your experience is extremely limited, the only position I could possibly offer is **asst.** to our **mdse. mgr.** in the shipping **dept.** As an **ex.** of what the job entails, you might be asked to ship a two **oz. pkg.** to Taiwan, or a three **lb. pkg.** to Timbuktu. Let me know what you think as soon as possible. I'm a very busy guy.

Sincerely,
Joe Quick, Pres.
Speedy Co., Inc.

Look back at all the boldfaced abbreviations in the selection. Try to say all the words written in abbreviated form.

TIP

An abbreviation is the shortened form of a word that ends with a period. Most are spelled with the first letters of the word, as in company > co. Some are spelled with a combination of letters from the word, as in package > pkg. Others are spelled with letters not found in the original word, as in ounce > oz. and pound > lb.

LIST WORDS

1. govt.
2. pres.
3. dept.
4. co.
5. inc.
6. subj.
7. ed.
8. vol.
9. biog.
10. no.
11. ex.
12. vs.
13. pt.
14. qt.
15. oz.
16. lb.
17. mgr.
18. asst.
19. pkg.
20. mdse.

Abbreviations

Write a **list word** that is an abbreviation for the word given.

1. manager _____
2. incorporated _____
3. merchandise _____
4. versus _____
5. assistant _____
6. department _____
7. ounce _____
8. volume _____
9. subject _____
10. quart _____
11. number _____
12. biography _____
13. pound _____
14. company _____
15. government _____
16. example _____
17. package _____
18. pint _____
19. edition _____
20. president _____

Abbreviations

Write a **list word** that is the abbreviation for the underlined word in each sentence.

1. The tour guide showed us an <u>example</u> of a fossil. _____

2. We found information about England in <u>volume</u> 6 of the encyclopedia. _____

3. The first <u>edition</u> of a classic would be priceless. _____

4. Martin wants to work for the <u>government</u> when he graduates. _____

5. Dr. Tripp introduced us to her young <u>assistant</u>. _____

6. The delivery service left the <u>package</u> on our doorstep. _____

7. I bought a <u>pint</u> of milk to go with my lunch. _____

8. Carlos applied for a job at my aunt's <u>company</u>. _____

9. Have you read the <u>biography</u> of Amelia Earhart? _____

10. Seth was elected <u>president</u> of the student council. _____

Solve the Code

Use the code to find the **list words** that will complete the sentences. Write the **list words** on the lines.

A B C D E F G H I J K L M N O P Q R S T U V W X Y Z

1. Is it true that an ___ ___. of prevention is worth a ___ ___. of cure?

2. He is the ___ ___ ___. of a printing company called Ink, ___ ___ ___.

3. The company softball game will feature the sales staff ___ ___. the art ___ ___ ___ ___.

4. When you buy the ___ ___ ___ ___. for the camping trip, can you include a 2-___ ___. water bottle?

5. George Washington has been the ___ ___ ___ ___. of a ___ ___. of books.

Spelling and Writing

Proofreading

The following made-up recipe has nine mistakes. Use the proofreading marks to fix each mistake. Then, write the misspelled **list words** on the lines.

Golden Coconut Bread
1/4 cup butter
1/4 cup milk
3 os. shredded coconut
1 pakg. yeast
3 cups flour

Mix ingredients together and cover. Set the bowl bowl aside and allow the dough to to rise. Then punch knead, and push the dough. Put it in a loaf pan and bake for 1 hour.
(Recipe from Breads vrs. Muffins, Second edi., New Com., Valley Books, Inc., Anytown New York.)

1. _____   2. _____

3. _____   4. _____

5. _____

Proofreading Marks

⬭ spelling mistake

⌃ add something

℮ take out something

Writing an Informative Paragraph

Why do you think people use abbreviations? Write your ideas in an informative paragraph. Be sure to explain why they are useful or why they create problems. Try to use as many **list words** as you can. Remember to proofread your paragraph and fix any mistakes.

_____
_____
_____
_____
_____

BONUS WORDS

blvd.

mo.

tsp.

hwy.

etc.

Lessons 31–35 · Review

In lessons 31 through 35, you learned how words are spelled when suffixes are added to words that end in single consonants, **e**, or **y**. You also learned how plurals are formed and how to spell homonyms, challenging words, and abbreviations.

Check Your Spelling Notebook

Look at the words in your spelling notebook. Which words for lessons 31 through 35 did you have the most trouble with? Write them here.

_____

_____

Practice writing your troublesome words with a partner. Take turns saying the base words for words with suffixes, the singular form for plural words, homonyms, and the complete words for abbreviations.

Lesson 31

 Before adding a suffix to a word, sometimes you need to double the final consonant, as in <u>referred</u>, or drop the final **e,** as in <u>organizing</u>.

Write a **list word** that means the same or almost the same as the word given. Not all the words will be used.

List Words

combining
approved
referred
crammed
evaporated
produced
occurred
advertising
controlled
exciting
hesitation
realized

1. happened _____

2. blending _____

3. understood _____

4. thrilling _____

5. accepted _____

6. crowded _____

7. created _____

8. uncertainty _____

9. mentioned _____

10. managed _____

Before adding a suffix or ending to a word that ends in a consonant and **y**, change the **y** to **i**, as in <u>jellies</u> and <u>magnified.</u> If the word ends in a vowel and **y**, add **ed** or **s** without changing the base word, as in <u>dismayed.</u>

List Words

jellies
theories
thirstily
steadily
waterways
remedies
decaying
modified
industries
attorneys
magnified
galaxies

Circle the correctly spelled **list word**. Write the word on the line. Not all the words will be used.

1. jellies   jellys   _____

2. decaing   decaying   _____

3. magnifyed   magnified   _____

4. attorneys   attornies   _____

5. waterways   waterwaies   _____

6. theorys   theories   _____

7. modified   modifyed   _____

8. steadyly   steadily   _____

9. industryes   industries   _____

10. remedies   remedyes   _____

 Some words are the same in both the singular and plural form. To form the plural of most words that end in **f** or **fe**, change the **f** or **fe** to **v** and add **es**. For some words, including words that end in **ff**, just add **s**. Some words that end in **o** take **es** to form the plural, while others just take an **s**.

List Words

tuxedos
patios
stereos
kangaroos
thieves
rodeos
tariffs
species
ponchos
mementos
spaghetti
mosquitoes

Write the **list words** that would be found between these dictionary guide words in alphabetical order. Not all the words will be used.

mariner/triumph

1. _____   2. _____

3. _____   4. _____

5. _____   6. _____

7. _____   8. _____

9. _____   10. _____

Words that sound the same, but are spelled differently and have different meanings, are homonyms. Some words have similar spellings and pronunciations, but different meanings.

List Words

through
weight
principal
ceiling
except
weather
coarse
sealing
patients
accept
desert
personnel

Study the relationship between the first two underlined words. Then, write a **list word** that has the same relationship with the third underlined word. Not all the words will be used.

1. tall is to short as smooth is to _____
2. feet is to height as pounds is to _____
3. stairs is to up as tunnel is to _____
4. ship is to crew as office is to _____
5. sell is to buy as give is to _____
6. side is to top as wall is to _____
7. wet is to lake as dry is to _____
8. team is to captain as school is to _____
9. population is to people as climate is to _____
10. lawyer is to clients as doctor is to _____

TIP Abbreviations are shortened forms of words formed with the first letters of the word or with a combination of letters in the word. Some are formed with letters that are not in the original word.

List Words

pres.
inc.
no.
asst.
dept.
vol.
govt.
mdse.
qt.
lb.
pkg.
ex.

Write the **list words** to complete each sentence. Not all the words will be used.

1. Please give me a 1 _____ _____ of beef.
2. She would like to be _____ of the student body _____.
3. Do you have an _____ of the _____ you are selling?
4. She works in the manufacturing _____ of Speedy Co., _____.
5. What _____ is _____ S of the encyclopedia?

Show What You Know

One word is misspelled in each set of **list words**. Fill in the circle next to the **list word** that is spelled incorrectly.

1. ○ qt.   ○ pursonal   ○ principle   ○ occurred   ○ jellies

2. ○ identified   ○ except   ○ attornies   ○ vs.   ○ exciting

3. ○ no.   ○ coarse   ○ embargoes   ○ seeling   ○ evaporated

4. ○ referred   ○ theeries   ○ rodeos   ○ govt.   ○ mosquitoes

5. ○ pres.   ○ portrayd   ○ mgr.   ○ galaxies   ○ tuxedos

6. ○ patience   ○ hesitashun   ○ ed.   ○ disguised   ○ species

7. ○ desert   ○ memorized   ○ sloppily   ○ biog.   ○ avocadoes

8. ○ oz.   ○ weather   ○ Eskimos   ○ unpayved   ○ ex.

9. ○ inc.   ○ patients   ○ companees   ○ realized   ○ approved

10. ○ threw   ○ mdse.   ○ spaghetti   ○ occupied   ○ tarrifs

11. ○ dept.   ○ patios   ○ dismayed   ○ produced   ○ cramed

12. ○ ceiling   ○ organizing   ○ remedyes   ○ beliefs   ○ dessert

13. ○ dicaying   ○ vol.   ○ steadily   ○ calculation   ○ stereos

14. ○ lb.   ○ course   ○ thieves   ○ modified   ○ handkerchievs

15. ○ graduated   ○ personnel   ○ surveying   ○ pcg.   ○ ponchos

16. ○ co.   ○ wait   ○ kangeroos   ○ magnified   ○ accept

17. ○ whether   ○ abreviated   ○ subj.   ○ thirstily   ○ mementos

18. ○ dominows   ○ broccoli   ○ waterways   ○ advertising   ○ asst.

19. ○ pt.   ○ disobeyed   ○ combineing   ○ industries   ○ controlled

20. ○ throgh   ○ principal   ○ equipped   ○ weight   ○ jackknives

Writing and Proofreading Guide

1. Choose a topic to write about.

2. Write your ideas. Don't worry about mistakes.

3. Now organize your writing so that it makes sense.

4. Proofread your work.
   Use these proofreading marks to make changes.

Proofreading Marks

⬭	spelling mistake
≡	capital letter
⊙	add period
⌃	add something
⌄	add apostrophe
ℓ	take out something
¶	indent paragraph
/	make small letter
⟨⟨ ⟩⟩	add quotation marks

the electronic keyboard is a ⟨remarkible⟩ musical ʳinstrument
that can ~~can~~ produce the sounds of drums⌃pianos⌃or violins ⊙

5. Write your final copy.

   The electronic keyboard is a remarkable musical instrument
   that can produce the sounds of drums, pianos, or violins.

6. Share your writing.

Using Your Dictionary

The *Spelling Workout* Dictionary shows you many things about your spelling words.

The **entry word** listed in alphabetical order is the word you are looking up.

The **sound-spelling** or **respelling** tells how to pronounce the word.

The **part of speech** is given as an abbreviation.

im·prove (im proov′) **v. 1** to make or become better [Business has *improved*.] **2** to make good use of [She *improved* her spare time by reading.] —**im·proved′, im·prov′ing**

Sample sentences or **phrases** show how to use the word.

Other **forms** of the word are given.

The **definition** tells what the word means. There may be more than one definition.

Pronunciation Key

SYMBOL	KEY WORDS	SYMBOL	KEY WORDS	SYMBOL	KEY WORDS	SYMBOL	KEY WORDS
a	ask, fat	o͝o	look, pull	b	bed, dub	t	top, hat
ā	ape, date	yo͞o	unite, cure	d	did, had	v	vat, have
ä	car, lot	o͞o	ooze, tool	f	fall, off	w	will, always
		yo͞o	cute, few	g	get, dog	y	yet, yard
e	elf, ten	ou	out, crowd	h	he, ahead	z	zebra, haze
er	berry, care			j	joy, jump		
ē	even, meet	u	up, cut	k	kill, bake	ch	chin, arch
		ʉ	fur, fern	l	let, ball	ŋ	ring, singer
i	is, hit			m	met, trim	sh	she, dash
ir	mirror, here	ə	a in ago	n	not, ton	th	thin, truth
ī	ice, fire		e in agent	p	put, tap	*th*	then, father
			e in father	r	red, dear	zh	s in pleasure
ō	open, go		i in unity	s	sell, pass		
ô	law, horn		o in collect				
oi	oil, point		u in focus				

An Americanism is a word or usage of a word that was born in this country. An open star (☆) before an entry word or definition means that the word or definition is an Americanism.

Aa

ab·bre·vi·ate (ə brē′vē āt) *v.* to make shorter by cutting out part [The word "Street" is often *abbreviated* to "St."] —**ab·bre′vi·at·ed, ab·bre′vi·at·ing**

ab·stract (ab strakt′ *or* ab′strakt) *adj.* **1** thought of apart from a particular act or thing [A just trial is a fair one, but justice itself is an *abstract* idea.] **2** formed with designs taken from real things, but not actually like any real object or being [an *abstract* painting]

a·bun·dance (ə bun′dəns) *n.* a great supply; an amount more than enough [Where there is an *abundance* of goods, prices are supposed to go down.]

ac·cel·er·a·tor (ak sel′ər āt′ ər) *n.* a thing that accelerates an action; especially, the foot pedal that can make an automobile go faster by feeding the engine more gasoline

ac·cept (ak sept′) *v.* **1** to take what is offered or given [Will you *accept* $20 for that old bicycle?] **2** to answer "yes" to [We *accept* your invitation.] **3** to believe to be true [to *accept* a theory]

ac·cess (ak′ses) *n.* **1** a way of approach [The *access* to the park is by this road.] **2** the right or ability to approach, enter, or use [Do the students have *access* to a good library?]

ac·com·plish (ə käm′plish) *v.* to do; carry out [The task was *accomplished* in one day.]

ac·cor·di·on (ə kôr′dē ən) *n.* a musical instrument with keys, metal reeds, and a bellows: it is played by pulling out and pressing together the bellows to force air through the reeds, which are opened by fingering the keys

ac·count (ə kount′) *v.* **1** to give a detailed record of money handled [Our treasurer can *account* for every penny spent.] **2** to give a satisfactory reason; explain [How do you *account* for your absence from school?] ◆*n.* **1** *often* **accounts,** *pl.* a statement of money received, paid, or owed; record of business dealings **2** a report or story [The book is an *account* of their travels.]

a·chieve·ment (ə chēv′mənt) *n.* **1** the act of achieving something [his *achievement* of a lifelong dream] **2** something achieved by skill, work, courage, etc. [The landing of spacecraft on the moon was a remarkable *achievement.*]

ac·knowl·edge (ak näl′ij) *v.* **1** to admit to be true [I *acknowledge* that you are right.] **2** to recognize the authority of [They *acknowledged* him as their king.] **3** to recognize and answer or express one's thanks for [She *acknowledged* my greeting by smiling. Have you written to your uncle to *acknowledge* his gift?] —**ac·knowl′edged, ac·knowl′edg·ing**

ac·quaint·ance (ə kwānt′ns) *n.* **1** knowledge of a thing or person got from one's own experience [She has some *acquaintance* with modern art.] **2** a person one knows but not as a close friend

ac·tiv·i·ty (ak tiv′ə tē) *n.* **1** the condition of being active; action; motion [There was not much *activity* in the shopping mall today.] **2** normal power of mind or body; liveliness; alertness [His mental *activity* at age eighty was remarkable.] **3** something that one does besides one's regular work [We take part in many *activities* after school.] —*pl.* **ac·tiv′i·ties**

ad·di·tion (ə dish′ən) *n.* **1** an adding of numbers to get a sum or total **2** a joining of one thing to another thing [The lemonade was improved by the *addition* of sugar.] **3** a thing or part added [The gymnasium is a new *addition* to our school.]

ad·just·ment (ə just′mənt) *n.* **1** a changing or settling of things to bring them into proper order or relation [She made a quick *adjustment* to her new job.] **2** a way or device by which parts are adjusted [An *adjustment* on our television set can make the picture brighter.]

ad·mit (ad mit′) *v.* **1** to permit or give the right to enter [One ticket *admits* two persons.] **2** to accept as being true; confess [Lucy will not *admit* her mistake.] —**ad·mit′ted, ad·mit′ting**

ad·o·les·cent (ad′ə les′ ənt) *adj.* growing up; developing from a child to an adult ◆*n.* a boy or girl between childhood and adulthood; teenage person

a·dult (ə dult′ *or* ad′ult) *adj.* grown up; having reached full size and strength [an *adult* person or plant] ◆*n.* **1** a man or woman who is fully grown up; mature person **2** an animal or plant that is fully developed —**a·dult′ hood**

ad·van·tage (ad van′tij) *n.* **1** a more favorable position; better chance [My speed gave me an *advantage* over them.] **2** a thing, condition, or event that can help one; benefit [What are the *advantages* of a smaller school?]

ad·ver·tise (ad′vər tīz) *v.* **1** to tell about a product in public and in such a way as to make people want to buy it [to *advertise* cars on television] **2** to announce or ask for publicly, as in a newspaper [to *advertise* a house for rent; to *advertise* for a cook] —**ad′ver·tised, ad′ver·tis·ing** —**ad′ver·tis′er** *n.*

ad·ver·tis·ing (ad′vər tīz′iŋ) *n.* **1** an advertisement or advertisements **2** the work of preparing advertisements and getting them printed or on radio and TV [*Advertising* is a major industry in this country.]

a	ask, fat
ā	ape, date
ä	car, lot
e	elf, ten
ē	even, meet
i	is, hit
ī	ice, fire
ō	open, go
ô	law, horn
oi	oil, point
σσ	look, pull
σ̄σ̄	ooze, tool
ou	out, crowd
u	up, cut
ʉ	fur, fern
ə	a in ago
	e in agent
	e in father
	i in unity
	o in collect
	u in focus
ch	chin, arch
ŋ	ring, singer
sh	she, dash
th	thin, truth
th	then, father
zh	s in pleasure

ad·vise (ad vīz′) *v.* 1 to give advice or an opinion to [The doctor *advised* me to have an operation.] 2 to notify; inform [The letter *advised* us of the time of the meeting.] —ad·vised′, ad·vis′ing

af·fec·tion (ə fek′shən) *n.* fond or tender feeling; warm liking

af·ford (ə fôrd′) *v.* 1 to have money enough to spare for: *usually used with* can *or* be able [Can we *afford* a new car?] 2 to be able to do something without taking great risks [I can *afford* to speak frankly.]

ag·ri·cul·tur·al (ag′ri kul′ chər əl) *adj.* of agriculture; of growing crops and raising livestock; farming

ail·ment (āl′mənt) *n.* an illness; sickness

al·li·ga·tor (al′ə gāt′ər) *n.* a large lizard like the crocodile, found in warm rivers and marshes of the U.S. and China

al·might·y (ôl mīt′ē) *adj.* having power with no limit; all-powerful

al·though (ôl *thō*′) *conj.* in spite of the fact that; even if; though [*Although* the sun is shining, it may rain later.]

an·a·lyze (an′ə līz) *v.* to separate or break up any thing or idea into its parts so as to examine them and see how they fit together [to *analyze* the causes of war] —an′a·lyz′er *n.*

an·cient (ān′chənt *or* ān′shənt) *adj.* 1 of times long past; belonging to the early history of people, before about 500 A.D. 2 having lasted a long time; very old [their *ancient* quarrel]

an·gle (aŋ′gəl) *n.* 1 the shape made by two straight lines meeting in a point, or by two surfaces meeting along a line 2 the way one looks at something; point of view [Consider the problem from all *angles*.] ◆*v.* to move or bend at an angle —an′gled, an′gling

an·nounce (ə nouns′) *v.* 1 to tell the public about; proclaim [to *announce* the opening of a new store] 2 to say; tell [Mother *announced* she wasn't going with us.] —an·nounced′, an·nounc′ing

an·ten·na (an ten′ə) *n.* 1 either of a pair of slender feelers on the head of an insect, crab, lobster, etc. —*pl.* an·ten·nae (an ten′ē) *or* an·ten′nas 2 a wire or set of wires used in radio and television to send and receive signals; aerial —*pl.* an·ten′nas

an·ti·bod·y (an′ti bäd′ e) *n.* a specialized protein that is formed in the body to neutralize a particular foreign substance that is harmful, making the body immune to it —*pl.* an′ti·bod′ies

an·tic·i·pate (an tis′ə pāt′) *v.* to look forward to; expect [We *anticipate* a pleasant trip.] —an·tic′i·pat·ed, an·tic′i·pat·ing —an·tic′i·pa′tion *n.*

an·ti·dote (an′ti dōt) *n.* 1 a substance that is taken to work against the effect of a poison 2 anything that works against an evil or unwanted condition [The party was a good *antidote* to the sadness we felt.]

☆an·ti·freeze (an′ti frēz′) *n.* a liquid with a low freezing point, such as alcohol, put in the water of automobile radiators to prevent freezing

an·tique (an tēk′) *adj.* very old; of former times; made or used a long time ago ◆*n.* a piece of furniture or silverware, a tool, etc. made many years ago [They sell *antiques* of colonial America.]

an·ti·sep·tic (an′ti sep′tik) *adj.* 1 preventing infection by killing germs 2 free from living germs; sterile [an *antiseptic* room] ◆*n.* any substance used to kill germs or stop their growth, as alcohol or iodine

an·ti·so·cial (an′ti sō′shəl) *adj.* not liking to be with other people [Are you so *antisocial* that you never have visitors?]

ap·par·el (ə per′əl) *n.* clothing; garments; dress [They sell only children's *apparel*.] ◆*v.* to dress; clothe [The king was *appareled* in purple robes.] —ap·par′eled *or* ap·par′elled, ap·par′el·ing *or* ap·par′el·ling

ap·pear (ə pir′) *v.* 1 to come into sight or into being [A ship *appeared* on the horizon. Leaves appear on the tree every spring.] 2 to seem; look [He *appears* to be in good health.] 3 to come before the public [The actor will *appear* on television. The magazine *appears* monthly.] —ap·peared′

ap·plause (ə plôz′ *or* ə pläz′) *n.* the act of showing that one enjoys or approves of something, especially by clapping one's hands

ap·point·ment (ə point′mənt) *n.* 1 the act of appointing or the fact of being appointed [the *appointment* of Jones as supervisor] 2 an arrangement to meet someone or be somewhere at a certain time [an *appointment* for lunch]

ap·pre·ci·ate (ə prē′shē āt′) *v.* 1 to think well of; understand and enjoy [I now *appreciate* modern art.] 2 to recognize and be grateful for [We *appreciate* all you have done for us.] —ap·pre′ci·at·ed, ap·pre′ci·at·ing —ap·pre′ci·a′tion *n.*

ap·proach (ə prōch′) *v.* to come closer or draw nearer [We saw three riders *approaching*. Vacation time *approaches*.] —ap·proach′a·ble *adj.*

ap·prove (ə prōōv′) *v.* 1 to think or say to be good, worthwhile, etc.; be pleased with: *often used with* of [She doesn't *approve* of smoking.] 2 to give one's consent to [Has the mayor *approved* the plans?] —ap·proved′, ap·prov′ing

ar·gu·ment (är′gyōō mənt) *n.* 1 the act of arguing; discussion in which people disagree; dispute 2 a reason given for or against something [What are your *arguments* for wanting to study mathematics?]

ar·range·ment (ə rānj′mənt) *n.* **1** the act of arranging or putting in order **2** the way in which something is arranged [a new *arrangement* of pictures on the wall] **3** a preparation; plan: *usually used in pl.*, **arrangements** [*Arrangements* have been made for the party.]

as·cend (ə send′) *v.* to go up; move upward; rise; climb [The procession *ascended* the hill.]

a·shamed (ə shāmd′) *adj.* feeling shame because something bad, wrong, or foolish was done [They were *ashamed* of having broken the window.]

as·sign·ment (ə sīn′mənt) *n.* **1** the act of assigning **2** something assigned, as a lesson

asst. *abbreviation for* **assistant**

as·sure (ə shoor′) *v.* **1** to make a person sure of something; convince [What can we do to *assure* you of our friendship?] **2** to tell or promise positively [I *assure* you I'll be there.] **3** to make a doubtful thing certain; guarantee [Their gift of money *assured* the success of our campaign.] —**as·sured′, as·sur′ing**

as·ter·isk (as′tər isk) *n.* a sign in the shape of a star (*) used in printing and writing to call attention to a footnote or other explanation or to show that something has been left out

as·ter·oid (as′tər oid) *n.* any of the many small planets that move in orbits around the sun between the orbits of Mars and Jupiter

as·tro·naut (as′trə nôt *or* as′trə nät) *n.* a person trained to make rocket flights in outer space

ath·lete (ath′lēt) *n.* a person who is skilled at games, sports, or exercises in which one needs strength, skill, and speed

at·tain (ə tān′) *v.* to get by working hard; gain; achieve [to *attain* success]

at·tor·ney (ə tur′nē) *n.* a lawyer —*pl.* **at·tor′neys**

auc·tion (ôk′shən *or* äk′shən) *n.* a public sale at which each thing is sold to the person offering to pay the highest price ►*v.* to sell at an auction [They *auctioned* their furniture instead of taking it with them.]

Aus·tral·ia (ô strāl′yə *or* ä strāl′yə) **1** an island continent in the Southern Hemisphere, southeast of Asia **2** a country made up of this continent and Tasmania —**Aus·tral′ian** *adj., n.*

au·then·tic (ô then′tik *or* ä then′tik) *adj.* **1** that can be believed; reliable; true [an *authentic* news report] **2** that is genuine; real [an *authentic* antique] —**au·then′ti·cal·ly** *adv.*

au·to·mat·ic (ôt′ə mat′ik *or* ät′ ə mat′ik) *adj.* **1** done without thinking about it, as though by a machine; unconscious [Breathing is usually *automatic*.] **2** moving or working by itself [*automatic* machinery] —**au′ to·mat′i·cal·ly** *adv.*

au·tumn (ôt′əm *or* ät′əm) *n.* the season of the year that comes between summer and winter; fall ►*adj.* of or like autumn —**au·tum·nal** (ô tum′n'l) *adj.*

a·vi·a·tor (ā′vē āt′ ər) *n.* a person who flies airplanes; pilot

☆**av·o·ca·do** (av′ ə kä′dō *or* äv′ ə kä′dō) *n.* a tropical fruit that is shaped like a pear and has a thick, green or purplish skin and a single large seed: its yellow, buttery flesh is used in salads, sauces, dips, etc. —*pl.* **av′o·ca′ dos**

a·void (ə void′) *v.* **1** to keep away from; get out of the way of; shun [to *avoid* crowds] **2** to keep from happening [Try to *avoid* spilling the milk.] —**a·void′ed** —**a·void′a·ble** *adj.* —**a·void′ance** *n.*

awe·some (ô′səm *or* ä′səm) *adj.* **1** causing one to feel awe [The burning building was an *awesome* sight.] **2** showing awe [He had an *awesome* look on his face.]

awn·ing (ôn′iŋ *or* än′iŋ) *n.* a covering made of canvas, metal, or wood fixed to a frame over a window, door, etc. to keep off the sun and rain

a·wry (ə rī′) *adv., adj.* **1** twisted to one side; askew [The curtains were blown *awry* by the wind.] **2** wrong; amiss [Our plans went *awry*.]

ax·le (ak′səl) *n.* **1** a rod on which a wheel turns, or one connected to a wheel so that they turn together **2** the bar joining two opposite wheels, as of an automobile

back·gam·mon (bak′gam ən) *n.* a game played on a special board by two people: the players have fifteen pieces each, which they move after throwing dice to get a number

bad·min·ton (bad′mint′ n *or* bad′mit′ n) *n.* a game like tennis, in which a cork with feathers in one end is batted back and forth across a high net by players using light rackets

bail (bāl) *n.* money left with a law court as a guarantee that an arrested person will appear for trial ►*v.* to have an arrested person set free by giving bail

bail·iff (bāl′if) *n.* **1** a sheriff's assistant **2** an officer who has charge of prisoners and jurors in a court

bank·rupt (baŋk′rupt) *adj.* not able to pay one's debts and freed by law from the need for doing so [Any property a *bankrupt* person may still have is usually divided among those to whom the person owes money.]

a	ask, fat
ā	ape, date
ä	car, lot
e	elf, ten
ē	even, meet
i	is, hit
ī	ice, fire
ō	open, go
ô	law, horn
oi	oil, point
͡oo	look, pull
o͞o	ooze, tool
ou	out, crowd
u	up, cut
ᵾ	fur, fern
ə	a in ago
	e in agent
	e in father
	i in unity
	o in collect
	u in focus
ch	chin, arch
ŋ	ring, singer
sh	she, dash
th	thin, truth
th	then, father
zh	s in pleasure

ban·quet (baŋ′kwət) *n.* a formal dinner or feast for many people: banquets, during which speeches are made, are often held to celebrate something or to raise money

bare·ly (ber′lē) *adv.* **1** only just; no more than; scarcely [It is *barely* a year old.] **2** in a bare way; meagerly [a *barely* furnished room, with only a bed in it].

be·lief (bē lēf′) *n.* **1** a believing or feeling that certain things are true or real; faith [You cannot destroy my *belief* in the honesty of most people.] **2** trust or confidence [I have *belief* in Pat's ability.] **3** anything believed or accepted as true; opinion [What are her political *beliefs*?]

be·lieve (bē lēv′) *v.* **1** to accept as true or real [Can we *believe* that story?] **2** to have trust or confidence [I know you will win; I *believe* in you.] —**be·lieved′, be·liev′ing** —**be·liev′a·ble** *adj.* —**be·liev′er** *n.*

bi·an·nu·al (bī an′yōō əl) *adj.* coming twice a year —**bi·an′nu·al·ly** *adv.*

bi·fo·cals (bī′fō kəlz) *pl. n.* eyeglasses in which each lens has two parts, one for reading and seeing nearby objects and the other for seeing things far away

bil·lion (bil′yən) *n., adj.* a thousand millions (1,000,000,000)

bin·oc·u·lars (bi näk′yə lərz) *pl. n.* a pair of small telescopes fastened together for use with both eyes [Field glasses are a kind of *binoculars*.]

bio. *abbreviation for* **biographical** *or* **biography**

bi·ol·o·gy (bī äl′ə jē) *n.* the science of plants and animals; the study of living things and the way they live and grow —**bi·ol′o·gist** *n.*

bi·plane (bī′plān) *n.* the earlier type of airplane with two main wings, one above the other

☆**bis·cuit** (bis′kit) *n.* a small bread roll made of dough quickly raised with baking powder

bi·sect (bī sekt′ *or* bī′sekt) *v.* **1** to cut into two parts [Budapest is *bisected* by the Danube River.] **2** to divide into two equal parts [A circle is *bisected* by its diameter.]

bit·ter (bit′ər) *adj.* **1** having a strong, often unpleasant taste [The seed in a peach pit is *bitter*.] **2** full of sorrow, pain, or discomfort [Poor people often suffer *bitter* hardships.] —**bit′ter·ness** *n.*

bi·week·ly (bī′wēk′lē) *adj., adv.* once every two weeks

bleak (blēk) *adj.* **1** open to wind and cold; not sheltered; bare [the *bleak* plains] **2** cold and cutting; harsh [a *bleak* wind] **3** not cheerful; gloomy [a *bleak* story] **4** not hopeful or promising [a *bleak* future]

blvd. *abbreviation for* **boulevard**

boil (boil) *v.* **1** to bubble up and become steam or vapor by being heated [Water *boils* at 100°C.] **2** to heat a liquid until it bubbles up in this way [to *boil* water] **3** to cook in a boiling liquid [to *boil* potatoes] —**boiled**

bor·ough (bur′ō) *n.* **1** in some States, a town that has a charter to govern itself **2** one of the five main divisions of New York City

bor·row (bär′ō *or* bôr′ō) *v.* **1** to get to use something for a while by agreeing to return it later [You can *borrow* that book from the library.] **2** to take another's word, idea, etc. and use it as one's own [The Romans *borrowed* many Greek myths.] —**bor′row·er** *n.*

bough (bou) *n.* a large branch of a tree

boul·der (bōl′dər) *n.* any large rock made round and smooth by weather and water

boun·ti·ful (boun′tə fəl) *adj.* **1** giving much gladly; generous [a *bountiful* patron] **2** more than enough; plentiful [a *bountiful* harvest] —**boun′ti·ful·ly** *adv.*

bowl·ing (bōl′iŋ) *n.* a game in which each player rolls a heavy ball along a wooden lane (**bowling alley**), trying to knock down ten wooden pins at the far end

brave (brāv) *adj.* willing to face danger, pain, or trouble; not afraid; full of courage —**brav′er, brav′est** ◆*v.* to face without fear; defy [We *braved* the storm.] —**braved, brav′ing** —**brave′ly** *adv.* —**brave′ness** *n.*

brawn·y (brôn′ē *or* brän′ē) *adj.* strong and muscular —**brawn′i·er, bran′i·est** —**brawn′i·ness** *n.*

break·a·ble (brāk′ə bəl) *adj.* that can be broken or that is likely to break

brief (brēf) *adj.* **1** not lasting very long; short in time [a *brief* visit] **2** using just a few words; not wordy; concise [a *brief* news report] —**brief′ly** *adv.* —**brief′ness** *n.*

bright (brīt) *adj.* **1** shining; giving light; full of light [a *bright* star; a *bright* day] **2** very strong or brilliant in color or sound [a *bright* red; the *bright* tones of a cornet] **3** lively; cheerful [a *bright* smile] **4** having a quick mind; clever [a *bright* child] —**bright′est** ◆*adv.* in a bright manner [stars shining *bright*] —**bright′ly** *adv.* —**bright′ness** *n.*

broc·co·li (bräk′ə lē) *n.* a vegetable whose tender shoots and loose heads of tiny green buds are cooked for eating

bro·chure (brō shoor′) *n.* a pamphlet, now especially one that advertises something

bruise (brōōz) *v.* **1** to hurt a part of the body, as by a blow, without breaking the skin [Her *bruised* knee turned black-and-blue.] **2** to hurt the outside of [Some peaches fell and were *bruised*.] —**bruised, bruis′ing** ◆*n.* an injury to the outer part or flesh that does not break the skin but darkens it in color

budg·et (buj′ət) *n.* a careful plan for spending the money that is received in a certain period ◆*v.* **1** to plan the spending of money; make a budget **2** to plan in detail how to spend [I *budget* my time as well as my money.]

buf·fet (bə fā′ *or* bŏŏ fā′) *n.* platters of food on a buffet or table from which people serve themselves

build·ing (bil′diŋ) *n.* **1** anything that is built with walls and a roof; a structure, as a house, factory, or school **2** the act or work of one who builds

bun·ga·low (buŋ′gə lō) *n.* a small house with one story and an attic

cal·ci·um (kal′sē əm) *n.* a chemical element that is a soft, silver-white metal: it is found combined with other elements in the bones and teeth of animals and in limestone, marble, chalk, etc.

cal·cu·late (kal′kyŏŏ lāt′) *v.* **1** to find out by using arithmetic; compute [*Calculate* the amount of cloth you will need for the skirt.] **2** to find out by reasoning; estimate [Try to *calculate* the effect of your decision.] —**cal′cu·lat·ed, cal′cu·lat·ing**

cal·cu·la·tion (kal′kyŏŏ lā′ shən) *n.* **1** the act of calculating **2** the answer found by calculating **3** careful or shrewd thought or planning

cam·er·a (kam′ər ə) *n.* **1** a closed box for taking pictures: the light that enters when a lens or hole at one end is opened by a shutter and forms an image on the film or plate at the other end **2** that part of a TV transmitter which picks up the picture to be sent and changes it to electrical signals

cam·paign (kam pān′) *n.* a series of planned actions for getting something done [a *campaign* to get someone elected] ◆*v.* to take part in a campaign —**cam·paign′er** *n.*

Ca·na·di·an (kə nā′dē ən) *adj.* of Canada or its people ◆*n.* a person born or living in Canada

can·ta·loupe or **can·ta·loup** (kan′tə lōp) *n.* a muskmelon, especially a kind that has a hard, rough skin and sweet, juicy, orange-colored flesh

can·vas (kan′vəs) *n.* **1** a strong, heavy cloth of hemp, cotton, or linen, used for tents, sails, oil paintings, etc. **2** an oil painting on canvas

ca·pac·i·ty (kə pas′i tē) *n.* **1** the amount of space that can be filled; room for holding [a jar with a *capacity* of 2 quarts] **2** the ability to be, learn, or become; skill or fitness [the *capacity* to be an actor] —*pl.* —**ca·pac′i·ties**

cap·i·tal (kap′it′l) *adj.* where the government is located [a *capital* city] *See also* **capital letter** ◆*n.* **1** same as **capital letter 2** a city or town where the government of a state or nation is located

capital letter the form of a letter that is used to begin a sentence or a name [THIS IS PRINTED IN *CAPITAL* LETTERS.]

Cap·i·tol (kap′it′l) the building in which the U.S. Congress meets, in Washington, D.C. ◆*n.* usually **capitol** the building in which a State legislature meets

car·bo·hy·drate (kär′ bō hī′drāt) *n.* any of a group of substances made up of carbon, hydrogen, and oxygen, including the sugars and starches: carbohydrates are an important part of our diet

car·bon (kär′bən) *n.* a chemical element that is not a metal, found in all plant and animal matter: diamonds and graphite are pure carbon, while coal and charcoal are forms of impure carbon

car·bu·ret·or (kär′bə rāt′ər) *n.* the part of a gasoline engine that mixes air with gasoline spray to make the mixture that explodes in the cylinders

care·ful (ker′fəl) *adj.* **1** taking care so as not to have mistakes or accidents; cautious [Be *careful* in crossing streets.] **2** done or made with care [*careful* work] —**care′ful·ly** *adv.* —**care′ful·ness** *n.*

car·i·ca·ture (kər′i kə chər) *n.* a picture or imitation of a person or thing in which certain features or parts are exaggerated in a joking or mocking way ◆*v.* to make or be a caricature of [Cartoonists often *caricature* the president.] —**car′i·ca·tured, car′i·ca·tur·ing** —**car′i·ca·tur·ist** *n.*

car·ni·val (kär′ni vəl) *n.* an entertainment that travels from place to place, with sideshows, amusement rides, refreshments, etc.

car·tridge (kär′trij) *n.* **1** the metal or cardboard tube that holds the gunpowder and the bullet or shot for use in a firearm. **2** a small container used in a larger device, as one holding ink for a pen **3** a roll of camera film in a case **4** a unit holding the needle for a phonograph

cas·tle (kas′əl) *n.* a large building or group of buildings that was the home of a king or noble in the Middle Ages: castles had thick walls, moats, etc. to protect them against attack

cas·u·al (kazh′ŏŏ əl) *adj.* **1** happening by chance; not planned [a *casual* visit] **2** not having any particular purpose [a *casual* glance; a *casual* remark] **3** for wear at times when dressy clothes are not needed [*casual* sports clothes] —**cas′u·al·ly** *adv.* —**cas′u·al·ness** *n.*

ca·ter (kā′tər) *v.* to provide food and service [Smith's business is *catering* for large parties.] —**ca′ter·er** *n.*

a	ask, fat
ā	ape, date
ä	car, lot
e	elf, ten
ē	even, meet
i	is, hit
ī	ice, fire
ō	open, go
ô	law, horn
oi	oil, point
ŏŏ	look, pull
ōō	ooze, tool
ou	out, crowd
u	up, cut
ʉ	fur, fern
ə	a in ago
	e in agent
	e in father
	i in unity
	o in collect
	u in focus
ch	chin, arch
ŋ	ring, singer
sh	she, dash
th	thin, truth
th	then, father
zh	s in pleasure

cau·li·flow·er (kôl′ə flou ər *or* käl′ə flou ər) *n.* a kind of cabbage with a head of white, fleshy flower clusters growing tightly together

ceil·ing (sēl′iŋ) *n.* the inside top part of a room, opposite the floor

cel·e·brate (sel′ə brāt) *v.* **1** to honor a victory, the memory of something, etc. in some special way [to *celebrate* a birthday with a party; to *celebrate* the Fourth of July with fireworks] **2** to have a good time: *used only in everyday talk* [Let's *celebrate* when we finish painting the garage.] —**cel′e·brat·ed, cel′e·brat·ing** —**cel′e·bra′tion** *n.*

cel·lo (chel′ō) *n.* a musical instrument like a violin but larger and having a deeper tone: *its full name is* **violoncello** —*pl.* **cel′los** *or* **cel·li** (chel′ē)

cha·grin (shə grin′) *n.* a feeling of being embarrassed and annoyed because one has failed or has been disappointed ◆*v.* to embarrass and annoy [Our hostess was *chagrined* when the guest to be honored failed to appear.]

chal·lenge (chal′ənj) *v.* **1** to question the right or rightness of; refuse to believe unless proof is given [to *challenge* a claim; to *challenge* something said or the person who says it] **2** to call to take part in a fight or contest; dare [He *challenged* her to a game of chess.] **3** to call for skill, effort, or imagination [That puzzle will really *challenge* you.] —**chal′lenged, chal′leng·ing** ◆*n.* **1** the act of challenging [I accepted his *challenge* to a race.] **2** something that calls for much effort; hard task [Climbing Mt. Everest was a real *challenge*.]

change·a·ble (chān′jə bəl) *adj.* changing often or likely to change [*changeable* weather]

check·ers (chek′ərz) *pl. n.* a game played on a checkerboard by two players, each of whom tries to capture all 12 pieces of the other player: *used with a singular verb*

chem·is·try (kem′is trē) *n.* the science in which substances are examined to find out what they are made of, how they act under different conditions, and how they are combined or separated to form other substances

chess (ches) *n.* a game played on a chessboard by two players: each has 16 pieces (called **chess′men**) which are moved in trying to capture the other's pieces and checkmate the other's king

chis·el (chiz′əl) *n.* a tool having a strong blade with a sharp edge for cutting or shaping wood, stone, or metal ◆*v.* to cut or shape with a chisel —**chis′eled** *or* **chis′elled, chis′el·ing** *or* **chis′el·ling** —**chis′el·er** *or* **chis′el·ler** *n.*

chives (chīvz) *pl. n.* a plant related to the onion, having slender, hollow leaves that are chopped up and used for flavoring

cho·les·ter·ol (kə les′tər ôl) *n.* a waxy substance found in the body and in certain foods: when there is much of it in the blood, it is thought to cause hardening of the arteries

cho·rus (kôr′əs) *n.* **1** a group of people trained to speak or sing together [Ancient Greek plays usually had a *chorus* which explained what the actors were doing.] **2** singers and dancers who work together as a group and not as soloists, as in a musical show **3** the part of a song that is repeated after each verse; refrain [The *chorus* of "The Battle Hymn of the Republic" begins "Glory, glory, hallelujah!"] ◆*v.* to speak or sing together or at the same time [The Senators *chorused* their approval.]

chrome (krōm) *n.* chromium, especially when it is used to plate steel or other metal

chute (shoot) *n.* **1** a part of a river where the water moves swiftly **2** a waterfall **3** a long tube or slide in which things are dropped or slid down to a lower place [a laundry *chute*]

cir·cuit (sur′kət) *n.* **1** the act of going around something; course of journey in a circle [The moon's *circuit* of Earth takes about 28 days.] **2** the complete path of an electric current; also, any hookup, wiring, etc. that is connected into this path

cir·cu·la·tion (sur′kyə lā′shən) *n.* **1** free movement around from place to place [The fan kept the air in *circulation*.] **2** the movement of blood through the veins and arteries **3** the average number of copies of a magazine or newspaper sent out or sold in a certain period [Our school paper has a weekly *circulation* of 630.]

cir·cum·fer·ence (sər kum′fər əns) *n.* **1** the line that bounds a circle or other rounded figure or area **2** the length of such a line [The *circumference* of the pool is 70 feet.]

clause (klôz *or* kläz) *n.* a group of words that includes a subject and a verb, but that forms only part of a sentence [In the sentence "She will visit us if she can," "She will visit us" is a *clause* that could be a complete sentence, and "if she can" is a *clause* that depends on the first *clause*.]

clean·ly (klen′lē) *adj.* always keeping clean or kept clean —**clean′li·ness** *n.*

clev·er (klev′ər) *adj.* **1** quick in thinking or learning; smart; intelligent **2** showing skill or fine thinking [a *clever* move in chess] —**clev′er·ly** *adv.* —**clev′er·ness** *n.*

close (klōz) *v.* **1** to make no longer open; shut [*Close* the door.] **2** to bring or come to a finish; end [to *close* a speech] —**closed, clos′ing** ◆*n.* an end; finish

clothes (klōz *or* klō*th*z) *pl. n.* cloth or other material made up in different shapes and styles to wear on the body; dresses, suits, hats, underwear, etc.; garments

Co. *or* **co.** *abbreviation for* **company, county**

coarse (kôrs) *adj.* **1** made up of rather large particles; not fine [*coarse* sand] **2** rough or harsh to the touch [*coarse* cloth] **3** not polite or refined; vulgar; crude [a *coarse* joke] —**coars´est** —**coarse´ly** *adv.* —**coarse´ness** *n.*

co·coa (kō´kō) *n.* **1** a powder made from roasted cacao seeds, used in making chocolate **2** a drink made from this powder by adding sugar and hot water or milk

cof·fee (kôf´ē *or* käf´e) *n.* a dark-brown drink made by brewing the roasted and ground seeds of a tropical plant in boiling water

co·logne (kə lōn´) *n.* a sweet-smelling liquid like perfume, but not so strong

col·umn (käl´əm) *n.* **1** a long, generally round, upright support; pillar: columns usually stand in groups to hold up a roof or other part of a building, but they are sometimes used just for decoration **2** any long, upright thing like a column [a *column* of water; the spinal *column*] **3** any of the long sections of print lying side by side on a page and separated by a line or blank space [Each page of this book has two *columns*.]

com·bi·na·tion (käm´bi nā´shən) *n.* **1** the act of combining or joining [He succeeded by a *combination* of hard work and luck.] **2** the series of numbers or letters that must be turned to in the right order to open a kind of lock called a ☆**combination lock** [Most safes have a *combination lock*.]

com·bine (kəm bīn´) *v.* to come or bring together; join; unite [to *combine* work with pleasure; to *combine* chemical elements] —**com·bined´, com·bin´ing**

com·mo·tion (kə mō´shən) *n.* a noisy rushing about; confusion [There was a great *commotion* as the ship began to sink.]

com·mu·ni·cate (kə myōō´nə kāt´) *v.* to make known; give or exchange information [to *communicate* by telephone; to *communicate* ideas by the written word] —**com·mu´ni·cat·ed, com·mu´ni·cat·ing**

com·mu·ni·ca·tion (kə myōō´ni kā´shən) *n.* **1** the act of communicating [the *communication* of disease; the *communication* of news] **2** a way or means of communicating [The hurricane broke down all *communication* between the two cities.] **3** information, message, letter, etc. [They received the news in a *communication* from their lawyer.]

com·pact (kəm pakt´ *or* käm´pakt) *adj.* closely and firmly packed together [Tie the clothes in a neat, *compact* bundle.] ◆*n.* (käm´pakt) ☆a model of automobile smaller and cheaper than the standard model

com·pa·ny (kum´pə nē) *n.* a group of people; especially, a group joined together in some work or activity [a *company* of actors; a business *company*] —*pl.* **com´pa·nies**

com·pare (kəm per´) *v.* **1** to describe as being the same; liken [The sound of thunder can be *compared* to the roll of drums.] **2** to examine certain things in order to find out how they are alike or different [How do the two cars *compare* in size and price?] —**com·pared´, com·par´ing**

com·pel (kəm pel´) *v.* to make do something; force [Many men were *compelled* by the draft to serve in the armed forces.] —**com·pelled´, com·pel´ling**

com·pet·i·tor (kəm pet´i tər) *n.* a person who competes; rival [business *competitors*]

com·plaint (kəm plānt´) *n.* **1** the act of complaining or finding fault **2** something to complain about [The tenants gave a list of their *complaints* to the landlord.]

com·plete (kəm plēt´) *adj.* **1** having no parts missing; full; whole [a *complete* deck of cards] **2** finished; ended [No one's education is ever really *complete*.] **3** thorough; perfect [I have *complete* confidence in my doctor.] ◆*v.* to make complete; finish or make whole, full, perfect, etc. [When will the new road be *completed*?] —**com·plet´ed, com·plet´ing** —**com·plete´ly** *adv.*

com·po·si·tion (käm´pə zish´ən) *n.* **1** the act, work, or style of composing something **2** something composed, as a piece of writing or a musical work **3** the parts or materials of a thing and the way they are put together [We shall study the *composition* of this gas.]

com·po·sure (kəm pō´zhər) *n.* calmness of mind; self-control; serenity

com·pound (käm´pound) *n.* anything made up of two or more parts or materials; mixture ◆*adj.* made up of two or more parts ["Handbag" is a *compound* word.]

con·ceal (kən sēl´) *v.* to hide or keep secret; put or keep out of sight [I *concealed* my amusement. The thief *concealed* the stolen jewelry in a pocket.] —**con·cealed´**

con·ceit (kən sēt´) *n.* too high an opinion of oneself; vanity [His *conceit* shows when he talks about how bright he is.] —**con·ceit´ed** *adj.*

con·ces·sion·aire (kən sesh ə ner´) *n.* the owner or operator of a business, such as a refreshment stand

con·demn (kən dem´) *v.* **1** to say that a person or thing is wrong or bad [We *condemn* cruelty to animals.] **2** to declare to be guilty; convict [A jury tried and *condemned* them.] —**con·dem·na·tion** (kän´dem nā´shən) *n.*

con·fer·ence (kän´fər əns) *n.* a meeting of people to discuss something [A *conference* on education was held in Washington.]

con·fet·ti (kən fet´ē) *pl. n. used with a singular verb*: bits of colored paper thrown about at carnivals and parades [*Confetti* was all over the street.]

con·fir·ma·tion (kän´fər mā´shən) *n.* **1** the act of confirming, or making sure **2** something that confirms or proves

a	ask, fat
ā	ape, date
ä	car, lot
e	elf, ten
ē	even, meet
i	is, hit
ī	ice, fire
ō	open, go
ô	law, horn
oi	oil, point
oo	look, pull
ōō	ooze, tool
ou	out, crowd
u	up, cut
ʉ	fur, fern
ə	a in ago
	e in agent
	e in father
	i in unity
	o in collect
	u in focus
ch	chin, arch
ŋ	ring, singer
sh	she, dash
th	thin, truth
th	then, father
zh	s in pleasure

157

con·fuse (kən fyo͞oz′) **v. 1** to mix up, especially in the mind; put into disorder; bewilder [You will *confuse* us with so many questions.] **2** to fail to see or remember the difference between; mistake [You are *confusing* me with my twin.] —**con·fused′, con·fus′ing** —**con·fus·ed·ly** (kən fyo͞oz′id lē) *adv.*

con·ju·gate (kän′jə gāt) **v.** to list the different forms of a verb in person, number, and tense [*Conjugate* "to be," beginning "I am, you are, he is."] —**con′ju·gat·ed, con′ju·gat·ing** —**con′ju·ga′tion** *n.*

con·science (kän′shəns) **n.** a sense of right and wrong; feeling that keeps one from doing bad things [My *conscience* bothers me after I tell a lie.]

con·scious (kän′shəs) **adj.** aware of one's own feelings or of things around one [*conscious* of a slight noise]

con·sum·er (kən so͞om′ər) **n.** a person or thing that consumes; especially, a person who buys goods for his own needs and not to sell to others or to use in making other goods for sale

con·tain·er (kən tān′ər) **n.** a thing for holding something; box, can, bottle, pot, etc.

con·trol (kən trōl′) **v. 1** to have the power of ruling, guiding, or managing [A thermostat *controls* the heat.] **2** to hold back; curb [*Control* your temper!] —**con·trolled′, con·trol′ling** ◆*n.* **1** power to direct or manage [He's a poor coach, with little *control* over the team.] **2** a part or thing that controls a machine [the *controls* of an airplane] —**con·trol′la·ble** *adj.*

con·ven·tion (kən ven′shən) **n.** a meeting of members or delegates from various places, held every year or every few years [a political *convention*; a national *convention* of English teachers]

con·ver·sa·tion (kän′vər sā′shən) **n.** a talk or a talking together

con·vert·i·ble (kən vʉrt′ə bəl) **adj.** that can be converted [Matter is *convertible* into energy.] ◆*n.* ☆an automobile with a top that can be folded back

con·vey (kən vā′) **v. 1** to take from one place to another; carry or transport [The cattle were *conveyed* in trucks to the market.] **2** to make known; give [Please *convey* my best wishes to them.] —**con·veyed′**

corps (kôr) **n. 1** a section or a special branch of the armed forces [the Marine *Corps*] **2** a group of people who are joined together in some work or organization [a press *corps*]

cor·re·spond·ence (kôr′ə spän′dens) **n. 1** the writing and receiving of letters [to engage in *correspondence*] **2** the letters written or received [The *correspondence* concerning the new contract is in the file.]

coun·sel (koun′səl) **n. 1** the act of talking together in order to exchange ideas or opinions; discussion [They took *counsel* before making the decision.] **2** the lawyer or lawyers who are handling a case ◆*v.* to give advice to; advise [a person who *counsels* students] —**coun′seled** or **coun′selled, coun′sel·ing** or **coun′sel·ling**

coun·se·lor or **coun·sel·lor** (koun′sə lər) **n. 1** a person who advises; advisor **2** a lawyer **3** a person in charge of children at a camp

coun·ter·act (koun tər akt′) **v.** to act against; to stop or undo the effect of [The rains will help *counteract* the dry spell.]

coun·ter·at·tack (koun′tər ə tak) **n.** an attack made in return for another attack ◆*v.* to attack so as to answer the enemy's attack

coun·ter·bal·ance (koun′tər bal′əns) **n.** a weight, power, or force that balances or acts against another

coun·ter·feit (koun′tər fit) **adj.** made in imitation of the real thing so as to fool or cheat people [*counterfeit* money] ◆*n.* a thing that is counterfeit ◆*v.* to make an imitation of in order to cheat [to *counterfeit* money] —**coun′ter·feit·er**

coun·ter·part (koun′tər pärt) **n. 1** a person or thing that is very much like another [He is his father's *counterpart*.] **2** a thing that goes with another thing to form a set [This cup is the *counterpart* to that saucer.]

course (kôrs) **n. 1** a going on from one point to the next; progress in space or time [the *course* of history; the *course* of a journey] **2** a way or path along which something moves; channel, track, etc. [a golf *course*; race*course*] **3** a part of a meal served at one time [The main *course* was roast beef.] **4** a complete series of studies [I took a business *course* in high school.] **5** any of these studies [a mathematics *course*] —**coursed, cours′ing**

cow·ard (kou′ərd) **n.** a person who is unable to control his fear and so shrinks from danger or trouble

cram (kram) **v. 1** to pack full or too full [Her suitcase is *crammed* with clothes.] **2** to stuff or force [He *crammed* the papers into a drawer.] **3** to study many facts in a hurry, as for a test —**crammed, cram′ming**

cray·on (krā′ən *or* krā′än) **n.** a small stick of chalk, charcoal, or colored wax, used for drawing or writing ◆*v.* to draw with crayons

cra·zy (krā′zē) **adj. 1** mentally ill; insane **2** very foolish or mad [a *crazy* idea] **3** very eager or enthusiastic: *used only in everyday talk* [I'm *crazy* about the movies.] —**cra′zi·er, cra′zi·est** —**cra′zi·ly** *adv.* —**cra′zi·ness** *n.*

cre·a·tion (krē ā′shən) *n.* **1** the act of creating **2** the whole world and everything in it; universe **3** anything created or brought into being

cre·a·tive (krē ā′tiv) *adj.* creating or able to create; inventive; having imagination and ability —**cre·a·tiv·i·ty** (krē′ā tiv′ə tē) *n.*

crepe or **crêpe** (krāp) *n.* **1** a thin, crinkled cloth **2** (krāp *or* krep) a very thin pancake, rolled up or folded with a filling: *usually* crêpe

cres·cent (kres′ənt) *n.* **1** the shape of the moon in its first or last quarter **2** anything shaped like this, as a curved bun or roll ◆*adj.* shaped like a crescent

croc·o·dile (kräk′ə dīl) *n.* a large lizard like the alligator, that lives in and near tropical rivers: it has a thick, tough skin, a long tail, large jaws, and pointed teeth

crois·sant (krə sänt′) *n.* a rich, flaky bread roll made in the form of a crescent

cro·quet (krō kā′) *n.* an outdoor game in which the players use mallets to drive a wooden ball through hoops in the ground

cru·el (krōo′əl) *adj.* **1** liking to make others suffer; having no mercy or pity [The *cruel* Pharaoh made slaves of the Israelites.] **2** causing pain and suffering [*cruel* insults; a *cruel* winter] —**cru·el·est** —**cru·el·ly** *adv.*

cruise (krōoz) *v.* **1** to sail or drive about from place to place, as for pleasure or in searching for something **2** to move smoothly at a speed that is not strained [The airplane *cruised* at 300 miles per hour.] —**cruised, cruis′ing** ◆*n.* a ship voyage from place to place for pleasure

crumb (krum) *n.* a tiny piece broken off, as of bread or cake

crutch (kruch) *n.* a support used under the arm by a lame person to help in walking —*pl.* **crutch′es**

crys·tal (kris′təl) *n.* **1** a clear, transparent quartz that looks like glass **2** a very clear, sparkling glass **3** something made of such glass, as a goblet or bowl **4** any of the regularly shaped pieces into which many substances are formed when they become solids: a crystal has a number of flat surfaces in an orderly arrangement [Salt, sugar, and snow are made up of *crystals*.] ◆*adj.* made of crystal

cul·ture (kul′chər) *n.* **1** improvement by study or training, especially of the mind, manners, and taste; refinement **2** the ideas, skills, arts, tools, and way of life of a certain people in a certain time; civilization [the *culture* of the Aztecs] —**cul′tur·al** *adj.* —**cul′tur·al·ly** *adv.*

cur·few (kʉr′fyōo) *n.* a time in the evening beyond which certain persons or all people must not be on the streets [Our town has a nine o'clock *curfew* for children.]

☆**cur·ren·cy** (kʉr′ən sē) *n.* the money in common use in any country; often, paper money —*pl.* **cur′ren·cies**

cus·tom (kus′təm) *n.* **1** a usual thing to do; habit [It is my *custom* to have tea after dinner.] **2** something that has been done for a long time and so has become the common or regular thing to do [the *custom* of eating turkey on Thanksgiving] **3 customs,** *pl.* taxes collected by a government on goods brought in from other countries; also, the government agency that collects these taxes ◆*adj.* made or done to order [*custom* shoes]

cym·bal (sim′bəl) *n.* a round brass plate, used in orchestras and bands, that makes a sharp, ringing sound when it is hit: cymbals can be used in pairs that are struck together

cy·press (sī′prəs) *n.* an evergreen tree with cones and dark leaves

Dd

damp (damp) *adj.* slightly wet; moist [*damp* clothes; *damp* weather] ◆*n.* a slight wetness; moisture [Rains caused *damp* in the basement.] —**damp′ly** *adv.* —**damp′ness** *n.*

dare (der) *v.* **1** to face bravely or boldly; defy [The hunter *dared* the dangers of the jungle.] **2** to call on someone to do a certain thing in order to show courage; challenge [She *dared* me to swim across the lake.] —**dared, dar′ing** ◆*n.* a challenge to prove that one is not afraid [I accepted her *dare* to swim across the lake.]

dar·ing (der′iŋ) *adj.* bold enough to take risks; fearless ◆*n.* bold courage

de·bate (dē bāt′) *v.* **1** to give reasons for or against; argue about something, especially in a formal contest between two opposite sides [The Senate *debated* the question of foreign treaties.] **2** to consider reasons for and against [I *debated* the problem in my own mind.] —**de·bat′ed, de·bat′ing** ◆*n.* the act of debating something; discussion or formal argument —**de·bat′er** *n.*

de·brief (dē brēf′) *v.* to question someone who has ended a mission, to get information [The astronaut was *debriefed* after the space flight.]

debt (det) *n.* **1** something that one owes to another [a *debt* of $25; a *debt* of gratitude] **2** the condition of owing [I am greatly in *debt* to you.]

de·cay (dē kā′) *v.* **1** to become rotten by the action of bacteria [The fallen apples *decayed* on the ground.] **2** to fall into ruins; become no longer sound, powerful, rich, beautiful, etc. [Spain's power *decayed* after its fleet was destroyed.] —**de·cay′ing** ◆*n.* a rotting or falling into ruin

a	ask, fat
ā	ape, date
ä	car, lot
e	elf, ten
ē	even, meet
i	is, hit
ī	ice, fire
ō	open, go
ô	law, horn
oi	oil, point
oo	look, pull
o͞o	ooze, tool
ou	out, crowd
u	up, cut
ʉ	fur, fern
ə	a in ago
	e in agent
	e in father
	i in unity
	o in collect
	u in focus
ch	chin, arch
ŋ	ring, singer
sh	she, dash
th	thin, truth
th	then, father
zh	s in pleasure

de·cent (dē′sənt) *adj.* **1** proper and fitting; not to be ashamed of; respectable [*decent* manners; *decent* language] **2** fairly good; satisfactory [a *decent* wage] **3** kind; generous; fair [It was *decent* of you to lend me your car.] —**de′cent·ly** *adv.*

de·cep·tive (dē sep′tiv) *adj.* deceiving; not what it seems to be —**de·cep′tive·ly** *adv.*

dec·i·bel (des′ə bəl) *n.* a unit for measuring the relative loudness of sound

de·cline (dē klīn′) *v.* **1** to bend or slope downward [The lawn *declines* to the sidewalk.] **2** to become less in health, power, or value; decay [A person's strength usually *declines* in old age.] **3** to refuse something, especially in a polite way [I am sorry I must *decline* your invitation.] ◆*n.* **1** the process or result of becoming less, smaller, or weaker; decay [a *decline* in prices] **2** the last part [the *decline* of life] **3** a downward slope [We slid down the *decline*.]

dec·o·ra·tion (dek′ə rā′ shən) *n.* **1** anything used for decorating; ornament [*decorations* for the birthday party] **2** a medal, ribbon, etc. given as a sign of honor

de·crease (dē krēs′ or dē′krēs) *v.* to make or become gradually less or smaller [She has *decreased* her weight by dieting. The pain is *decreasing*.] —**de·creased′, de·creas′ing** ◆*n.* a decreasing or growing less [a *decrease* in profits]

ded·i·cate (ded′i kāt′) *v.* **1** to set aside for a special purpose [The doctor has *dedicated* her life to cancer research.] **2** to say at the beginning of a book, etc. that it was written in honor of, or out of affection for, a certain person [He *dedicated* his novel to his wife.] —**ded′i·cat′ed, ded′i·cat′ing** —**ded′i·ca′tion** *n.*

de·fi·cien·cy (dē fish′ən sē) *n.* an amount short of what is needed; shortage [A *deficiency* of vitamin C causes scurvy.] —*pl.* **de·fi′cien·cies**

de·lete (dē lēt′) *v.* to take out or cross out something printed or written [Her name has been *deleted* from the list of members.] —**de·let′ed, de·let′ing** —**de·le·tion** (di lē′shən) *n.*

de·liv·er·y (dē liv′ər ē) *n.* the act of delivering; a transferring or distributing [daily *deliveries* to customers; the *delivery* of a prisoner into custody] —*pl.* **de·liv′er·ies**

den·im (den′im) *n.* a coarse cotton cloth that will take hard wear and is used for work clothes or play clothes

de·pend (dē pend′) *v.* **1** to be controlled or decided by [The attendance at the game *depends* on the weather.] **2** to put one's trust in; be sure of [You can't *depend* on the weather.] **3** to rely for help or support [They *depend* on their parents for money.] —**de·pend′ed**

de·pos·it (dē päz′it) *v.* **1** to place for safekeeping, as money in a bank **2** to give as part payment or as a pledge [They *deposited* $500 on a new car.] **3** to lay down [I *deposited* my books on the chair. The river *deposits* tons of mud at its mouth.] —**de·pos′it·ed** ◆*n.* **1** something placed for safekeeping, as money in a bank **2** something left lying, as sand, clay, or minerals deposited by the action of wind, water, or other forces of nature

dept. *abbreviation for* **department**

depth (dep*th*) *n.* **1** the fact of being deep, or how deep a thing is; deepness [the *depth* of the ocean; a closet five feet in *depth*; the *depth* of a color; the great *depth* of their love] **2** the middle part [the *depth* of winter]

de·scend (dē send′) *v.* **1** to move down to a lower place [to *descend* from a hilltop; to *descend* a staircase] **2** to become lesser or smaller [Prices have *descended* during the past month.] **3** to come from a certain source [They are *descended* from pioneers.] —**de·scend′ing**

des·ert (dez′ərt) *n.* a dry sandy region with little or no plant life ◆*adj.* **1** of or like a desert **2** wild and not lived in [a *desert* island]

de·serve (də zurv′) *v.* to have a right to; be one that ought to get [This matter *deserves* thought. You *deserve* a scolding.] —**de·served′, de·serv′ing** —**de·serv′ed·ly** *adv.*

de·serv·ing (də zur′viŋ) *adj.* that ought to get help or a reward [a *deserving* student]

de·sign·er (də zī′nər) *n.* a person who designs or makes original plans [a dress *designer*]

de·sir·a·ble (də zīr′ə bəl) *adj.* worth wanting or having; pleasing, excellent, beautiful, etc. —**de·sir′a·bil′i·ty** *n.* —**de·sir′a·bly** *adv.*

de·spair (də sper′) *n.* a giving up or loss of hope [Sam is in *despair* of ever getting a vacation.] ◆*v.* to lose or give up hope [The prisoner *despaired* of ever being free again.]

☆**des·sert** (də zurt′) *n.* something sweet served at the end of a meal, as fruit, pie, or cake

de·struc·tive (dē struk′tiv) *adj.* destroying or likely to destroy [a *destructive* windstorm]

de·vel·op (dē vel′əp) *v.* **1** to make or become larger, fuller, better, etc.; grow or expand [The seedling *developed* into a tree. Reading *develops* one's knowledge.] **2** to bring or come into being and work out gradually; evolve [Dr. Salk *developed* a vaccine for polio. Mold *developed* on the cheese.] **3** to treat an exposed photographic film or plate with chemicals, so as to show the picture

di·ag·o·nal (dī ag′ə nəl) *adj.* **1** slanting from one corner to the opposite corner, as of a square **2** going in a slanting direction [a tie with *diagonal* stripes] ◆*n.* a diagonal line, plane, course, or part —**di·ag′o·nal·ly** *adv.*

dic·tion·ar·y (dik′shə ner′ē) *n.* a book in which the words of a language, or of some special field, are listed in alphabetical order with their meanings, pronunciations, and other information [a school *dictionary*] —*pl.* **dic·tion·ar′ies**

die·sel (dē′zəl *or* dē′səl) *n. often* **Diesel 1** a kind of internal-combustion engine that burns fuel oil by using heat produced by compressing air; *also called* **diesel engine** or **diesel motor 2** a locomotive or motor vehicle with such an engine

dif·fer·ence (dif′ər əns *or* dif′rəns) *n.* **1** the state of being different or unlike [the *difference* between right and wrong] **2** a way in which people or things are unlike [a *difference* in size] **3** the amount by which one quantity is greater or less than another [The *difference* between 11 and 7 is 4.]

dif·fuse (di fyoos′) *adj.* **1** spread out; not centered in one place [This lamp gives *diffuse* light.] **2** using more words than are needed; wordy [a *diffuse* style of writing] ◆*v.* (di fyooz′) **1** to spread out in every direction; scatter widely [to *diffuse* light] **2** to mix together [to *diffuse* gases or liquids]

di·gest (di jest′ *or* dī jest′) *v.* to change food in the stomach and intestines into a form that can be used by the body [Small babies cannot *digest* solid food.] —**di·gest′i·ble** *adj.*

di·no·saur (dī′nə sôr) *n.* any of a group of reptiles that lived millions of years ago: dinosaurs had four legs and a long, tapering tail, and some were almost 100 feet long

dis·ap·point (dis ə point′) *v.* to fail to give or do what is wanted, expected, or promised; leave unsatisfied [I am *disappointed* in the weather. You promised to come, but *disappointed* us.]

dis·ap·point·ment (dis′ə point′mənt) *n.* **1** a disappointing or being disappointed [one's *disappointment* over not winning] **2** a person or thing that disappoints [The team is a *disappointment* to us.]

dis·ci·pline (dis′ə plin) *n.* **1** training that teaches one to obey rules and control one's behavior [the strict *discipline* of army life] **2** the result of such training; self-control; orderliness [The pupils showed perfect *discipline*.] ◆*v.* **1** to train in discipline [Regular chores help to *discipline* children.] **2** to punish —**dis′ci·plined, dis′ci·plin·ing**

dis·count (dis′kount) *n.* an amount taken off a price, bill, or debt [He got a 10% *discount* by paying cash, so the radio cost $90 instead of $100.] ◆*v.* (dis kount′) **1** to take off a certain amount as a discount from a price, bill, etc. **2** to tend not to believe

dis·ease (di zēz′) *n.* a condition of not being healthy; sickness; illness [Chicken pox is a common childhood *disease*. Some fungi cause *disease* in animals and plants.] —**dis·eased′** *adj.*

dis·guise (dis gīz′) *v.* **1** to make seem so different as not to be recognized [to *disguise* oneself with a false beard; to *disguise* one's voice] **2** to hide so as to keep from being known [She *disguised* her dislike of him by being very polite.] —**dis·guised′, dis·guis′ing** ◆*n.* any clothes, makeup, way of acting, etc. used to hide who or what one is

dis·may (dis mā′) *v.* to fill with fear or dread so that one is not sure of what to do [We were *dismayed* at the sight of the destruction.] —**dis·mayed′** ◆*n.* loss of courage or confidence when faced with trouble or danger [The doctor's report filled her with *dismay*.]

dis·o·bey (dis′ ō bā′) *v.* to fail to obey or refuse to obey —**dis·o·beyed′**

dis·tort (di stôrt′) *v.* **1** to twist out of its usual shape or look [The old mirror gave a *distorted* reflection.] **2** to change so as to give a false idea [The facts were *distorted*.] —**dis·tor′tion** *n.*

dis·turb·ance (di stʉr′bəns) *n.* **1** a disturbing or being disturbed **2** anything that disturbs **3** noisy confusion; uproar; disorder

di·vi·sor (də vī′zər) *n.* the number by which another number is divided [In 6 ÷ 3 = 2, the number 3 is the *divisor*.]

dom·i·no (däm′ə nō) *n.* a small, oblong piece of wood, plastic, etc. marked with dots on one side: a set of these pieces is used in playing the game called **dominoes**, in which the halves are matched —*pl.* **dom′i·noes** *or* **dom′i·nos**

doubt (dout) *v.* to think that something may not be true or right; be unsure of; question [I *doubt* that those are the correct facts. Never *doubt* my love.] ◆*n.* a doubting; being unsure of something [I have no *doubt* that you will win.] —**doubt′er** *n.*

dough·nut (dō′nut) *n.* a small, sweet cake fried in deep fat, usually shaped like a ring

down·stream (doun′strēm) *adv., adj.* in the direction in which a stream is flowing

draw·back (drô′bak *or* drä′bak) *n.* a condition that acts against one; hindrance; disadvantage

drought (drout) *or* **drouth** (drouth) *n.* a long period of dry weather, with little or no rain

drow·sy (drou′zē) *adj.* **1** sleepy or half asleep **2** making one feel sleepy [*drowsy* music] —**drow′si·er, drow′si·est** —**drow′si·ly** *adv.* —**drow′si·ness** *n.*

du·ti·ful (doot′ə fəl *or* dyoot′ə fəl) *adj.* doing or ready to do one's duty; having a proper sense of duty [a *dutiful* parent] —**du′ti·ful·ly** *adv.*

a	ask, fat
ā	ape, date
ä	car, lot
e	elf, ten
ē	even, meet
i	is, hit
ī	ice, fire
ō	open, go
ô	law, horn
oi	oil, point
oo	look, pull
o͞o	ooze, tool
ou	out, crowd
u	up, cut
ʉ	fur, fern
ə	a in ago
	e in agent
	e in father
	i in unity
	o in collect
	u in focus
ch	chin, arch
ŋ	ring, singer
sh	she, dash
th	thin, truth
th	then, father
zh	s in pleasure

ear·nest (ʉr'nəst) *adj.* not light or joking; serious or sincere [an *earnest* wish] —**ear'nest·ly** *adv.* —**ear'nest·ness** *n.*

earn (ʉrn) *v.* **1** to get as pay for work done [She *earns* $10 an hour.] **2** to get or deserve because of something done [He *earned* a medal for swimming.] **3** to get as profit [Your savings *earn* 5% interest.] —**earn'ing** —**earn'ings** *pl. n.*

ear·ring (ir'riŋ) *n.* an ornament worn on or in the lobe of the ear

earth·en·ware (ʉrth'ən wer) *n.* the coarser sort of dishes, vases, jars, etc. made of baked clay

ea·sel (ē'zəl) *n.* a standing frame for holding an artist's canvas, a chalkboard, etc.

east·ward (ēst'wərd) *adv., adj.* in the direction of the east [an *eastward* journey; to travel *eastward*]

ech·o (ek'ō) *n.* sound heard again when sound waves bounce back from a surface —*pl.* **ech'oes** ◆*v.* —**ech'oed, ech'o·ing**

e·clipse (e klips) *n.* a hiding of all or part of the sun by the moon when it passes between the sun and the earth (called a **solar eclipse**); also, a hiding of the moon by the earth's shadow (called a **lunar eclipse**) ◆*v.* to cause an eclipse of; darken —**e·clipsed', e·clips'ing**

e·col·o·gy (ē käl'ə jē) *n.* the science that deals with the relations between all living things and the conditions that surround them —**e·col'o·gist** *n.*

ed. *abbreviation for:* **1** edition *or* editor —*pl.* **eds. 2** education

ed·u·ca·tion (ej'ə kā'shən) *n.* **1** the act or work of educating or training people; teaching [a career in *education*] **2** the things a person learns by being taught; schooling or training [a high-school *education*]

ef·fec·tive (ə fek'tiv) *adj.* **1** making a certain thing happen; especially, bringing about the result wanted [an *effective* remedy] **2** in force or operation; active [The law becomes *effective* Monday.] **3** making a strong impression on the mind; impressive [an *effective* speaker] —**ef·fec'tive·ly** *adv.*

ef·fi·cient (ə fish'ənt) *adj.* bringing about the result or effect wanted with the least waste of time, effort, or materials [an *efficient* method of production; an *efficient* manager] —**ef·fi'cien·cy** *n.*

E·gyp·tian (ē jip'shən) *adj.* of Egypt, its people, or their culture ◆*n.* **1** a person born or living in Egypt **2** the language of the ancient Egyptians: modern Egyptians speak Arabic

e·lec·tric·i·ty (ē lek'tris'i tē) *n.* a form of energy that comes from the movement of electrons and protons: it can be produced by friction (as by rubbing wax with wool), by chemical action (as in a storage battery), or by induction (as in a dynamo or generator): electricity is used to produce light, heat, power, etc. electricity moving in a stream, as through a wire, is called **electric current**

em·bank·ment (im baŋk'mənt) *n.* a long mound or wall of earth, stone, etc. used to keep back water, hold up a roadway, etc.

em·bar·go (em bär'gō) *n.* a government order that forbids certain ships to leave or enter its ports —*pl.* **em·bar'goes** ◆*v.* to put an embargo upon —**em·bar'goed, em·bar'go·ing**

em·bat·tle (em bat'l) *v.* to prepare for battle —**em·bat'tled, em·bat'tling**

em·bel·lish (em bel'ish) *v.* to decorate or improve by adding something [to *embellish* a talk with details] —**em·bel'lish·ment** *n.*

em·bit·ter (em bit'ər) *v.* to make bitter; make feel angry or hurt [He was *embittered* by her remark.]

em·bla·zon (em blā'zən) *v.* **1** to decorate with bright colors or in a rich, showy way [The bandstand was *emblazoned* with bunting.] **2** to mark with an emblem [The shield was *emblazoned* with a golden lion.]

em·broi·der·y (em broi'dər ē) *n.* **1** the art or work of embroidering **2** an embroidered decoration —*pl.* **em·broi'der·ies**

em·pha·size (em'fə sīz) *v.* to give special force or attention to; stress [I want to *emphasize* the importance of honesty.] —**em'pha·sized, em'pha·siz·ing**

em·ploy·ment (e ploi'mənt) *n.* **1** the condition of being employed **2** one's work, trade, or profession

em·pow·er (em pou'ər) *v.* to give certain power or rights to; authorize [The warrant *empowered* the police to search the house.]

emp·ty (emp'tē) *adj.* having nothing or no one in it; not occupied; vacant [an *empty* jar; an *empty* house] —**emp'ti·er, emp'ti·est** ◆*v.* **1** to make or become empty [The auditorium was *emptied* in ten minutes.] **2** to take out or pour out [*Empty* the dirty water in the sink.] **3** to flow out; discharge [The Amazon *empties* into the Atlantic.] —**emp'tied, emp'ty·ing** —**emp'ti·ly** *adv.* —**emp'ti·ness** *n.* —*pl.* **emp'ties**

en·com·pass (en kum'pəs) *v.* **1** to surround on all sides; enclose or encircle [a lake *encompassed* by mountains] **2** to have in it; contain or include [A dictionary *encompasses* much information.]

en·cour·age (en kʉr'ij) *v.* **1** to give courage or hope to; make feel more confident [Praise *encouraged* her to try harder.] **2** to give help to; aid; promote [Rain *encourages* the growth of plants.] —**en·cour'aged, en·cour'ag·ing** —**en·cour'age·ment** *n.*

en·dan·ger (en dān′jər) **v.** to put in danger or peril [to *endanger* one's life]

en·dow (en dou′) **v.** 1 to provide with some quality or thing [a person *endowed* with musical talent; a land *endowed* with natural resources] 2 to provide a gift of money to a college, hospital, museum, etc., that will bring a regular income to help support it —**en·dow′ment n.**

en·gage (en gāj′) **v.** 1 to promise to marry [Harry is *engaged* to Grace.] 2 to promise or undertake to do something [She *engaged* to tutor the child after school.] 3 to draw into; involve [She *engaged* him in conversation.] —**en·gaged′, en·gag′ing**

Eng·lish (iŋ′glish) **adj.** of England, its people, language, etc. ◆**n.** 1 the language spoken in England, the U.S., Canada, Australia, New Zealand, Liberia, etc. 2 a course in school for studying the English language or English literature

en·grave (en grāv′) **v.** 1 to carve or etch letters, designs, etc. on [a date *engraved* on a building] 2 to cut or etch a picture, lettering, etc. into a metal plate, wooden block, etc. to be used for printing; also, to print from such a plate, block, etc. [an *engraved* invitation] —**en·graved′, en·grav′ing** —**en·grav′er n.**

en·light·en (en līt′n) **v.** to get someone to have knowledge or know the truth; get rid of ignorance or false beliefs; inform —**en·light′en·ment n.**

en·list (en list′) **v.** 1 to join or get someone to join; especially, to join some branch of the armed forces [She *enlisted* in the navy. This office *enlisted* ten new recruits.] 2 to get the support of [Try to *enlist* your parents' help.] —**en·list′ment n.**

en·roll or **en·rol** (en rōl′) **v.** 1 to write one's name in a list, as in becoming a member; register [New students must *enroll* on Monday.] 2 to make someone a member [We want to *enroll* you in our swim club.] —**en·rolled′, en·roll′ing**

en·roll·ment or **en·rol·ment** (en rōl′mənt) **n.** 1 the act of enrolling 2 the number of people enrolled

en·sure (en shoor′) **v.** 1 to make sure or certain [Good weather will *ensure* a large attendance.] 2 to make safe; protect [Seat belts help to *ensure* you against injury in a car accident.] —**en·sured′, en·sur′ing**

e·qui·lat·er·al (ē′kwi lat′ər əl) **adj.** having all sides equal in length

e·quip (ē kwip′) **v.** to provide with what is needed; outfit [The soldiers were *equipped* for battle. The car is *equipped* with power brakes.] —**e·quipped′, e·quip′ping**

☆**es·ca·la·tor** (es′kə lāt′ ər) **n.** a stairway whose steps are part of an endless moving belt, for carrying people up or down

es·cape (e skāp′) **v.** 1 to break loose; get free, as from prison 2 to keep from getting hurt, killed, etc.; keep safe from; avoid [Very few people *escaped* the plague.] —**es·caped′, es·cap′ing** ◆**n.** 1 the act of escaping [The prisoners made their plans for an *escape*.] 2 a way of escaping [The fire closed in and there seemed to be no *escape*.]

Es·ki·mo (es′kə mō) **n.** 1 a member of a group of people who live mainly in the arctic regions of the Western Hemisphere —**pl. Es′ki·mos** or **Es′ki·mo** 2 the language of the Eskimos ◆**adj.** of the Eskimos

es·say (es′ā) **n.** a short piece of writing on some subject, giving the writer's personal ideas

es·teem (e stēm′) **v.** to have a good opinion of; regard as valuable; respect [I *esteem* his praise above all other.] ◆**n.** good opinion; high regard; respect [to hold someone in high *esteem*]

etc. *abbreviation for* **et cetera**

e·vap·o·rate (ē vap′ə rāt) **v.** 1 to change into vapor [Heat *evaporates* water. The perfume in the bottle has *evaporated*.] 2 to disappear like vapor; vanish [Our courage *evaporated* when we saw the lion.] 3 to make thicker by heating so as to take some of the water from [to *evaporate* milk] —**e·vap′o·rat·ed, e·vap′o·rat·ing** —**e·vap′o·ra′tion n.**

ex. *abbreviation for* **example, extra**

ex·cel·lence (ek′sə ləns) **n.** the fact of being better or greater; extra goodness [We all praised the *excellence* of their singing.]

ex·cept (ek sept′) **prep.** leaving out; other than; but [Everyone *except* you liked the movie.] ◆**v.** to leave out; omit; exclude [Only a few of the students were *excepted* from her criticism.] ◆**conj.** were it not that; only; *used only in everyday talk* [I'd go with you *except* I'm tired.]

ex·cit·ing (ek sīt′iŋ) **adj.** causing excitement; stirring; thrilling [an *exciting* story]

ex·haust (eg zôst′ *or* eg zäst′) **v.** 1 to use up completely [Our drinking water was soon *exhausted*.] 2 to let out the contents of; make completely empty [The leak soon *exhausted* the gas tank.] 3 to use up the strength of; tire out; weaken [They are *exhausted* from playing tennis.] —**ex·haust′ed** ◆**n.** the used steam or gas that comes from the cylinders of an engine; especially, the fumes from the gasoline engine in an automobile

ex·hib·it (eg zib′it) **v.** to show or display to the public [to *exhibit* stamp collections] ◆**n.** 1 something exhibited to the public [an art *exhibit*] 2 something shown as evidence in a court of law

ex·ist·ence (eg zis′təns) **n.** 1 the condition of being; an existing 2 life or a way of life [a happy *existence*] —**ex·ist′ent adj.**

a	ask, fat
ā	ape, date
ä	car, lot
e	elf, ten
ē	even, meet
i	is, hit
ī	ice, fire
ō	open, go
ô	law, horn
oi	oil, point
oo	look, pull
oo	ooze, tool
ou	out, crowd
u	up, cut
ʉ	fur, fern
ə	a in ago
	e in agent
	e in father
	i in unity
	o in collect
	u in focus
ch	chin, arch
ŋ	ring, singer
sh	she, dash
th	thin, truth
th	then, father
zh	s in pleasure

ex·pe·ri·ence (ek spir′ē əns) *n.* **1** the fact of living through a happening or happenings [*Experience* teaches us many things.] **2** something that one has done or lived through [This trip was an *experience* that I'll never forget.] **3** skill that one gets by training, practice, and work [a lawyer with much *experience*] ◆*v.* to have the experience of [to *experience* success] —**ex·pe′ri·enced, ex·pe′ri·enc·ing**

ex·pla·na·tion (eks′ plə nā′shən) *n.* **1** the act of explaining [This plan needs an *explanation*.] **2** something that explains [This long nail is the *explanation* for the flat tire.] **3** a meaning given in explaining [different *explanations* of the same event]

ex·ploit (eks′ploit) *n.* a daring act or bold deed [the *exploits* of Robin Hood] ◆*v.* (ek sploit′) to use in a selfish way; take unfair advantage of [Children were *exploited* when they had to work in factories.] —**ex′ploi·ta′tion** *n.*

ex·plore (ek splôr′) *v.* **1** to travel in a region that is unknown or not well known, in order to find out more about it [to *explore* a wild jungle] **2** to look into or examine carefully [to *explore* a problem] —**ex·plored′, ex·plor′ing** —**ex′plo·ra′tion; ex·plor′er** *n.*

ex·po·sure (ek spō′zhər) *n.* **1** the fact of being exposed [tanned by *exposure* to the sun] **2** the time during which film in a camera is exposed to light; also, a section of film that can be made into one picture [Give this film a short *exposure*. There are twelve *exposures* on this film.]

ex·tra·ter·res·tri·al (eks′trə tər res′trē əl) *adj.* being, happening, or coming from a place not the earth [a science-fiction story about *extraterrestrial* beings]

ex·treme (ek strēm′) *adj.* **1** to the greatest degree; very great [*extreme* pain] **2** far from what is usual; also, very far from the center of opinion [She holds *extreme* political views.] ◆*n.* either of two things that are as different or as far from each other as possible [the *extremes* of laughter and tears] —**ex·treme′ly** *adv.*

eye·sight (ī′sīt) *n.* **1** the ability to see; sight; vision [keen *eyesight*] **2** the distance a person can see [Keep within *eyesight*!]

fab·ric (fab′rik) *n.* a material made from fibers or threads by weaving, knitting, etc., as any cloth, felt, lace, etc.

fa·cial (fā′shəl) *adj.* of or for the face ◆☆*n.* a treatment intended to make the skin of the face look better, as by massage and putting on creams and lotions

faith·ful (fāth′fəl) *adj.* **1** remaining loyal; constant [*faithful* friends] **2** showing a strong sense of duty or responsibility [*faithful* attendance] —**faith′ful·ly** *adv.* —**faith′ful·ness** *n.*

fal·low (fal′ō) *adj.* plowed but left unplanted during the growing season [Farmers let the land lie *fallow* at times to kill weeds, make the soil richer, etc.] ◆*n.* land that lies fallow

fan·ci·ful (fan′si fəl) *adj.* **1** full of fancy; having or showing a quick and playful imagination [*fanciful* costumes for the Halloween party] **2** not real; imaginary [a *fanciful* idea that horseshoes bring luck]

fas·ci·nate (fas′ə nāt) *v.* to hold the attention of by being interesting or delightful; charm [The puppet show *fascinated* the children.] —**fas′ci·nat·ed, fas′ci·nat·ing** —**fas′ci·na′tion** *n.*

fas·ten (fas′ən) *v.* **1** to join or become joined; attach [The collar is *fastened* to the shirt.] **2** to make stay closed or in place, as by locking or shutting [*Fasten* the door.] —**fas′ten·er** *n.*

fel·low·ship (fel′ō ship′) *n.* **1** friendship; companionship **2** a group of people having the same activities or interests **3** money given to a student at a university or college to help him or her study for a higher degree

fen·der (fen′dər) *n.* a metal piece over the wheel of a car, bicycle, etc. that protects against splashing water or mud

fes·ti·val (fes′tə vəl) *n.* **1** a day or time of feasting or celebrating; happy holiday [The Mardi Gras in New Orleans is a colorful *festival*.] **2** a time of special celebration or entertainment [Our town holds a maple sugar *festival* every spring.] ◆*adj.* of or for a festival [*festival* music]

fetch (fech) *v.* to go after and bring back; get [The dog *fetched* my slippers.] —**fetched**

fidg·et (fij′it) *v.* to move about restlessly [Children sometimes *fidget* if they have to sit still too long.]

fierce (firs) *adj.* **1** wild or cruel; violent; raging [a *fierce* dog; a *fierce* wind] **2** very strong or eager [a *fierce* effort] —**fierc′er, fierc′est** —**fierce′ly** *adv.* —**fierce′ness** *n.*

fif·teen (fif′tēn′) *n., adj.* five more than ten; the number 15

filth·y (fil′thē) *adj.* full of filth; disgusting **filth′i·er, filth′i·est**

firm (furm) *adj.* **1** that does not easily give way when pressed; solid [*firm* muscles] **2** that cannot be moved easily; fixed; stable [He stood as *firm* as a rock.] **3** that stays the same; not changing; constant [a *firm* friendship] —**firm´est** —**firm´ly** *adv.* —**firm´ness** *n.*

flash·bulb (flash´bulb) *n.* a lightbulb that gives a short, bright light for taking photographs

flo·rist (flôr´ist) *n.* a person whose business is selling flowers, house plants, etc.

flour·ish (flur´ish) *v.* to grow strongly and well; be successful or healthy; prosper [Daisies *flourish* in full sun.]

fo·li·age (fō´lē ij) *n.* the leaves of a tree or plant, or of many trees or plants

fol·ly (fä´lē) *n.* a lack of good sense; foolishness

fore·close (fôr klōz´) *v.* to end a mortgage and become the owner of the mortgaged property [A bank can *foreclose* a mortgage if payments on its loan are not made in time.] —**fore·closed´, fore·clos´ing** —**fore·clo´sure** *n.*

fore·ground (fôr´ground) *n.* the part of a scene or picture that is or seems to be nearest to the one looking at it

for·eign·er (fôr´in ər *or* fär´in ər) *n.* a person from another country, thought of as an outsider

fore·knowl·edge (fôr´nä´lij) *n.* knowledge of something before it happens

fore·most (fôr´mōst) *adj.* first in position or importance [the *foremost* writers of their time] ◆*adv.* before all else [to be first and *foremost* a dancer]

fore·sight (fôr´sīt) *n.* **1** a foreseeing **2** the power to foresee **3** a looking forward **4** a looking ahead and planning for the future

fore·warn (fôr wôrn´) *v.* to warn ahead of time [We were *forewarned* we wouldn't get tickets later.] —**fore·warn´ing** *n.*

foun·da·tion (foun dā´shən) *n.* **1** the part at the bottom that supports a wall, house, etc.; base **2** the basis on which an idea, belief, etc. rests

found·er (foun´dər) *n.* a person who founds, or establishes [the *founder* of a city]

fra·grant (frā´grənt) *adj.* having a sweet or pleasant smell

☆**frank·furt·er** (frank´fər tər) *n.* a smoked sausage of beef or beef and pork; wiener

freight (frāt) *n.* a load of goods shipped by train, truck, ship, or airplane ◆*v.* to carry or send by freight [Cars are often *freighted* by trains or trucks to where they are sold.]

fre·quen·cy (frē´kwən sē) *n.* **1** the fact of being frequent, or happening often **2** the number of times something is repeated in a certain period [a *frequency* of 1,000 vibrations per second]: the frequency of radio waves is measured in hertz —*pl.* **fre´quen·cies**

fruit·ful (frootˈfəl) *adj.* **1** bearing much fruit [a *fruitful* tree] **2** producing a great deal [Mozart was a *fruitful* composer.] —**fruitˈful·ly** *adv.* —**fruitˈful·ness** *n.*

gal·ax·y (gal´ək sē) ◆*n.* any vast group of stars —*pl.* **gal´ax·ies**

gal·ler·y (gal´ər ē) *n.* **1** a balcony, especially the highest balcony in a theater, with the cheapest seats **2** the people who sit in these seats **3** a place for showing or selling works of art —*pl.* **gal´ler·ies**

gawk (gôk *or* gäk) *v.* to stare in a stupid way [The crowd *gawked* at the overturned truck.]

gear (gir) *n.* **1** *often* **gears,** *pl.* a part of a machine consisting of two or more wheels having teeth that fit together so that when one wheel moves the others are made to move [The *gears* pass on the motion of the engine to the wheels of the car.] **2** tools and equipment needed for doing something [My *gear* for fishing consists of a rod, lines, and flies.] ◆*v.* to adjust or make fit [Our new cafeteria is *geared* to handle more students.]

gen·tle (jent´l) *adj.* **1** mild, soft, or easy; not rough [a *gentle* touch] **2** tame; easy to handle [a *gentle* horse] **3** gradual; not sudden [a *gentle* slope] **4** courteous, kindly, or patient [a *gentle* nature] —**gen´tler, gen´tlest**

gen·u·ine (jen´yσoin) *adj.* **1** really being what it seems to be; not false; true [a *genuine* diamond] **2** sincere or honest [*genuine* praise] —**gen´u·ine·ly** *adv.* —**gen´u·ine·ness** *n.*

ge·ol·o·gy (jē ä´lə jē) *n.* the study of the earth's crust and of the way in which its layers were formed: it includes the study of rocks and fossils —**ge·ol´o·gist** *n.*

gloom·y (gl$\overline{oo}$m´ē) *adj.* **1** dark or dim [a *gloomy* dungeon] **2** having or giving a feeling of deep sadness [a *gloomy* mood; a *gloomy* story] —**gloom´i·er, gloom´i·est** —**gloom´i·ly** *adv.* —**gloom´i·ness** *n.*

glo·ri·fy (glôr´ə fī) *v.* **1** to give glory to; cause to be famous and respected [Our town *glorified* the hero by building a statue.] **2** to praise in worship [to *glorify* God] **3** to make seem better than is really so [to *glorify* war] —**glo´ri·fied, glo·ri·fy´ing**

gnarled (närld) *adj.* full of gnarls or knobs; twisted and knotty [a *gnarled* tree; *gnarled* hands]

gnome (nōm) *n.* a dwarf in folk tales who lives inside the earth and guards the treasures there

govt. *or* **Govt.** *abbreviation for* **government**

a	ask, fat
ā	ape, date
ä	car, lot
e	elf, ten
ē	even, meet
i	is, hit
ī	ice, fire
ō	open, go
ô	law, horn
oi	oil, point
$\overline{oo}$	look, pull
$\overline{oo}$	ooze, tool
ou	out, crowd
u	up, cut
u	fur, fern
ə	a in ago
	e in agent
	e in father
	i in unity
	o in collect
	u in focus
ch	chin, arch
ŋ	ring, singer
sh	she, dash
th	thin, truth
th	then, father
zh	s in pleasure

gra·cious (grā′shəs) *adj.* **1** kind, polite, and charming [a *gracious* host and hostess] **2** full of grace, comfort, and luxury [*gracious* living]

grad·u·ate (gra′jōō ət) *n.* a person who has finished a course of study at a school or college and has been given a diploma or degree ►*v.* (gra′jōō āt′) **1** to make or become a graduate of a school or college **2** to mark off with small lines for measuring [A thermometer is a tube *graduated* in degrees.] —**grad′u·at·ed, grad′u·at·ing** —**grad′u·a′tion** *n.*

greas·y (grē′sē *or* grē′zē) *adj.* **1** smeared with grease [*greasy* hands] **2** full of grease [*greasy* food] **3** like grease; oily [a *greasy* salve] —**greas′i·er, greas′i·est** —**greas′i·ly** *adv.* —**greas′i·ness** *n.*

greed·y (grēd′ē) *adj.* wanting or taking all that one can get with no thought of what others need [The *greedy* little boy ate all the cookies.] **greed′i·er, greed′i·est** —**greed′i·ly** *adv.* —**greed′i·ness** *n.*

greet·ing (grēt′iŋ) *n.* **1** the act or words of one who greets **2** *often* **greetings**, *pl.* a message of regards from someone not present

growth (grōth) *n.* **1** the act of growing; a becoming larger or a developing **2** the amount grown; increase [a *growth* of two inches over the summer] **3** something that grows or has grown [He shaved off the two weeks' *growth* of beard. A tumor is an abnormal *growth* in the body.]

guar·an·tee (′ger ən tē′ *or* ger′ən tē′) *n.* **1** a promise to replace something sold if it does not work or last as it should [a one-year *guarantee* on the clock] **2** a promise or assurance that something will be done [You have my *guarantee* that we'll be on time.] ►*v.* **1** to give a guarantee or guaranty for **2** to promise or assure [I cannot *guarantee* that she will be there.] —**guar′·an·teed′, guar′·an·tee′ing**

guess (ges) *v.* **1** to judge or decide about something without having enough facts to know for certain [Can you *guess* how old he is?] **2** to judge correctly by doing this [She *guessed* the exact number of beans in the jar.] **3** to think or suppose [I *guess* you're right.] ►*n.* a judgment formed by guessing; surmise [Your *guess* is as good as mine.] —**guess′er** *n.*

guilt·y (gil′tē) *adj.* **1** having done something wrong; being to blame for something [She is often *guilty* of telling lies.] **2** judged in court to be a wrongdoer [The jury found him *guilty* of robbery.] **3** caused by a feeling of guilt [a *guilty* look] —**guilt′i·er, guilt′i·est** —**guilt′i·ly** *adv.* —**guilt′i·ness** *n.*

gui·tar (gi tär′) *n.* a musical instrument with six strings: it is played by plucking the strings with the fingers or with a guitar pick. —**gui·tar′ist** *n.*

gym·na·si·um (jim nā′zē əm) *n.* a building or room with equipment for doing exercises and playing games

hand·ker·chief (haŋ′kər chif) *n.* a small piece of cloth for wiping the nose, eyes, or face, or worn as a decoration

hap·py (hap′ē) *adj.* **1** feeling or showing pleasure or joy; glad; contended [a *happy* child; a *happy* song] **2** lucky; fortunate [The story has a *happy* ending.] —**hap′pi·er, hap′pi·est** —**hap′pi·ly** *adv.* —**hap′pi·ness** *n.*

hatch·et (hach′ət) *n.* a small ax with a short handle

haz·ard·ous (haz′ər dəs) *adj.* dangerous; risky

head·ache (hed′āk) *n.* a pain in the head

health·y (hel′thē) *adj.* **1** having good health; well [a *healthy* child] **2** showing good health [a *healthy* appetite] **3** good for one's health; healthful [a *healthy* climate] —**health′i·er, health′i·est** —**health′i·ness** *n.*

height (hīt) *n.* **1** the distance from the bottom to the top; tallness [the *height* of a building; a child four feet in *height*] **2** the highest point or degree [to reach the *height* of fame]

hem·i·sphere (hem′i sfir′) *n.* **1** half of a sphere or globe [The dome of the church was in the shape of a *hemisphere*.] **2** any of the halves into which the earth's surface is divided in geography

he·ro (hir′ō *or* hē′rō) *n.* **1** a person who is looked up to for having done something brave or noble [Washington was the *hero* of the American Revolution.] **2** the most important person in a novel, play, or movie, especially if the person is good or noble —*pl.* **he′roes**

hes·i·ta·tion (hez′i tā′shən) *n.* **1** the act of hesitating, as because of doubt, fear, etc.; unsure or unwilling feeling [I agreed without *hesitation*.] **2** a pausing for a moment [talk filled with *hesitations*]

hex·a·gon (hek′sə gän) *n.* a flat figure with six angles and six sides

hon·or·a·ble (än′ər ə bəl) *adj.* **1** worthy of being honored [an *honorable* trade] **2** honest, upright, and sincere [*honorable* intentions] **3** bringing honor [*honorable* mention] —**hon′or·a·bly** *adv.*

hor·i·zon·tal (hôr′ə zänt′l) *adj.* parallel to the horizon; not vertical; level; flat [The top of a table is *horizontal*; its legs are vertical.] ►*n.* a horizontal line, plane, etc. —**hor′i·zon′tal·ly** *adv.*

horse·rad·ish (hôrs'rad'ish) *n.* **1** a plant with a long, white root, that has a sharp, burning taste **2** a relish made by grating this root

house·hold (hous'hōld) *n.* **1** all the persons who live in one house, especially a family **2** the home and its affairs [to manage a *household*]

Hud·son (hud'sən) a river in eastern New York: its mouth is at New York City

hus·band (huz'bənd) *n.* the man to whom a woman is married

hwy. *abbreviation for* **highway**

hymn (him) *n.* **1** a song praising or honoring God **2** any song of praise

hy·phen·ate (hī'fən āt) *v.* to join or write with a hyphen —**hy'phen·at·ed, hy'phen·at·ing** —**hy'phen·a'tion** *n.*

hyp·no·tize (hip'nə tīz) *v.* to put someone into a state of hypnosis or a condition like it —**hyp'no·tized, hyp'no·tiz·ing** —**hyp'no·tist** *n.*

i·ci·cle (ī'sik əl) *n.* a hanging stick of ice formed by water freezing as it drips down

I·da·ho (ī'də hō) a state in the northwestern part of the U.S.: *abbreviated* **Ida., ID**

i·den·ti·fy (ī den'tə fī) *v.* **1** to think of or treat as the same [The Roman god Jupiter is *identified* with the Greek god Zeus.] **2** to show or prove to be a certain person or thing [She was *identified* by a scar on her chin.] —**i·den'ti·fied, i·den'ti·fy·ing**

ig·ni·tion (ig nish'ən) *n.* **1** the act of setting on fire or catching fire **2** the switch, spark plugs, etc. that set fire to the mixture of gases in the cylinders of a gasoline engine

il·le·gal (i lē'gəl) *adj.* not legal; not allowed by law; against the law —**il·le'gal·ly** *adv.*

il·leg·i·ble (il lej'ə bəl) *adj.* hard to read or impossible to read, as because badly written or printed —**il·leg'i·bly** *adv.*

Il·li·nois (il'ə noi') a state in the north central part of the U.S.: *abbreviated* **Ill., IL**

il·lit·er·ate (il lit'ər ət) *adj.* **1** not educated; especially, not knowing how to read or write **2** showing a lack of education [an *illiterate* letter] ◆*n.* a person who does not know how to read or write —**il·lit'er·a·cy**

il·log·i·cal (il läj'i kəl) *adj.* not logical; showing poor reasoning —**il·log'i·cal·ly** *adv.*

il·lu·mi·nate (il lōō'mə nāt') *v.* **1** to give light to; light up [Candles *illuminated* the room.] **2** to make clear; explain [The teacher *illuminated* the meaning of the poem.] —**il·lu'mi·nat'ed, il·lu'mi·nat'ing**

im·ma·te·ri·al (im'ə tir'ē əl) *adj.* **1** of no importance [The cost is *immaterial* if the quality is good.] **2** not made of matter; spiritual

im·ma·ture (im ə toor' *or* im ə choor') *adj.* not mature; not fully grown or developed [*immature* fruit; *immature* judgment] —**im'ma·tu'ri·ty** *n.*

☆**im·mi·grant** (im'ə grənt) *n.* a person who comes into a foreign country to make a new home

im·mor·tal (im môrt''l) *adj.* **1** never dying; living forever [The Greek gods were thought of as *immortal* beings.] **2** having fame that will last a long time [Shakespeare is an *immortal* poet.] ◆*n.* a being that lasts forever —**im·mor·tal·i·ty** (i'môr tal'ə tē) —**im·mor'tal·ly** *adv.*

im·pair (im per') *v.* to make worse, less, or weaker; damage [The disease *impaired* her hearing.]

im·pa·tient (im pā'shənt) *adj.* **1** not patient; not willing to put up with delay, annoyance, etc. [Some parents become *impatient* when their children cry.] **2** eager to do something or for something to happen [Rita is *impatient* to go swimming.] —**im·pa'tient·ly** *adv.*

im·per·fect (im pur'fikt) *adj.* not perfect; having some fault or flaw [an *imperfect* diamond]

im·po·lite (im pə līt') *adj.* not polite; rude —**im·po·lite'ly** *adv.* —**im·po·lite'ness** *n.*

im·prac·ti·cal (im prak'ti kəl) *adj.* not practical; not useful, efficient, etc.

im·print (im print') *v.* **1** to mark by pressing or stamping [The paper was *imprinted* with the state seal.] **2** to fix firmly [Her face is *imprinted* in my memory.] ◆*n.* (im'print) a mark made by pressing; print [the *imprint* of a dirty hand on the wall]

im·prop·er (im präp'ər) *adj.* **1** not proper or suitable; unfit [Sandals are *improper* shoes for tennis.] **2** not true; wrong; incorrect [an *improper* street address] **3** not decent; in bad taste [*improper* jokes] —**im·prop'er·ly** *adv.*

in·a·bil·i·ty (in'ə bil'ə tē) *n.* the condition of being unable; lack of ability or power

inc. *abbreviation for* **included, income, incorporated, increase**

in·ca·pa·ble (in kā'pə bəl) *adj.* **1** not capable; not having the ability or power needed [*incapable* of helping] **2** not able to undergo; not open to [*incapable* of change] —**in'ca·pa·bil'i·ty** *n.*

in·cred·i·ble (in kred'ə bəl) *adj.* so great, unusual, etc. that it is hard or impossible to believe [an *incredible* story; *incredible* speed] —**in·cred'i·bly** *adv.*

in·def·i·nite (in def'ə nit) *adj.* **1** having no exact limits [an *indefinite* area] **2** not clear or exact in meaning; vague [*indefinite* instructions] **3** not sure or positive; uncertain [*indefinite* plans] —**in·def'i·nite·ly** *adv.*

a	ask, fat
ā	ape, date
ä	car, lot
e	elf, ten
ē	even, meet
i	is, hit
ī	ice, fire
ō	open, go
ô	law, horn
oi	oil, point
σσ	look, pull
o͞o	ooze, tool
ou	out, crowd
u	up, cut
ʉ	fur, fern
ə	a in ago
	e in agent
	e in father
	i in unity
	o in collect
	u in focus
ch	chin, arch
ŋ	ring, singer
sh	she, dash
th	thin, truth
th	then, father
zh	s in pleasure

in·di·rect (in′də rekt′) *adj.* **1** not direct or straight; by a longer way; roundabout [an *indirect* route] **2** not straight to the point [an *indirect* reply] —**in′di·rect′ly** *adv.*

in·dus·try (in′dəs trē) *n.* **1** any branch of business or manufacturing [the steel *industry*; the motion-picture *industry*] **2** all business and manufacturing [Leaders of *industry* met in Chicago.] —*pl.* **in′dus·tries**

in·flate (in flāt′) *v.* to cause to swell out by putting in air or gas; blow up [to *inflate* a balloon] —**in·flat′a·ble** *adj.*

in·for·ma·tion (in′ fər mā′shən) *n.* **1** an informing or being informed [This is for your *information* only.] **2** something told or facts learned; news or knowledge; data [An encyclopedia gives *information* about many things.] **3** a person or service that answers certain questions [Ask *information* for the location of the shoe department.]

in·spec·tion (in spek′shən) *n.* **1** the act or process of looking at carefully **2** an official examination or review [The *inspection* of the troops was postponed.]

in·struc·tor (in struk′tər) *n.* **1** a teacher ☆**2** a college teacher ranking below an assistant professor

in·stru·ment (in′strə mənt) *n.* **1** a tool or other device for doing very exact work, for scientific purposes, etc. [surgical *instruments*] **2** a device used in making musical sound, as a flute, violin, piano, etc.

in·su·late (in′sə lāt) *v.* to separate or cover with a material that keeps electricity, heat, or sound from escaping [electric wire *insulated* with rubber; a furnace *insulated* with asbestos] —**in′su·lat·ed, in′su·lat·ing**

in·su·la·tor (in′sə lāt′ ər) *n.* anything that insulates; especially, a device of glass or porcelain, for insulating electric wires

in·sure (in shoor′) *v.* to get or give insurance on [We *insured* our car against theft. Will your company *insure* my house against storms?] —**in·sured′, in·sur′ing** —**in·sur′a·ble** *adj.*

in·tel·li·gent (in tel′ə jənt) *adj.* having or showing intelligence, especially high intelligence —**in·tel′li·gent·ly** *adv.*

in·tol·er·ant (in tä′lər ənt) *adj.* not tolerant; not willing to put up with ideas or beliefs that are different from one's own, or not willing to put up with people of other races or backgrounds —**in·tol′er·ance** *n.*

in·trude (in trood′) *v.* to force oneself or one's thoughts on others without being asked or wanted [I don't like to *intrude* when you are so busy.] —**in·trud′ed, in·trud′ing** —**in·tru′sion** *n.*

in·ven·tion (in ven′shən) *n.* **1** the act of inventing [the *invention* of television] **2** something invented [the many *inventions* of Edison] **3** the ability to invent [a novelist who shows great *invention* in telling a story]

in·ves·ti·gate (in ves′tə gāt′) *v.* to search into so as to learn the facts; examine in detail [to *investigate* an accident] —**in·ves′ti·gat′·ed, in·ves′ti·gat·ing** —**in·ves′ti·ga′tion** *n.* —**in·ves′ti·ga′tor** *n.*

ir·ra·tion·al (ir rash′ən əl) *adj.* that does not make sense; not rational; absurd [an *irrational* fear of the dark] —**ir·ra′tion·al·ly** *adv.*

ir·reg·u·lar (ir reg′yə lər) *adj.* **1** not regular; not like the usual rule, way, or custom [an *irregular* diet] **2** not straight, even, or the same throughout [an *irregular* design] —**ir·reg′u·lar·ly** *adv.*

ir·rel·e·vant (ir rel′ə vənt) *adj.* having nothing to do with the subject; not to the point [That remark about the candidate's height was *irrelevant* to the issues of the campaign.]

ir·re·spon·si·ble (ir′ rē spän′sə bəl) *adj.* not responsible; not showing a sense of duty; doing as one pleases —**ir′re·spon′si·bly** *adv.*

is·sue (ish′oo *or* ish′yoo) *n.* **1** a thing or group of things sent or given out [the July *issue* of a magazine] **2** a problem to be talked over [The candidates will debate the *issues.*] ◆*v.* **1** to put forth or send out [The city *issues* bonds. The general *issued* an order.] **2** to give or deal out; distribute [The teacher *issued* new books.] —**is′sued, is′su·ing**

i·vo·ry (ī′vər ē *or* ī′vrē) *n.* **1** the hard, white substance that forms the tusks of the elephant, walrus, etc. **2** any substance like ivory, as the white plastic used on piano keys **3** the color of ivory; creamy white —*pl.* **i′vo·ries** ◆*adj.* **1** made of or like ivory **2** having the color of ivory; creamy-white

Jj

☆**jack·knife** (jak′nīf) *n.* **1** a large pocketknife **2** a dive in which the diver touches the feet with the hands while in the air —*pl.* **jack′ knives** ◆*v.* to bend at the middle as in a jackknife dive —**jack′ knifed, jack′ knif·ing**

Jef·fer·son (jef′ər sən), **Thomas** 1743–1826; the third president of the United States, from 1801 to 1809

jel·ly (jel′ē) *n.* **1** a soft, firm food that looks smooth and glassy, and is easily cut, spread, etc.: jelly is made from cooked fruit syrup, meat juice, or gelatin **2** any substance like this —*pl.* **jel′lies** ◆*v.* to become, or make into, jelly —**jel′lied, jel′ly·ing**

jew·el·er *or* **jew·el·ler** (joo′l′ər) *n.* a person who makes, sells, or repairs jewelry, watches, etc.

jock·ey (jäk′ē) *n.* a person whose work is riding horses in races

jour·nal·ism (jʉr′nəl iz əm) *n.* the work of gathering, writing, or editing the news for publication in newspapers or magazines or for broadcasting on radio or television

jour·nal·ist (jʉr′nəl ist) *n.* a person whose work is journalism, as a reporter, news editor, etc. —**jour′nal·is′tic** *adj.*

juic·y (jo͞o′sē) *adj.* full of juice [a *juicy* plum] —**juic′i·er, juic′i·est**

ju·ror (jo͞or′ər *or* jʉr′ər) *n.* a member of a jury

ju·ven·ile (jo͞o′və nəl *or* jo͞o′və nīl) *adj.* 1 young or youthful 2 of, like, or for children or young people [*juvenile* ideas; *juvenile* books] ◆*n.* a child or young person

kan·ga·roo (kaŋ gə r o͞o′) *n.* an animal of Australia with short forelegs and strong, large hind legs, with which it makes long leaps: the female carries her young in a pouch in front —*pl.* **kan·ga·roos′**

Ken·ne·dy (ken′ə dē) **John F.** 1917–1963; the 35th president of the United States, from 1961 to 1963: he was assassinated

Ken·tuck·y (kən tuk′ē) a state in the eastern central part of the U.S.: *abbreviated* **Ky., KY**

key·board (kē′bôrd) *n.* the row or rows of keys of a piano, organ, typewriter, etc.

kin·dling (kind′liŋ) *n.* bits of dry wood or the like, for starting a fire

kitch·en (kich′ən) *n.* a room or place for preparing and cooking food

kneel (nēl) *v.* to rest on a knee or knees [Some people *kneel* when they pray.] —**knelt** or **kneeled, kneel′ing**

knelt (nelt) *a past tense and past participle of* **kneel**

☆**knick·ers** (nik′ərz) *pl. n.* short, loose trousers gathered in just below the knees

knot·hole (nät′hol) *n.* a hole in a board or tree trunk where a knot has fallen out

knowl·edge (nä′lij) *n.* 1 the fact or condition of knowing [*Knowledge* of the murder spread through the town.] 2 what is known or learned, as through study or experience [a scientist of great *knowledge*] 3 all that is known by all people

knuck·le (nuk′əl) *n.* a joint of the finger, especially one connecting a finger to the rest of the hand

Ko·re·a (kô rē′ə) a country in eastern Asia, divided into two republics, North Korea and South Korea —**Ko·re′an** *adj., n.*

lan·guage (laŋ′gwij) *n.* 1 human speech or writing that stands for speech [People communicate by means of *language*.] 2 the speech of a particular nation, group, etc. [the Greek *language*; the Navaho *language*] 3 any means of passing on one's thoughts or feelings to others [sign *language*]

laugh·a·ble (laf′ə bəl) *adj.* causing laughter; funny; ridiculous [a *laughable* costume]

launch (lônch *or* länch) *v.* 1 to throw, hurl, or send off into space [to *launch* a rocket] 2 to cause to slide into the water; set afloat [to *launch* a new ship] —**launched** ◆*n.* the act of launching a ship, spacecraft, etc.

laun·dry (lôn′drē *or* län′drē) *n.* 1 a place where laundering is done 2 clothes, linens, etc. that have been, or are about to be, washed and ironed —*pl.* **laun′dries**

law-a·bid·ing (lô′ə bīd′iŋ *or* lä′ə bīd′iŋ) *adj.* obeying the law [*law-abiding* citizens]

lb. *abbreviation for* **pound** —*pl.* **lbs.**

lec·ture (lek′chər) *n.* 1 a talk on some subject to an audience or class 2 a long or tiresome scolding ◆*v.* 1 to give a lecture 2 to scold —**lec′tured, lec′tur·ing** —**lec′tur·er** *n.*

leg·is·la·tion (lej′ is lā′shən) *n.* 1 the act or process of making laws 2 the laws made

lei·sure·ly (lē′zhər lē *or* lezh′ər lē) *adj.* without hurrying; slow [a *leisurely* walk] ◆*adv.* in a slow, unhurried way [We talked *leisurely*.]

light·ning (līt′niŋ) *n.* a flash of light in the sky caused by the passing of electricity from one cloud to another or between a cloud and the earth

lik·a·ble or **like·a·ble** (līk′ə bəl) *adj.* easy to like because pleasing, friendly, etc.

lim·it·ed (lim′it əd) *adj.* 1 having a limit or limits; restricted in some way [This offer is good for a *limited* time only.] ☆2 making only a few stops [a *limited* bus]

lim·ou·sine (lim ə zēn′ *or* lim′ə zēn) *n.* 1 a large automobile driven by a chauffeur, who is sometimes separated from the passengers by a glass window ☆2 a buslike sedan used to carry passengers to or from an airport

Lin·coln (liŋ′kən) **Abraham** 1809–1865; 16th president of the United States, from 1861 to 1865: he was assassinated

lis·ten (lis′ən) *v.* to pay attention in order to hear; try to hear [*Listen* to the rain. *Listen* when the counselor speaks.] —**lis′ten·ing** —**lis′ten·er** *n.*

live·li·hood (līv′lē hood′) *n.* a means of living, or of supporting oneself [She earns her *livelihood* as a teacher.]

lock·smith (läk′smith) *n.* a person whose work is making or repairing locks and keys

a	ask, fat
ā	ape, date
ä	car, lot
e	elf, ten
ē	even, meet
i	is, hit
ī	ice, fire
ō	open, go
ô	law, horn
oi	oil, point
o͞o	look, pull
o͞o	ooze, tool
ou	out, crowd
u	up, cut
ʉ	fur, fern
ə	a in ago
	e in agent
	e in father
	i in unity
	o in collect
	u in focus
ch	chin, arch
ŋ	ring, singer
sh	she, dash
th	thin, truth
th	then, father
zh	s in pleasure

169

lounge (lounj) *v.* to move, sit, or lie in an easy or lazy way; loll —**lounged, loung´ing** ◆*n.* a room with comfortable furniture where people can lounge —**loung´er**

lunch·eon (lun´chən) *n.* a lunch; especially, a formal lunch with others

lus·cious (lush´əs) *adj.* **1** having a delicious taste or smell; full of flavor [a *luscious* steak] **2** very pleasing to see, hear, etc. [the *luscious* sound of violins] —**lus´cious·ly** *adv.*

lux·u·ry (luk´shər ē *or* lug´zhər ē) *n.* **1** the use and enjoyment of the best and most costly things that give one the most comfort and pleasure [a life of *luxury*] **2** anything that gives one such comfort, usually something one does not need for life or health [Jewels are *luxuries*.] —*pl.* **lux´u·ries**

ma·chin·e·ry (mə shēn´ər ē) *n.* **1** machines in general [the *machinery* of a factory] **2** the working parts of a machine [the *machinery* of a printing press] —*pl.* **ma·chin´er·ies**

ma·chin·ist (mə shēn´ist) *n.* **1** a person who is skilled in working with machine tools **2** a person who makes, repairs, or runs machinery

mag·i·cal (maj´i kəl) *adj.* of or like magic —**mag´i·cal·ly** *adv.*

mag·nif·i·cent (mag nif´ə sənt) *adj.* rich, fine, noble, beautiful, etc. in a grand way; splendid [a *magnificent* castle; a *magnificent* idea]

mag·ni·fy (mag´nə fī) *v.* to make look or seem larger or greater than is really so [This lens *magnifies* an object to ten times its size. He *magnified* the seriousness of his illness.] —**mag´ni·fied, mag´ni·fy·ing**

main·stay (mān´stā) *n.* **1** the line that runs forward from the upper part of the mainmast, helping to hold it in place **2** the main or chief support [She was the *mainstay* of her family.]

main·te·nance (mānt´n əns) *n.* **1** a maintaining or being maintained; upkeep or support [Taxes pay for the *maintenance* of schools.] **2** a means of support; livelihood [a job that barely provides a *maintenance*]

mal·let (mal´ət) *n.* **1** a wooden hammer made with a short handle for use as a tool **2** a wooden hammer made with a long handle for playing croquet or with a long, flexible handle for playing polo

man·age·a·ble (man´ij ə bəl) *adj.* that can be managed, controlled, or done

man·u·fac·tur·er (man´yoo fak´chər ər) *n.* a person or company that manufactures; especially, a factory owner

mar·tial (mär´shəl) *adj.* **1** having to do with war or armies [*martial* music] **2** showing a readiness or eagerness to fight [*martial* spirit]

mas·ter·piece (mas´tər pēs) *n.* **1** a thing made or done with very great skill; a great work of art **2** the best thing that a person has ever made or done ["The Divine Comedy" was Dante's *masterpiece*.]

match (mach) *n.* **1** any person or thing equal to or like another in some way [Joan met her *match* in chess when she played Joe.] **2** two or more people or things that go well together [That suit and tie are a good *match*.] **3** a game or contest between two persons or teams [a tennis *match*] ◆*v.* **1** to go well together [Do your shirt and tie *match*?] **2** to make or get something like or equal to [Can you *match* this cloth?] **3** to be equal to [I could never *match* that lawyer in an argument.]

may·on·naise (mā ə nāz´ *or* mā´ə nāz) *n.* a thick, creamy salad dressing made of egg yolks, olive oil, lemon juice or vinegar, and seasoning

mdse. *abbreviation for* **merchandise**

meas·ure (mezh´ər) *v.* **1** to find out the size, amount, or extent of, as by comparing with something else [*Measure* the child's height with a yardstick. How do you *measure* a person's worth?] **2** to set apart or mark off a certain amount or length of [*Measure* out three pounds of sugar.] —**meas´ured, meas´ur·ing** ◆*n.* **1** the size, amount, or extent of something, found out by measuring [The *measure* of the bucket is 15 liters.] **2** a system of measuring [Liquid *measure* is a system of measuring liquids.]

me·chan·ic (mə kan´ik) *n.* a worker skilled in using tools or in making, repairing, and using machinery [an automobile *mechanic*]

med·i·cine (med´ə sən) *n.* **1** any substance used in or on the body to treat disease, lessen pain, heal, etc. **2** the science of treating and preventing disease

mel·low (mel´ō) *adj.* **1** soft, sweet, and juicy from ripeness [a *mellow* apple] **2** having a good flavor from being aged; not bitter [a *mellow* wine] **3** rich, soft, and pure; not harsh [the *mellow* tone of a cello] **4** made gentle and kind by age or experience [a *mellow* teacher]

me·men·to (mə men´tō) *n.* an object kept to remind one of something; souvenir [This toy is a *memento* of my childhood.] —*pl.* **me·men´tos** *or* **me·men´toes**

☆**mem·o·rize** (mem´ər īz) *v.* to fix in one's memory exactly or word for word; learn by heart —**mem´o·rized, mem´o·riz·ing** —**mem´o·ri·za´tion** *n.*

Mex·i·can (mek′si kən) *adj.* of Mexico, its people, their dialect of Spanish, or their culture ➤*n.* a person born or living in Mexico

mgr. *abbreviation for* **manager**

mi·cro·phone (mī′krə fōn) *n.* a device for picking up sound that is to be made stronger, as in a theater, or sent over long distances, as in radio: microphones change sound into electric waves, which go into electron tubes and are changed back into sound by loudspeakers

mid·point (mid′point) *n.* a point in the middle or at the center

mid·sum·mer (mid′sum′ər) *n.* **1** the middle of summer **2** the period around June 21

Mid·west·ern (mid′wes′tərn) *adj.* of, in, or having to do with the Middle West

mil·dew (mil′dōō *or* mil′dyōō) *n.* a fungus that appears as a furry, white coating on plants or on damp, warm paper, cloth, etc. ➤*v.* to become coated with mildew

mil·lion·aire (mil yə ner′) *n.* a person who has at least a million dollars, pounds, etc.

mi·nor·i·ty (mī nôr′ə tē *or* mi nôr′ə tē) *n.* **1** the smaller part or number; less than half [A *minority* of the Senate voted for the law.] **2** a small group of people of a different race, religion, etc. from the main group of which it is a part —*pl.* **mi·nor′i·ties**

mis·cal·cu·late (mis kal′kyōō lāt′) *v.* to make a mistake in figuring or planning; misjudge [Our manager *miscalculated* the pitcher's strength and we lost the game.]

mis·cel·la·ne·ous (mis′ə lā′nē əs) *adj.* of many different kinds; mixed; varied [A *miscellaneous* collection of objects filled the shelf.]

mis·chief (mis′chif) *n.* **1** harm or damage [Gossip can cause great *mischief*.] **2** action that causes harm, damage, or trouble. **3** a playful trick; prank **4** playful, harmless spirits [a child full of *mischief*]

mis·chie·vous (mis′chə vəs) *adj.* **1** causing some slight harm or annoyance, often in fun; naughty [a *mischievous* act] **2** full of playful tricks; teasing [a *mischievous* child] **3** causing harm or damage; injurious [*mischievous* slander]

mis·pro·nounce (mis prə nouns′) *v.* to pronounce in a wrong way [Some people *mispronounce* "cavalry" as "calvary."] —**mis·pro·nounced′, mis·pro·nounc′ing** —**mis·pro·nun·ci·a·tion** (mis′prə nun′sē ā′shən) *n.*

mis·tle·toe (mis′əl tō) *n.* an evergreen plant with waxy white, poisonous berries, growing as a parasite on certain trees

mis·un·der·stand (mis′un dər stand′) *v.* to understand in a way that is wrong; give a wrong meaning to —**mis·un·der·stood** (mis′un der stood′), **mis′under·stand′ing**

mo. *abbreviation for* **month**

mo·bile (mō′bəl *or* mō′bīl *or* mō′bēl) *adj.* that can be moved quickly and easily [a *mobile* army] ➤*n.* (mō′bēl) a kind of sculpture made of flat pieces, rods, etc. that hang balanced from wires so as to move easily in air currents —**mo·bil·i·ty** (mō bil′ə tē)

mod·i·fy (mäd′ə fī) *v.* **1** to make a small or partial change in [Exploration has *modified* our maps of Antarctica.] **2** to make less harsh, strong, etc. [to *modify* a jail term] **3** to limit the meaning of; describe or qualify [In the phrase "old man" the adjective "old" *modifies* the noun "man."] —**mod′i·fied, mod′i·fy·ing** —**mod′i·fi·ca′tion, mod′i·fi′er** *n.*

mois·ten (mois′ən) *v.* to make or become moist

mon·o·gram (män′ə gram) *n.* initials, especially of a person's name, put together in a design and used on clothing, stationery, and so on

mon·o·rail (män′ə rāl′) *n.* **1** a railway having cars that run on a single rail, or track, and are hung from it or balanced on it **2** this track

mon·o·syl·la·ble (män′ō sil′ə bəl) *n.* a word of one syllable, as "he" or "thought" —**mon·o·syl·lab·ic** (män′ e si lab′ik) *adj.*

mo·not·o·nous (mə nät′n əs) *adj.* **1** going on and on in the same tone [a *monotonous* voice] **2** having little or no change; boring or tiresome [a *monotonous* trip; *monotonous* work]

mon·soon (män sōōn′) *n.* **1** a wind of the Indian Ocean and southern Asia, blowing from the southwest from April to October, and from the northeast the rest of the year **2** the rainy season, when this wind blows from the southwest

mor·al (môr′əl) *adj.* **1** having to do with right and wrong in conduct [Cheating is a *moral* issue.] **2** good or right according to ideas of being decent and respectable [She was a *moral* woman all her life.] ➤*n.* **1** a lesson about what is right and wrong, taught by a story or event [the *moral* of a fable] **2** **morals**, *pl.* standards of behavior having to do with right and wrong; ethics

mos·qui·to (mə skēt′ō) *n.* a small insect with two wings: the female bites animals to suck their blood: some mosquitoes spread diseases, as malaria —*pl.* **mos·qui′toes** or **mos·qui′tos**

mouth·ful (mouth′fool) *n.* **1** as much as the mouth can hold **2** as much as is usually put into the mouth at one time —*pl.* **mouth′fuls**

a	ask, fat
ā	ape, date
ä	car, lot
e	elf, ten
ē	even, meet
i	is, hit
ī	ice, fire
ō	open, go
ô	law, horn
oi	oil, point
ōō	look, pull
ōō	ooze, tool
ou	out, crowd
u	up, cut
ʉ	fur, fern
ə	a in ago
	e in agent
	e in father
	i in unity
	o in collect
	u in focus
ch	chin, arch
ŋ	ring, singer
sh	she, dash
th	thin, truth
th	then, father
zh	s in pleasure

mud·dy (mud′ē) *adj.* full of mud or smeared with mud [a *muddy* yard; *muddy* boots] —**mud′di·er, mud′di·est** ◆*v.* to make or become muddy —**mud′died, mud′dy·ing**

mu·ral (myoor′əl) *n.* a picture or photograph, especially a large one, painted or put on a wall ◆*adj.* of or on a wall [a *mural* painting]

mus·cle (mus′əl) *n.* **1** the tissue in an animal's body that makes up the fleshy parts: muscle can be stretched or tightened to move the parts of the body **2** any single part or band of this tissue [The biceps is a *muscle* in the upper arm.] **3** strength that comes from muscles that are developed; brawn

my·thol·o·gy (mi thäl′ə jē) *n.* **1** myths as a group; especially, all the myths of a certain people [Roman *mythology*] —*pl.* **my·thol′o·gies 2** the study of myths —**myth·o·log·i·cal** (mith′ e läj′i kəl) *adj.*

nar·rate (ner′āt) *v.* to give the story of in writing or speech; tell what has happened [Our guest *narrated* her adventures.] —**nar′rat·ed, nar′rat·ing** —**nar′ra·tor** *n.*

na·tion (nā′shən) *n.* **1** a group of people living together in a certain region under the same government; state; country [the Swiss *nation*] **2** a group of people sharing the same history, language, customs, etc. [the Iroquois *nation*]

nau·se·a (nô′zhə *or* nä′zhə *or* nô′zhē ə) *n.* a feeling of sickness in the stomach that makes a person want to vomit

ne·go·ti·ate (ni gō′shē āt′) *v.* to talk over a problem, business deal, dispute, etc. in the hope of reaching an agreement [to *negotiate* a contract] —**ne·go′ti·at·ed, ne·go′ti·at·ing** —**ne·go′ti·a′tion, ne·go′ti·a′tor** *n.*

neigh·bor·ly (nā′bər lē) *adj.* friendly, kind, helpful, etc. [It was very *neighborly* of you to shovel the snow from my walk.] —**neigh′bor·li·ness** *n.*

niece (nēs) *n.* **1** the daughter of one's brother or sister **2** the daughter of one's brother–in–law or sister–in–law

No. *or* **no.** *abbreviation for* **number**

nois·y (noi′zē) *adj.* **1** making noise [a *noisy* bell] **2** full of noise [a *noisy* theater] —**nois′i·er, nois′i·est** —**nois′i·ly** *adv.* —**nois′i·ness** *n.*

no·tice·a·ble (nōt′is ə bəl) *adj.* easily seen; likely to be noticed; remarkable [*noticeable* improvement] —**no′tice·a·bly** *adv.*

nour·ish (nʉr′ish) *v.* to feed; provide with the things needed for life and growth [Water and sunlight *nourished* the plants.] —**nour′ish·ing** *adj.*

nui·sance (noo′səns *or* nyoo′səns) *n.* an act, thing, or person that causes trouble or bother [It's such a *nuisance* to put on boots just to go next door.]

numb (num) *adj.* not able to feel, or feeling very little [*numb* with cold] ◆*v.* to make numb [The cold *numbed* his toes.]

nu·tri·tion (noo trish′ən *or* nyoo trish′ən) *n.* **1** the process by which an animal or plant takes in food and uses it in living and growing **2** food; nourishment **3** the study of the foods people should eat for health and well–being —**nu·tri′tion·al** *adj.*

o·boe (ō′bō) *n.* a woodwind instrument whose mouthpiece has a double reed —**o′bo·ist**

ob·serv·a·to·ry (äb zʉrv′ə tôr′ē) *n.* a building with telescopes and other equipment in it for studying the stars, weather conditions, etc. —*pl.* **ob·serv′a·to′ries**

ob·serve (əb zʉrv′) *v.* **1** to see, watch, or notice [I *observed* that the child was smiling.] **2** to examine and study carefully [to *observe* an experiment] —**ob·served′, ob·serv′ing** —**ob·serv′er** *n.*

ob·vi·ous (äb′vē əs) *adj.* easy to see or understand; plain; clear [an *obvious* rust stain; an *obvious* danger] —**ob′vi·ous·ly** *adv.* —**ob′vi·ous·ness** *n.*

oc·ca·sion (ə kā′zhən) *n.* **1** a suitable time; good chance; opportunity [Did you have *occasion* to visit with them?] **2** a particular time [We've met on several *occasions.*] **3** a special time or happening [Independence Day is an *occasion* to celebrate.]

oc·cu·py (äk′yoo pī′) *v.* **1** to live in [to *occupy* a house] **2** to take up; fill [The store *occupies* the entire building.] **3** to keep busy; employ [Many activities *occupy* his time.] —**oc′cu·pied, oc′cu·py·ing**

oc·cur (ə kʉr′) *v.* **1** to come into one's mind [The idea never *occurred* to me.] **2** to happen; take place [That event *occurred* years ago.] —**oc·curred′, oc·cur′ring**

oc·ta·gon (äk′tə gän) *n.* a flat figure having eight angles and eight sides

of·fi·cer (ôf′i sər *or* äf′i sər) *n.* **1** a person holding some office, as in a business, club, or government **2** a member of a police force **3** a person who commands others in an army, navy, etc. [Generals and lieutenants are commissioned *officers.*]

172

of·fi·cial (ə fish′əl) **n. 1** a person who holds an office, especially in government ☆**2** a person who sees to it that the rules are followed in a game, as a referee or umpire ◆**adj. 1** of or having to do with an office [an *official* record; *official* duties] **2** coming from a person who has authority [an *official* request] **3** fit for an important officer; formal [an *official* welcome] —**of·fi′cial·ly adv.**

oint·ment (ɔint′mənt) **n.** an oily cream rubbed on the skin to heal it or make it soft and smooth; salve

or·gan·ize (ôr′gə nīz) **v.** to arrange or place according to a system [The library books are *organized* according to their subjects.] —**or′gan·ized, or′gan·iz·ing** —**or′gan·iz′er n.**

o·rig·i·nal·i·ty (ə rij′ ə nal′ə tē) **n.** the quality or condition of being fresh, new, or creative

or·phan·age (ôr′fən ij) **n.** a home for taking care of a number of orphans

out·ra·geous (ɔut rā′jəs) **adj. 1** doing great injury or wrong [*outrageous* crimes] **2** so wrong or bad that it hurts or shocks [an *outrageous* lie] —**out·ra′geous·ly adv.**

o·ver·due (ō vər doo′ or ō vər dyoo′) **adj.** delayed past the time set for payment, arrival, etc. [an *overdue* bill; a bus long *overdue*]

o·ver·e·mo·tion·al (ō′vər ē mō′shə nəl) **adj.** too full of emotion or strong feeling [an *overemotional* speech]

o·ver·flow (ō vər flō′) **v. 1** to flow across; flood [Water *overflowed* the streets.] **2** to have its contents flowing over [The sink is *overflowing*.] ◆**n.** (ō′vər flō) the act of overflowing

o·ver·grown (ō′vər grōn′) **adj. 1** covered with foliage or weeds [a lawn that is badly *overgrown*] **2** having grown too large or too fast [an *overgrown* child]

o·ver·joyed (ō vər jɔid′) **adj.** filled with great joy

o·ver·pro·tect (ō′vər prə tekt′) **v.** to protect more than is necessary or helpful, especially by trying to keep someone from the normal hurts and disappointments of life

o·ver·sen·si·tive (ō′vər sn′sə tiv) **adj.** too quick to feel, notice, or respond to

o·ver·weight (ō′vər wāt′) **n.** more weight than is needed or allowed; extra weight ◆**adj.** (ō vər wāt′) weighing more than is normal or proper; too heavy

oys·ter (ɔis′tər) **n.** a shellfish with a soft body enclosed in two rough shells hinged together: some are used as food, and pearls are formed inside others

oz. *abbreviation for* **ounce** —*pl.* **oz.** or **ozs.**

pain·ful (pān′fəl) **adj.** causing pain; hurting; unpleasant [a *painful* wound] —**pain′ful·ness n.**

pam·phlet (pam′flət) **n.** a thin booklet with a paper cover

pap·ri·ka (pə prē′kə) **n.** a red seasoning made by grinding certain peppers

par·a·chute (per′ə shoot) **n.** a large cloth device that opens up like an umbrella and is used for slowing down a person or thing dropping from an airplane —**par′a·chut·ist n.** ◆**v.** to jump with or drop by a parachute —**par′a·chut·ed, par′a·chut·ing**

par·al·lel·o·gram (par′ ə lel′ə gram) **n.** a figure having four sides, with the opposite sides parallel and of equal length

par·ent (per′ənt) **n. 1** a father or mother **2** any animal or plant as it is related to its offspring —**par′ent·hood**

pa·ren·the·is (pə ren′thə sis) **n. 1** a word, phrase, etc. put into a complete sentence as an added note or explanation and set off, as between curved lines, from the rest of the sentence **2** either or both of the curved lines ( ) used to set off such a word, phrase, etc. —*pl.* **pa·ren·the·ses** (pə ren′thə sēz)

par·tial (pär′shəl) **adj. 1** of or in only a part; not complete or total [a *partial* eclipse of the sun] **2** favoring one person or side more than another; biased [A judge should not be *partial*.] —**par′tial·ly adv.**

par·tic·i·pate (pär tis′ə pāt) **v.** to take part with others; have a share [Sue *participated* in the school play.] —**par·tic′i·pat·ed, par·tic′i·pat·ing** —**par·tic′i·pa′tion, par·tic′i·pa′tor n.**

pas·sive (pas′iv) **adj. 1** not active, but acted upon [Spectators have a *passive* interest in sports.] **2** not resisting; yielding; submissive [The *passive* child did as he was told.] —**pas′sive·ly adv.**

pa·tience (pa′shəns) **n.** the fact of being patient or the ability to be patient

pa·tient (pā′shənt) **adj.** able to put up with pain, trouble, delay, boredom, etc. without complaining [The *patient* children waited in line for the theater to open.] ◆**n.** a person under the care of a doctor —**pa′tient·ly adv.**

☆**pa·ti·o** (pat′ē ō or pät′ē ō) **n. 1** in Spain and Spanish America, a courtyard around which a house is built **2** a paved area near a house, with chairs, tables, etc. for outdoor lounging, dining, etc. —*pl.* **pa′ti·os**

pa·trol (pə trōl′) **v.** to make regular trips around a place in order to guard it [The watchman *patrolled* the area all night.] —**pa·trolled′, pa·trol′ling n. 1** the act of patrolling **2** a person or group that patrols

a	ask, fat
ā	ape, date
ä	car, lot
e	elf, ten
ē	even, meet
i	is, hit
ī	ice, fire
ō	open, go
ô	law, horn
ɔi	oil, point
oo	look, pull
ōō	ooze, tool
ɔu	out, crowd
u	up, cut
ʉ	fur, fern
ə	a in ago
	e in agent
	e in father
	i in unity
	o in collect
	u in focus
ch	chin, arch
ŋ	ring, singer
sh	she, dash
th	thin, truth
th	then, father
zh	s in pleasure

173

pause (pôz *or* päz) *n.* a short stop, as in speaking or working ◆*v.* to make a pause; stop for a short time [He *paused* to catch his breath.] —**paused, paus′ing**

pave (pāv) *v.* to cover the surface of a road, walk, etc., as with concrete or asphalt —**paved, pav′ing** —**pave the way**, to make the way ready for something; prepare

per·ceive (pər sēv′) *v.* **1** to become aware of through one of the senses, especially through seeing [to *perceive* the difference between two shades of red] **2** to take in through the mind [I quickly *perceived* the joke.] —**per·ceived′, per·ceiv′ing**

per·cep·tion (pər sep′shən) *n.* **1** the act of perceiving or the ability to perceive [Jan's *perception* of color is poor.] **2** knowledge or understanding got by perceiving [She has a clear *perception* of her duty.]

per·pen·dic·u·lar (pʉr′ pən dik′yoo lər) *adj.* **1** at right angles [The wall should be *perpendicular* to the floor.] **2** straight up and down; exactly upright [a *perpendicular* flagpole ◆*n.* a line that is at right angles to the horizon, or to another line or plane [The Leaning Tower of Pisa leans away from the *perpendicular.*]

per·son·al (pʉr′sə nəl) *adj.* of one's own; private; individual [a *personal* opinion; a *personal* secretary]

per·son·nel (pʉr sə nel′) *n.* persons employed in any work, service, etc. [office *personnel*]

per·spec·tive (pər spek′tiv) *n.* **1** the way things look from a given point according to their size, shape, distance, etc. [*Perspective* makes things far away look small.] **2** the art of picturing things so that they seem close or far away, big or small, etc., just as they look to the eye when viewed from a given point **3** a certain point of view in understanding or judging things or happenings, especially one that shows them in their true relations to one another [Working in a factory will give you a new *perspective* on labor problems.]

pew·ter (pyoot′ər) *n.* **1** a grayish alloy of tin with lead, brass, or copper **2** things made of pewter, especially dishes, tableware, etc. ◆*adj.* made of pewter

phe·nom·e·non (fə näm′ə nän) *n.* **1** any fact, condition, or happening that can be seen, heard, and described in a scientific way, such as an eclipse **2** an unusual or remarkable event or thing [Rain is a *phenomenon* in the desert.] —*pl.* **phe·nom·e·na** (fə näm′ə nə) or (for sense **2** usually) **phe·nom′e·nons**

pho·to·graph (fōt′ə graf) *n.* a picture made with a camera ◆*v.* **1** to take a photograph of **2** to look a certain way in photographs [She *photographs* taller than she is.] — **pho′to·graphed**

phrase (frāz) *n.* a group of words that is not a complete sentence, but that gives a single idea, usually as a separate part of a sentence ["Drinking fresh milk," "with meals," and "to be healthy" are *phrases.*] ◆*v.* to say or write in a certain way [He *phrased* his answer carefully.] —**phrased, phras′ing**

phy·si·cian (fi zish′ən) *n.* a doctor of medicine, especially one who is not mainly a surgeon

pic·co·lo (pik′ə lō) *n.* a small flute that sounds notes an octave higher than an ordinary flute does —*pl.* **pic′co·los**

pierce (pirs) *v.* **1** to pass into or through; penetrate [The needle *pierced* her finger. A light *pierced* the darkness.] **2** to make a hole through; perforate; bore [to *pierce* one's ears for earrings] **3** to make a sharp sound through [A shriek *pierced* the air.] —**pierced, pierc′ing**

pig·ment (pig′mənt) *n.* **1** coloring matter, usually a powder, mixed with oil, water, etc. to make paints **2** the matter in the cells and tissues that gives color to plants and animals

pi·ta (pē′tə) *n.* a round, flat bread of the Middle East: it can be split open to form a pocket for a filling of meat, vegetables, etc.

☆**piz·za** (pēt′sə) *n.* an Italian dish made by baking a thin layer of dough covered with tomatoes, spices, cheese, etc.

pkg. *abbreviation for* **package** *or* **packages**

plain·tiff (plān′tif) *n.* the person who starts a suit against another in a court of law

plan·et (plan′ət) *n.* any of the large heavenly bodies that revolve around the sun and shine as they reflect the sun's light: the planets, in their order from the sun, are Mercury, Venus, Earth, Mars, Jupiter, Saturn, Uranus, Neptune, and Pluto —**plan·e·tar·y** (plan′ə ter′ē) *adj.*

plaque (plak) *n.* **1** a thin, flat piece of metal, wood, etc. with decoration or lettering on it **2** a thin film that forms on the teeth and hardens into tartar if not removed

play·wright (plā′rīt) *n.* a person who writes plays; dramatist

pledge (plej) *n.* **1** a promise or agreement [the *pledge* of allegiance to the flag] **2** something promised, especially money to be given as to a charity ◆*v.* **1** to promise to give [to *pledge* $100 to a building fund] **2** to bind by a promise [He is *pledged* to marry her.] —**pledged, pledg′ing**

plumb·er (plum′ər) *n.* a person whose work is putting in and repairing the pipes and fixtures of water and gas systems in a building

pol·y·gon (päl′i gän′) *n.* a flat, closed figure made up of straight lines, especially one having more than four angles and sides

pon·cho (pän′chō) *n.* a cloak like a blanket with a hole in the middle for the head: it is worn as a raincoat, etc., originally in South America —*pl.* **pon′chos**

por·trait (pôr′trit) *n.* a drawing, painting, or photograph of a person, especially of the face

por·tray (pôr trā′) *v.* 1 to make a picture of, as in a painting 2 to make a picture in words; describe [The writer *portrays* life in New York.] 3 to play the part of in a play, movie, etc. [The actress *portrayed* a scientist.] —**por·trayed′**

po·si·tion (pə zish′ən) *n.* 1 the way in which a person or thing is placed or arranged [a sitting *position*] 2 the place where a person or thing is; location [The ship radioed its *position*.] 3 a job or office; post [She has a *position* with the city government.] ◆*v.* to put in a certain position [They *positioned* themselves around the house.]

post·script (pōst′skript) *n.* a note added below the signature of a letter

post·war (pōst′wôr′) *adj.* after the war

po·ten·tial (po ten′shel) *adj.* that can be, but is not yet; possible [a *potential* leader; a *potential* source of trouble] ◆*n.* power or skill that may be developed [a baseball team with *potential*] —**po·ten′tial·ly** *adv.*

poul·try (pōl′trē) *n.* fowl raised for food; chickens, turkeys, ducks, geese, etc.

prac·ti·cal (prak′ti kəl) *adj.* 1 that can be put to use; useful and sensible [a *practical* idea; *practical* shoes] 2 dealing with things in a sensible and realistic way [Wouldn't it be more *practical* to paint it yourself than pay to have it painted?]

praise (prāz) *v.* 1 to say good things about; give a good opinion of [to *praise* someone's work] 2 to worship, as in song [to *praise* God] —**praised, prais′ing** ◆*n.* a praising or being praised; words that show approval

praise·wor·thy (prāz′wur·*th*ē) *adj.* deserving praise; that should be admired

pre·cau·tion (prē kô′shən *or* prē kä′shən) *n.* care taken ahead of time, as against danger, failure, etc. [She took the *precaution* of locking the door before she left.] —**pre·cau′tion·ar′y** *adj.*

pre·cede (prē sed′) *v.* to go or come before in time, order, or rank [She *preceded* him into the room.]

pre·dict (prē dikt′) *v.* to tell what one thinks will happen in the future [I *predict* that you will win.] —**pre·dict′ed** —**pre·dict′a·ble** *adj.*

pre·fer (prē fur′) *v.* to like better; choose first [He *prefers* baseball to football] —**pre·ferred′, pre·fer′ring**

pre·lude (prel′yood *or* prā′lood) *n.* a part that comes before or leads up to what follows [The strong wind was a *prelude* to the thunderstorm.]

Pres. *abbreviation for* **President**

pre·scrip·tion (prē skrip′shən) *n.* 1 an order or direction 2 a doctor's written instructions telling how to prepare and use a medicine; also, a medicine made by following such instructions

pre·sume (prē zoom′ *or* prē zyoom′) *v.* 1 to be so bold as to; dare [I wouldn't *presume* to tell you what to do.] 2 to take for granted; suppose [I *presume* you know what you are doing.] —**pre·sumed′, pre·sum′ing**

☆**pret·zel** (pret′s'l) *n.* a slender roll of dough, usually twisted in a knot, sprinkled with salt, and baked until hard

pre·vent (prē vent′) *v.* 1 to stop or hinder [A storm *prevented* us from going.] 2 to keep from happening [Careful driving *prevents* accidents.] —**pre·vent′ed** —**pre·vent′a·ble** *or* **pre·vent′i·ble** *adj.*

pre·vi·ous (prē′vē əs) *adj.* happening before in time or order; earlier [at a *previous* meeting; on the *previous* page] —**pre′vi·ous·ly** *adv.*

prin·ci·pal (prin′sə pəl) *adj.* most important; chief; main [the *principal* crop of a State] ◆*n.* the head of a school

prin·ci·ple (prin′sə pəl) *n.* 1 a rule, truth, etc. upon which others are based [the basic *principles* of law] 2 a rule used in deciding how to behave [It is against her *principles* to lie.]

pro·ceed (prō sēd′) *v.* 1 to go on, especially after stopping for a while [After eating, we *proceeded* to the next town.] 2 to begin and go on doing something [I *proceeded* to build a fire.] 3 to move along or go on [Things *proceeded* smoothly.]

proc·ess (prä′ses) *n.* 1 a series of changes by which something develops [the *process* of growth in a plant] 2 a method of making or doing something, in which there are a number of steps [the refining *process* used in making gasoline from crude oil] 3 the act of doing something, or the time during which something is done [I was in the *process* of writing a report when you called.] ◆*v.* to prepare by a special process [to *process* cheese] —**proc′essed**

pro·duce (prə doos′ *or* prə dyoos′) *v.* 1 to bring forth; bear; yield [trees *producing* apples; a well that *produces* oil] 2 to make or manufacture [a company that *produces* bicycles] —**pro·duced′, pro·duc′ing** ◆*n.* (prō′doos) something that is produced, especially fruits and vegetables for marketing —**pro·duc′er**

pro·found (prō found′) *adj.* 1 showing great knowledge, or thought [the *profound* remarks of the judge] 2 deeply felt; intense [*profound* grief] 3 thorough [*profound* changes]

prog·ress (präg′res) *n.* 1 a moving forward [the boat's slow *progress* down the river] 2 a developing or improving [She shows *progress* in learning French.] ◆*v.* (prō gres′) 1 to move forward; go ahead 2 to develop or improve; advance [Science has helped us to *progress*.]

pro·jec·tor (prə jek′tər) *n.* a machine for projecting pictures or movies on a screen

a	ask, fat
ā	ape, date
ä	car, lot
e	elf, ten
ē	even, meet
i	is, hit
ī	ice, fire
ō	open, go
ô	law, horn
oi	oil, point
oo	look, pull
ōo	ooze, tool
ou	out, crowd
u	up, cut
ʉ	fur, fern
ə	a in ago
	e in agent
	e in father
	i in unity
	o in collect
	u in focus
ch	chin, arch
ŋ	ring, singer
sh	she, dash
th	thin, truth
th	then, father
zh	s in pleasure

175

prompt (prämpt) *adj.* **1** quick in doing what should be done; on time [He is *prompt* in paying his bills.] **2** done, spoken, etc. without waiting [We would like a *prompt* reply.] ◆*v.* **1** to urge or stir into action [Tyranny *prompted* them to revolt.] **2** to remind of something that has been forgotten [to *prompt* an actor when a line has been forgotten] —**prompt´ly** *adv.* —**prompt´ness** *n.*

pro·noun (prō´noun) *n.* a word used in the place of a noun: *I, us, you, they, he, her, it* are some pronouns

pro·nounce (prə nouns´) *v.* **1** to say or make the sounds of [How do you *pronounce* "leisure"?] **2** to say or declare in an official or serious way [I now *pronounce* you husband and wife.] —**pro·nounced´, pro·nounc´ing**

pro·pel (prə pel´) *v.* to push or drive forward [Some rockets are *propelled* by liquid fuel.] —**pro·pelled´, pro·pel´ling**

pros·e·cute (präs´ə kyo͞ot) *v.* to put on trial in a court of law on charges of crime or wrongdoing —**pros´e·cut·ed, pros´e·cut·ing**

pros·e·cu·tor (präs´ə kyo͞ot´ər) *n.* a person who prosecutes; especially, a lawyer who works for the state in prosecuting persons charged with crime

pro·te·in (prō´tēn) *n.* a substance containing nitrogen and other elements, found in all living things and in such foods as cheese, meat, eggs, beans, etc.: it is a necessary part of an animal's diet

pro·vi·sion (prō vizh´ən) *n.* **1** a providing or supplying **2** something provided or arrangements made for the future [Her savings are a *provision* for her old age.] **3** provisions, *pl.* a supply or stock of food

pro·voke (prō vōk´) *v.* **1** to excite to some action or feeling [to *provoke* a fight] **2** to annoy or make angry [It *provoked* me to see litter on the lawn.] **3** to stir up [to *provoke* interest]

pt. *abbreviation for* **part, pint, point** —*pl.* **pts.**

pur·pose (pur´pəs) *n.* **1** what one plans to get or do; aim; goal [I came for the *purpose* of speaking to you.] **2** the reason or use for something [a room with no *purpose*] —**pur´pose·ful, pur´pose·less** *adj.*

pur·sue (pər so͞o´ *or* pər syo͞o´) *v.* **1** to follow in order to catch or catch up to [to *pursue* a runaway horse] **2** to carry out or follow; go on with [She is *pursuing* a career in acting.] **3** to try to find; seek [to *pursue* knowledge] —**pur·sued´, pur·su´ing** —**pur·su´er** *n.*

qt. *abbreviation for* **quart** *or* **quarts**

quad·ri·lat·er·al (kwäd´ rə lat´ər əl) *adj.* having four sides ◆*n.* a flat figure with four sides and four angles

qual·i·fy (kwôl´ə fī *or* kwä´lə fī) *v.* to make or be fit or suitable, as for some work or activity [Your training *qualifies* you for the job. Does he *qualify* for the team?] —**qual´i·fied, qual´i·fy·ing**

qual·i·ty (kwôl´ə tē *or* kwä´lə tē) *n.* **1** any of the features that make a thing what it is; characteristic [Coldness is one *quality* of ice cream.] **2** degree of excellence [a poor quality of paper] —*pl.* **qual´i·ties**

quan·ti·ty (kwänt´ə tē) *n.* **1** an amount or portion [large *quantities* of food] **2** a large amount [The factory makes toys in *quantity*.] —*pl.* **quan´ti·ties**

ques·tion·naire (kwes chən ner´) *n.* a written or printed list of questions used in gathering information from people

quilt (kwilt) *n.* a covering for a bed, made of two layers of cloth filled with down, wool, etc. and stitched together in lines or patterns to keep the filling in place ◆*v.* **1** to make in the form of a quilt [a *quilted* potholder] ☆**2** to make quilts —**quilt´ed**

quiz (kwiz) *n.* a short test given to find out how much one has learned —*pl.* **quiz´zes** ◆*v.* **1** to ask questions of [The police *quizzed* the suspect.] **2** to test the knowledge of with a quiz [The teacher *quizzed* the class.] —**quizzed, quiz´zing**

quo·ta·tion (kwō tā´shən) *n.* **1** the act of quoting **2** the words or section quoted [Sermons often have *quotations* from the Bible.]

quo·tient (kwō´shənt) *n.* the number got by dividing one number into another [In 32 ÷ 8 = 4, the number 4 is the *quotient*.]

Rr

ra·di·ance (rā´de əns) *n.* the quality or condition of being radiant; brightness

re·al·ize (rē´ə līz) *v.* to understand fully [I *realize* that good marks depend upon careful work.] —**re´al·ized, re´al·iz·ing** —**re´al·i·za´tion** *n.*

reas·on·a·ble (rē´zən ə bəl) *adj.* **1** using or showing reason; sensible [a *reasonable* person; a *reasonable* decision] **2** not too high or too low; fair [a *reasonable* price; a *reasonable* salary] —**rea´son·a·bly** *adv.*

re·ceipt (rē sēt′) *n.* **1** the act of receiving [We are in *receipt* of your letter.] **2** a written or printed statement that something has been received [My landlord gave me a *receipt* when I paid my rent.]

re·cent (rē′sənt) *adj.* of a time just before now; made or happening a short time ago [*recent* news] —**re′cent·ly** *adv.*

rec·i·pe (res′ə pē) *n.* a list of ingredients and directions for making something to eat or drink [a *recipe* for cookies]

re·cruit (rē krōōt′) *n.* a person who has recently joined an organization, group, or, especially, the armed forces ➤*v.* **1** to enlist new members in [to *recruit* an army] **2** to get to join [Our nature club *recruited* six new members.]

re·fer (rē fʉr′) *v.* **1** to speak of or call attention; mention [You seldom *refer* to your injury.] **2** to go for facts, help, etc. [Columbus had no accurate maps to *refer* to.] **3** to tell to go to a certain person or place for help, service, information, etc. [Our neighbor *referred* me to a good doctor.] —**re·ferred′, re·fer′ring**

re·frig·er·a·tor (rē frij′ər āt′ ər) *n.* a box or room in which the air is kept cool to keep food, etc. from spoiling

reg·u·la·tion (reg yə lā′shən) *n.* **1** the act of regulating or the condition of being regulated [the *regulation* of the sale of alcohol] **2** a rule or law that regulates or controls [safety *regulations*]

re·hearse (rē hʉrs′) *v.* **1** to go through a play, speech, etc. for practice, before giving it in public **2** to repeat in detail [They *rehearsed* all their troubles to me.] —**re·hearsed′, re·hears′ing** —**re·hears′al** *n.*

reign (rān) *n.* the rule of a king, queen, emperor, etc.; also, the time of ruling [laws made during the *reign* of Victoria] ➤*v.* to rule as a king, queen, etc. [Henry VIII *reigned* for 38 years.] —**reigned**

rein·deer (rān′dir) *n.* a large deer found in northern regions, where it is tamed and used for work or as food: both the male and female have antlers —*pl.* **rein′deer**

re·joice (rē jois′) *v.* to be or make glad or happy [We *rejoiced* at the news.] **re·joiced′, re·joic′ing** —**re·joic′ing** *n.*

re·late (rē lāt′) *v.* **1** to tell about; give an account of [*Relate* to us what you did.] **2** to connect in thought or meaning; show a relation between [to *relate* one idea to another] —**re·lat′ed, re·lat′ing**

re·lease (rē lēs′) *v.* to set free or relieve [*Release* the bird from the cage.] ➤*n.* the act of setting someone or something free [a *release* from prison]

re·li·a·ble (rē lī′ə bəl) *adj.* that can be trusted; dependable [This barometer gives a *reliable* weather forecast.] —**re·li·a·bil·i·ty** (ri lī′ə bil′ə tē) *n.* —**re·li·a·bly** *adv.*

re·lieve (rē lēv′) *v.* **1** to free from pain, worry, etc. [We were *relieved* when the danger passed.] **2** to set free from duty or work by replacing [The guard is *relieved* every four hours.] —**re·lieved′, re·liev′ing**

re·main·der (rē mān′dər) *n.* the part, number, etc. left over [I sold some of my books and gave the *remainder* to the library. When 3 is subtracted from 10, the *remainder* is 7.]

re·mark·a·ble (rē märk′ə bəl) *adj.* worth noticing because it is very unusual [the *remarkable* strength of Hercules] —**re·mark′a·bly** *adv.*

rem·e·dy (rem′ə dē) *n.* **1** a medicine or treatment that cures, heals, or relieves [a *remedy* for sunburn] **2** anything that corrects a wrong or helps make things better [a *remedy* for poor education] —*pl.* **rem′e·dies** ➤*v.* to cure, correct, make better, etc. [Some money would *remedy* her situation.] —**rem′e·died, rem′e·dy·ing**

re·peat·ed (ri pēt′əd) *adj.* said, made, or done again or often [*repeated* warnings] —**re·peat′ed·ly** *adv.*

re·quire (rē kwīr′) *v.* **1** to be in need of [Most plants *require* sunlight.] **2** to order, command, or insist upon [He *required* us to leave.] —**re·quired′, re·quir′ing**

re·search (rē′sʉrch′ *or* rē sʉrch′) *n.* careful, patient study in order to find out facts and principles about some subject [to carry on *research* into the causes of cancer] ➤*v.* to do research

re·sem·ble (rē zem′bəl) *v.* to be or look like [Rabbits *resemble* hares but are smaller.] —**re·sem′bled, re·sem′bling**

re·sign (rē zīn′) *v.* to give up one's office, position, membership, etc. [We *resigned* from the club.] —**re·signed′**

re·sist·ance (rē zis′təns) *n.* **1** the act of resisting **2** the power to resist or withstand [Her *resistance* to colds is low.] **3** the opposing of one force or thing to another [the fabric's *resistance* to wear]

re·solve (rē zälv′ *or* rē zôlv′) *v.* **1** to decide; make up one's own mind [I *resolved* to help them.] **2** to make clear; solve or explain [to *resolve* a problem] ➤*n.* firm purpose or determination [her *resolve* to be successful]

re·sound (rē zound′) *v.* **1** to echo or be filled with sound [The hall *resounded* with music.] **2** to make a loud, echoing sound; to be echoed [His laughter *resounded* throughout the cave.] —**re·sound′ing**

re·trieve (rē trēv′) *v.* **1** to get back; recover [to *retrieve* a kite from a tree] **2** to find and bring back [The spaniel *retrieved* the wounded duck.] —**re·trieved′, re·triev′ing**

re·veal (rē vēl′) *v.* **1** to make known what was hidden or secret [The map *revealed* the spot where the treasure was buried.] **2** to show [She took off her hat, *revealing* her golden hair.] —**re·vealed′**

a	ask, fat
ā	ape, date
ä	car, lot
e	elf, ten
ē	even, meet
i	is, hit
ī	ice, fire
ō	open, go
ô	law, horn
oi	oil, point
͝oo	look, pull
͞oo	ooze, tool
ou	out, crowd
u	up, cut
ʉ	fur, fern
ə	a in ago
	e in agent
	e in father
	i in unity
	o in collect
	u in focus
ch	chin, arch
ŋ	ring, singer
sh	she, dash
th	thin, truth
th	then, father
zh	s in pleasure

rev·e·nue (rev′ə nōō *or* rev′ə nyōō) *n.* money got as rent, profit, etc.; income; especially, the money a government gets from taxes, duties, etc.

re·vers·i·ble (rē vur′sə bəl) *adj.* that can be reversed; made so that either side can be used as the outer side [a *reversible* coat]

☆**ro·de·o** (rō′dē ō) *n.* a contest or show in which cowboys match their skill in riding horses, roping and throwing cattle, etc. —*pl.* **ro′de·os**

Roo·se·velt, Franklin D. (rō′zə velt) 1882–1945; 32d president of the United States, from 1933 to 1945

Roo·se·velt, Theodore 1858–1919; 26th president of the United States, from 1901 to 1909

rough·en (ruf′ən) *v.* to make or become rough [to *roughen* a smooth surface with a coarse file]

row·boat (rō′bōt) *n.* a boat made to be rowed

sauce·pan (sôs′pan *or* säs′pan) *n.* a small metal pot with a long handle, used for cooking

sax·o·phone (sak′sə fōn) *n.* a woodwind musical instrument with a curved metal body: its mouthpiece has a single reed

scald (skôld) *v.* **1** to burn with hot liquid or steam **2** to use boiling liquid on, as to kill germs **3** to heat until it almost boils [to *scald* milk for a custard] —**scald′ing** ➡*n.* a burn caused by scalding

scam·per (skam′pər) *v.* to move quickly or in a hurry [squirrels *scampering* through the trees] —**scam′per·ing** ➡*n.* a quick run or dash

scat·ter (skat′ər) *v.* **1** to throw here and there; sprinkle [to *scatter* seed over a lawn] **2** to separate and send or go in many directions; disperse [The wind *scattered* the leaves. The crowd *scattered* after the game.] —**scat′tered**

sce·ner·y (sēn′ər ē) *n.* **1** the way a certain area looks; outdoor views [the *scenery* along the shore] **2** painted screens, hangings, etc. used on a stage for a play

sce·nic (sēn′ik) *adj.* **1** having to do with scenery or landscapes [the *scenic* wonders of the Rockies] **2** having beautiful scenery [a *scenic* route along the river] —**sce′ni·cal·ly** *adv.*

scent (sent) *n.* **1** a smell; odor [the *scent* of apple blossoms] **2** the sense of smell [Lions hunt partly by *scent.*] **3** a smell left by an animal [The dogs lost the fox's *scent* at the river.] ➡*v.* to smell [Our dog *scented* a cat.] —**scent′ed**

sched·ule (skej′ool *or* ske′joo əl) *n.* ☆**1** a list of the times at which certain things are to happen; timetable [a *schedule* of the sailings of an ocean liner] ☆**2** a timed plan for a project [The work is ahead of *schedule.*] ➡*v.* **1** to make a schedule of [to *schedule* one's hours of work] ☆**2** to plan for a certain time [to *schedule* a game for 3:00 P.M.] —**sched′uled, sched′ul·ing**

scheme (skēm) *n.* **1** a plan or system in which things are carefully put together [the color *scheme* of a painting] **2** a plan or program, often a secret or dishonest one [a *scheme* for getting rich quick] ➡*v.* to make secret or dishonest plans; to plot —**schemed, schem′ing**

schol·ar·ship (skä′lər ship) *n.* a gift of money to help a student continue his or her education

sci·en·tif·ic (sī′ən tif′ik) *adj.* **1** having to do with, or used in, science [a *scientific* study; *scientific* equipment] **2** using the rules and methods of science [*scientific* procedure] —**sci′en·tif′i·cal·ly** *adv.*

scis·sors (siz′ərz) *pl. n.* a tool for cutting, with two blades that are joined so that they slide over each other when their handles are moved: *also used with a singular verb: also called* **pair of scissors**

scour (skour) *v.* to clean by rubbing hard, especially with something rough or gritty [The cook *scoured* the greasy frying pan with soap and steel wool.]

scowl (skoul) *v.* to lower the eyebrows and the corners of the mouth in showing displeasure; look angry or irritated [She *scowled* upon hearing the bad news.] ➡*n.* a scowling look; an angry frown

scratch (skrach) *v.* **1** to mark or cut the surface of slightly with something sharp [Thorns *scratched* her legs. Our cat *scratched* the chair with its claws.] **2** to rub or scrape, as with the nails, to relieve itching [to *scratch* a mosquito bite] **3** to cross out by drawing lines through [She *scratched* out what he had written.] —**scratched** ➡*n.* **1** a mark or cut made in a surface by something sharp **2** a slight wound

scream (skrēm) *v.* **1** to give a loud, shrill cry, as in fright or pain [They *screamed* as the roller coaster hurtled downward.] **2** to make a noise like this [The sirens *screamed.* We *screamed* with laughter.] —**scream′ing** ➡*n.* a loud, shrill cry or sound; shriek

scrimp (skrimp) *v.* to spend or use as little as possible [to *scrimp* to save money]

sculp·ture (skulp′chər) *n.* **1** the art of carving wood, chiseling stone, casting or welding metal, modeling clay or wax, etc. into statues, figures, or the like **2** a statue, figure, etc. made in this way ➡*v.* to cut, chisel, form, etc. in making sculptures —**sculp′tured, sculp′tur·ing** —**sculp′tur·al** *adj.*

seal (sēl) *n.* **1** a piece of paper, wax, etc. with a design pressed into it, fixed to an official document to show that it is genuine: such wax designs were once also used to seal letters **2** something that closes or fastens tightly ➛*v.* to close or fasten tight [to *seal* cracks with putty; to *seal* a letter] —**seal´er** *n.*

search (sʉrch) *v.* **1** to look over or through in order to find something [We *searched* the house. The police *searched* the thief for a gun.] **2** to try to find [to *search* for an answer] —**search´ing** —**search´er** *n.*

sea·son·al (sē´zən əl) *adj.* of or depending on a season or the seasons [*seasonal* rains; *seasonal* work] —**sea´son·al·ly** *adv.*

se·cu·ri·ty (si kyʊr´ə tē) *n.* **1** the condition or feeling of being safe or sure; freedom from danger, fear, doubt, etc. **2** something that protects [Insurance is a *security* against loss.] **3** something given or pledged as a guarantee [A car may be used as *security* for a loan.] **4** securities, *pl.* stocks and bonds —*pl.* **se·cu´ri·ties**

Seine (sān *or* sen) a river in northern France: it flows through Paris into the English Channel

seize (sēz) *v.* to take hold of in a sudden, strong, or eager way; grasp [to *seize* a weapon and fight; to *seize* an opportunity] —**seized, seiz´ing**

se·lec·tion (sə lek´shən) *n.* **1** a selecting or being selected; choice **2** the thing or things chosen; also, things to choose from [a wide *selection* of colors]

sem·i·cir·cle (sem´i sʉr´kəl) *n.* a half circle —**sem·i·cir·cu·lar** (sem´i sʉr´kyə lər) *adj.*

sem·i·co·lon (sem´i kō´lən) *n.* a punctuation mark (;) used to show a pause that is shorter than the pause at the end of a sentence, but longer than the pause marked by the comma [The *semicolon* is often used to separate closely related clauses, especially when they contain commas.]

sem·i·fi·nal (sem´i fī´nəl) *n.* a round, match, etc. that comes just before the final one in a contest or tournament —**sem´i·fi´nal·ist**

sem·i·pre·cious (sem´i presh´əs) *adj.* describing gems that are of less value than the precious gems [The garnet is a *semiprecious* gem.]

ses·sion (sesh´ən) *n.* **1** the meeting of a court, legislature, class, etc. to do its work **2** the time during which such a meeting or series goes on **3** a school term or period of study, classes, etc.

sham·poo (sham pʊo´) *v.* to wash with foamy suds, as hair or a rug —**sham·pooed´, sham·poo´ing** ➛*n.* **1** the act of shampooing **2** a special soap, or soaplike product, that makes suds

sharp (shärp) *adj.* **1** having a thin edge for cutting, or a fine point for piercing [a *sharp* knife; a *sharp* needle] **2** easily seen; distinct; clear [a *sharp* contrast] **3** very strong; intense; stinging [a *sharp* wind; *sharp* pain] —**sharp´ly** *adv.* —**sharp´ness** *n.*

sheaf (shēf) *n.* **1** a bunch of cut stalks of wheat, rye, or straw tied up together in a bundle **2** a bundle of things gathered together [a *sheaf* of papers] —*pl.* **sheaves**

shoul·der (shōl´dər) *n.* **1** the part of the body to which an arm or foreleg is connected **2** shoulders, the two shoulders and the part of the back between them

shuf·fle·board (shuf´əl bôrd) *n.* a game in which the players use long sticks to slide disks along a smooth lane, trying to get them on numbered sections

shut·ter (shut´ər) *n.* **1** a cover for a window, usually swinging on hinges **2** a part on a camera that opens and closes in front of the lens to control the light going in

siege (sēj) *n.* the act or an instance of surrounding a city, fort, etc. by an enemy army in an attempt to capture it

sight·see·ing (sīt´sē´iŋ) *n.* the act of going about to see places and things of interest — **sight´se´er**

sig·na·ture (sig´nə chər) *n.* **1** a person's name as he or she has written it **2** a sign in music placed at the beginning of a staff to give the key or the time

☆**sil·ver·ware** (sil´vər wer) *n.* things, especially tableware, made of or plated with silver

sim·mer (sim´ər) *v.* to keep at or just below the boiling point, usually forming tiny bubbles with a murmuring sound [*Simmer* the stew about two hours.]

sim·ple (sim´pəl) *adj.* **1** easy to do or understand [a *simple* task; *simple* directions] **2** without anything added; plain [the *simple* facts; a *simple* dress] —**sim´pler, sim´plest**

sketch (skech) *n.* **1** a simple, rough drawing or design, usually done quickly and with little detail **2** a short outline, giving the main points ➛*v.* to make a sketch of; draw sketches —**sketch´ing**

☆**sleigh** (slā) *n.* a carriage with runners instead of wheels, for travel over snow or ice

slop·py (släp´ē) *adj.* not neat or careful; messy [*sloppy* clothes; a *sloppy* piece of work] —**slop´pi·er, slop´pi·est** —**slop´pi·ly** *adv.* —**slop´pi·ness** *n.*

smear (smir) *v.* **1** to cover with something greasy or sticky [to *smear* the actor's face with cold cream] **2** to rub or spread [*Smear* some grease on the axle.] **3** to make a mark or streak that is not wanted on something [He *smeared* the wet paint with his sleeve.] —**smeared** ➛*n.* **1** a mark or streak made by smearing **2** the act of smearing or slandering someone

a	ask, fat
ā	ape, date
ä	car, lot
e	elf, ten
ē	even, meet
i	is, hit
ī	ice, fire
ō	open, go
ô	law, horn
oi	oil, point
ʊo	look, pull
o͞o	ooze, tool
ou	out, crowd
u	up, cut
ʉ	fur, fern
ə	a in ago
	e in agent
	e in father
	i in unity
	o in collect
	u in focus
ch	chin, arch
ŋ	ring, singer
sh	she, dash
th	thin, truth
th	then, father
zh	s in pleasure

smooth (smōō*th*) *adj.* **1** having an even surface, with no bumps or rough spots [as *smooth* as marble; *smooth* water on the lake] **2** even or gentle in movement; not jerky or rough [a *smooth* airplane flight; a *smooth* ride; *smooth* sailing] **3** with no trouble or difficulty [*smooth* progress] —**smooth′er** ◆*v.* **1** to make smooth or even [*Smooth* the board with sandpaper.] **2** to make easy by taking away troubles, difficulties, etc. [She *smoothed* our way by introducing us to the other guests.] ◆*adv.* in a smooth way [The engine is running *smooth* now.] —**smooth′ly** *adv.*

so·cial (sō′shəl) *adj.* **1** of or having to do with human beings as they live together in a group or groups [*social* problems; *social* forces] **2** liking to be with others; sociable [A hermit is not a *social* person.] ◆*n.* a friendly gathering; party [a church *social*] —**so′cial·ly** *adv.*

so·di·um (sō′dē əm) *n.* a soft, silver-white metal that is a chemical element: it is found in nature only in compounds [Salt, baking soda, lye, etc. contain *sodium*]

sof·ten (sôf′ən *or* säf′ən) *v.* to make or become soft or softer —**sof′ten·er** *n.*

so·lar (sō′lər) *adj.* **1** of or having to do with the sun [a *solar* eclipse; *solar* energy] **2** depending on light or energy from the sun [*solar* heating]

sol·dier (sōl′jər) *n.* a person in an army, especially one who is not a commissioned officer ◆*v.* to serve as a soldier —**sol′dier·ly** *adj.*

sol·emn (säl′əm) *adj.* serious; grave; very earnest [a *solemn* face; a *solemn* oath] —**sol′emn·ly** *adv.*

so·lu·tion (sə lōō′shən) *n.* **1** the solving of a problem **2** an answer or explanation [to find the *solution* to a mystery]

soothe (sōō*th*) *v.* **1** to make quiet or calm by being gentle or friendly [The clerk *soothed* the angry customer with helpful answers.] **2** to take away some of the pain or sorrow of; ease [I hope this lotion will *soothe* your sunburn.] —**soothed, sooth′ing** —**sooth′ing·ly** *adv.*

so·pra·no (sə pran′ō *or* sə prä′nō) *n.* **1** the highest kind of singing voice of women, girls, or young boys **2** a singer with such a voice or an instrument with a range like this —*pl.* **so·pra′nos**

spa·ghet·ti (spə get′ē) *n.* long, thin strings of dried flour paste, cooked by boiling or steaming and served with a sauce

spear·mint (spir′mint) *n.* a common plant of the mint family, used for flavoring

spe·cies (spē′shēz *or* spē′sēz) *n.* a group of plants or animals that are alike in certain ways [The lion and tiger are two different *species* of cat.] —*pl.* **spe′cies**

spec·ta·tor (spek′tātər) *n.* a person who watches something without taking part; onlooker [We were *spectators* at the last game of the World Series.]

sports·man (spôrts′mən) *n.* **1** a man who takes part in or is interested in sports **2** a person who plays fair and does not complain about losing or boast about winning —*pl.* **sports′men** —**sports′man·like** *adj.* —**sports′man·ship** *n.*

square (skwer) *n.* **1** a flat figure with four equal sides and four right angles **2** anything shaped like this [Arrange the chairs in a *square*.] ◆*adj.* **1** having the shape of a square **2** forming a right angle [a *square* corner] —**squar′er, squar′est** ◆*v.* to mark off in squares, as a checkerboard —**squared, squar′ing**

squawk (skwôk *or* skäwk) *n.* a loud, harsh cry such as a chicken or parrot makes ◆*v.* to let out a squawk —**squawk′ing** —**squawk′er** *n.*

squeeze (skwēz) *v.* **1** to press hard or force together [*Squeeze* the sponge to get rid of the water.] **2** to get by pressing or by force [to *squeeze* juice from an orange; to *squeeze* money from poor people] —**squeezed, squeez′ing** ◆*n.* a squeezing or being squeezed; hard press —**squeez′er**

stair·way (ster′wā) *or* **stair·case** (ster′kās) *n.* a flight of steps, usually with a handrail

sta·tion·ar·y (stā′shə ner′ e) *adj.* **1** staying in the same place; not moving; fixed [A *stationary* bicycle is pedaled for exercise, but does not move from its base.] **2** not changing in condition or value; not increasing or decreasing [*stationary* prices]

stead·y (sted′ē) *adj.* not changing or letting up; regular [a *steady* gaze; a *steady* worker] —**stead′i·er, stead′i·est** —**stead′ied, stead′y·ing** —**stead′i·ly** *adv.* —**stead′i·ness** *n.*

ster·e·o (ster′ē ō′) *n.* a stereophonic record player, radio, sound system, etc. —*pl.* **ster′e·os′**

stew·ard (stōō′ərd *or* styōō′ərd) *n.* a person, especially on a ship or airplane, whose work is to look after the passengers' comfort

stiff (stif) *adj.* **1** that does not bend easily; firm [*stiff* cardboard] **2** not able to move easily [*stiff* muscles] —**stiff′ly** *adv.* **stiff′ness** *n.*

stitch (stich) *n.* one complete movement of a needle and thread into and out of the material in sewing —*pl.* **stitch′es** ◆*v.* to sew or fasten with stitches [to *stitch* a seam] —**stitched**

stow·a·way (stō′ə wā) *n.* a person who hides aboard a ship, plane, etc. for a free or secret ride

strain·er (strān′ər) *n.* a thing used for straining, as a sieve, filter, etc.

stretch (strech) *v.* 1 to draw out to full length, to a greater size, to a certain distance, etc.; extend [She *stretched* out on the sofa. Will this material *stretch*? *Stretch* the rope between two trees. The road *stretches* for miles through the hills.] 2 to pull or draw tight; strain [to *stretch* a muscle] —**stretch′es**
◆*n.* 1 a stretching or being stretched [a *stretch* of the arms] 2 an unbroken space, as of time or land; extent [a *stretch* of two years; a long *stretch* of beach]

strict (strikt) *adj.* 1 keeping to rules in a careful, exact way [a *strict* supervisor] 2 never changing; rigid [a *strict* rule]
—**strict′est** —**strict′ly** *adv.*
—**strict′ness** *n.*

sub·con·tract (sub′kän′trakt) *n.* a contract in which a company hires a second company to do part of a job that the first company has agreed to complete
◆*v.* to make a subcontract [to *subcontract* for plumbing and electrical work]

subj. *abbreviation for* **subject, subjunctive**

sub·ma·rine (sub′mə rēn) *n.* a kind of warship that can travel under the surface of water ◆*adj.* (sub mə rən′) that lives, grows, happens, etc. under the surface of the sea [Sponges are *submarine* animals.]

sub·scrip·tion (səb skrip′shən) *n.* 1 the act of subscribing or something that is subscribed 2 an agreement to take and pay for a magazine, theater tickets, etc. for a particular period of time

sub·stan·tial (səb stan′shəl) *adj.* 1 of or having substance; material; real or true [Your fears turned out not to be *substantial*.] 2 strong; solid; firm [The bridge didn't look very *substantial*.] 3 more than average or usual; large [a *substantial* share; a *substantial* meal] 4 wealthy or well-to-do [a *substantial* farmer] —**sub·stan′tial·ly** *adv.*

sub·sti·tute (sub′stə tōōt *or* sub′stə tyōōt) *n.* a person or thing that takes the place of another [He is a *substitute* for the regular teacher.] ◆*v.* to use as or be a substitute [to *substitute* vinegar for lemon juice; to *substitute* for an injured player]
—**sub′sti·tut·ed, sub′sti·tut·ing**
—**sub′sti·tu′tion** *n.*

suc·ceed (sək sēd′) *v.* 1 to manage to do or be what was planned; do or go well [I *succeeded* in convincing them to come with us.] 2 to come next after; follow [Carter *succeeded* Ford as president.]
—**suc·ceed′ed**

suc·cess·ful (sək ses′fəl) *adj.*
1 having success; turning out well [a *successful* meeting] 2 having become rich, famous, etc. [a *successful* architect]
—**suc·cess′ful·ly** *adv.*

su·crose (sōō′krōs) *n.* a sugar found in sugarcane, sugar beets, etc.

suf·fi·cient (sə fish′ənt) *adj.* as much as is needed; enough [Do you have *sufficient* supplies to last through the week?]
—**suf·fi′cient·ly** *adv.*

suit·a·ble (sōōt′ə bəl) *adj.* right for the purpose; fitting; proper [a *suitable* gift]
—**suit′a·bil′i·ty** *n.* —**suit′a·bly** *adv.*

su·per·fi·cial (sōō′ pər fish′əl) *adj.* of or on the surface; not deep [a *superficial* cut; a *superficial* likeness] —**su·per·fi·ci·al·i·ty** (sōō′ pər fish′ē al′ə tē) *n.*
—**su′per·fi′cial·ly** *adv.*

su·per·son·ic (sōō′ pər sän′ik) *adj.* 1 of or moving at a speed greater than the speed of sound 2 *another word for* **ultrasonic**

su·per·vise (sōō′pər vīz) *v.* to direct or manage, as a group of workers; be in charge of —**su′per·vised, su′per·vis·ing**

sur·round (sər round′) *v.* to form or arrange around on all or nearly all sides; enclose [The police *surrounded* the criminals. The house is *surrounded* with trees.]
—**sur·round′ing**

sur·vey (sər vā′) *v.* to measure the size, shape, boundaries, etc. of a piece of land by the use of special instruments [to *survey* a farm] ◆*n.* (sur′vā) 1 a general study covering the main facts or points [The *survey* shows that we need more schools. This book is a *survey* of American poetry.] 2 the act of surveying a piece of land, or a record of this [He was hired to make a *survey* of the lake shore.]
—*pl.* **sur′veys**

sur·vey·ing (sər vā′iŋ) *n.* the act, work, or science of one who surveys land

Swede (swēd) *n.* a person born or living in Sweden

Swiss (swis) *adj.* of Switzerland or its people. ◆*n.* a person born or living in Switzerland —*pl.* **Swiss**

sym·me·try (sim′ə trē) *n.* 1 an arrangement in which the parts on opposite sides of a center line are alike in size, shape, and position [The human body has *symmetry*.] 2 balance or harmony that comes from such an arrangement

☆**syn·the·siz·er** (sin′thə sī zər) *n.* an electronic musical instrument that makes sounds that cannot be made by ordinary instruments

a	ask, fat
ā	ape, date
ä	car, lot
e	elf, ten
ē	even, meet
i	is, hit
ī	ice, fire
ō	open, go
ô	law, horn
oi	oil, point
ळ	look, pull
ळ̄	ooze, tool
ou	out, crowd
u	up, cut
ʉ	fur, fern
ə	a in ago
	e in agent
	e in father
	i in unity
	o in collect
	u in focus
ch	chin, arch
ŋ	ring, singer
sh	she, dash
th	thin, truth
th	then, father
zh	s in pleasure

tab·u·late (tab′y$\overline{oo}$ lāt′) *v.* to arrange in tables or columns [to *tabulate* numbers] —**tab′u·lat·ed, tab′u·lat·ing** —**tab′u·la′tion, tab′u·la′tor** *n.*

tam·bou·rine (tam bə rēn′) *n.* a small, shallow drum with only one head and with jingling metal disks in the rim: it is shaken, struck with the hand, etc.

tar·iff (ter′if) *n.* **1** a list of taxes on goods imported or, sometimes, on goods exported **2** such a tax or its rate

taught (tôt *or* tät) *past tense and past participle of* **teach**

teach (tēch) *v.* **1** to show or help to learn how to do something; train [She *taught* us to skate.] **2** to give lessons to or in [Who *teaches* your class? He *teaches* French.] **3** to make or help to know or understand [The accident *taught* her to be careful.] —**taught, teach′ing** —**teach′a·ble** *adj.*

tech·ni·cal (tek′ni kəl) *adj.* **1** having to do with the useful or industrial arts or skills [A *technical* school has courses in mechanics, welding, etc.] **2** of or used in a particular science, art, profession, etc. [*technical* words; *technical* skill] —**tech′ni·cal·ly** *adv.*

tech·nique (tek nēk′) *n.* a way of using tools, materials, etc. and following rules in doing something artistic, in carrying out a scientific experiment, etc. [a violinist with good bowing *technique*]

tech·nol·o·gy (tek näl′ə jē) *n.* **1** the study of the industrial arts or applied sciences, as engineering, mechanics, etc. **2** science as it is put to use in practical work [medical *technology*] **3** a method or process for dealing with a technical problem —**tech·no·log·i·cal** (tek′nə läj′i k′l) *adj.* —**tech′no·log′i·cal·ly** *adv.* —**tech·nol′o·gist** *n.*

tex·tile (teks′tīl *or* teks′təl) *n.* a fabric made by weaving; cloth ◆*adj.* **1** having to do with weaving or woven fabrics [He works in the *textile* industry.] **2** woven [Linen is a *textile* fabric.]

tex·ture (teks′chər) *n.* **1** the look and feel of a fabric as caused by the arrangement, size, and quality of its threads [Corduroy has a ribbed *texture*.] **2** the general look and feel of any other kind of material; structure; makeup [Stucco has a rough *texture*.] ◆*v.* to cause to have a particular texture —**tex′tured, tex′tur·ing**

the·ol·o·gy (thē äl′ə jē) *n.* **1** the study of God and of religious beliefs **2** a system of religious beliefs —*pl.* (for sense **2** only) —**the·ol′o·gies**

the·o·ry (thē′ə rē *or* thir′ē) *n.* **1** an explanation of how or why something happens, especially one based on scientific study and reasoning [Albert Einstein's *theory* of relativity] **2** the general principles on which an art or science is based [music *theory*] **3** an idea, opinion, guess, etc. [My *theory* is that the witness lied.] —*pl.* **the′o·ries**

the·sau·rus (thi sôr′əs *or* thi si′əs) *n.* a book containing lists of synonyms or related words —*pl.* **the·sau·ri** (thi sôr′ī) or **the·sau′rus·es**

thick (thik) *adj.* **1** great in width or depth from side to side; not thin [a *thick* board] **2** as measured from one side through to the other [a wall ten inches *thick*] —**thick′est** ◆*adv.* in a thick way —**thick′ly**

thief (thēf) *n.* a person who steals, especially secretly —*pl.* **thieves** (thēvz)

thirst·y (thurs′tē) *adj.* **1** wanting to drink; feeling thirst [The spicy food made me *thirsty*.] **2** needing water; dry [*thirsty* fields] —**thirst′i·er, thirst′i·est** —**thirst′i·ly** *adv.* —**thirst′i·ness** *n.*

this·tle (this′el) *n.* a plant with prickly leaves and flower heads of purple, white, pink, or yellow

thor·ough (thur′ō) *adj.* **1** complete in every way; with nothing left out, undone, etc. [a *thorough* search; a *thorough* knowledge of the subject] **2** very careful and exact [a *thorough* worker] —**thor′ough·ly** *adv.*

threw (thr$\overline{oo}$) *past tense of* throw

through (thr$\overline{oo}$) *prep.* **1** in one side and out the other side of; from end to end of [The nail went *through* the board. We drove *through* the tunnel.] **2** from the beginning to the end of [We stayed in Maine *through* the summer.] ◆*adv.* **1** from the beginning to the end [to see a job *through*] **2** in a complete and thorough way; entirely [We were soaked *through* by the rain.] ◆*adj.* finished [Are you *through* with your homework?]

through·out (thr$\overline{oo}$ out′) *prep.* all the way through; in every part of [The fire spread *throughout* the barn.] ◆*adv.* in every part; everywhere [The walls were painted white *throughout*.]

throw (thrō) *v.* **1** to send through the air by a fast motion of the arm; hurl, toss, etc. [to *throw* a ball] **2** to make fall down; upset [to *throw* someone in wrestling] —**threw, thrown, throw′ing** ◆*n.* the act of throwing [The fast *throw* put the runner out at first base.]

tight (tīt) *adj.* **1** put together firmly or closely [a *tight* knot] **2** fitting too closely [a *tight* shirt] —**tight′er** —**tight′ly** *adv.* —**tight′ness** *n.*

ti·ny (tī′nē) *adj.* very small; minute —**ti′ni·er, ti′ni·est**

tip·toe (tip′tō) *n.* the tip of a toe ◆*v.* to walk on one's tiptoes in a quiet or careful way —**tip′toed, tip′toe·ing**

ti·tle (tīt′l) *n.* **1** the name of a book, chapter, poem, picture, piece of music, etc. **2** a word showing the rank, occupation, etc. of a person ["Baron," Ms.," and "Dr." are *titles*.] **3** a claim or right; especially, a legal right to own something, or proof of such a right [The *title* to the car is in my name.] ◆*v.* to give a title to; name —**ti′tled, ti′tling**

tol·er·ate (täl′ə rāt) *v.* to let something be done or go on without trying to stop it [I won't *tolerate* such talk.] —**tol′er·at·ed, tol′er·at·ing**

tomb·stone (tōōm′stōn) *n.* a stone put on a tomb telling who is buried there; gravestone

tough·en (tuf′ən) *v.* to make or become tough or tougher

trans·ac·tion (tran zak′shən *or* tran sak′shən) *n.* **1** the act or an instance of transacting **2** something transacted [The *transaction* was completed when all parties signed the contract.]

trans·fer (trans fʉr′ *or* trans′fər) *v.* **1** to move, carry, send, or change from one person or place to another [He *transferred* his notes to another notebook. Jill has *transferred* to a new school.] **2** to move a picture, design, etc. from one surface to another, as by making wet and pressing —**trans·ferred′, trans·fer′ring** ◆*n.* (trans′fər) a thing or person that is transferred [They are *transfers* from another school.] —**trans·fer′a·ble** or **trans·fer′ra·ble** *adj.*

trans·form·er (trans fôr′mər) *n.* **1** a person or thing that transforms **2** a device that changes the voltage of an electric current

☆**tran·sis·tor** (tran zis′tər *or* tran sis′tər) *n.* an electronic device, made up of semiconductor material, that controls the flow of electric current: transistors are small and last a long time

trans·mis·sion (trans mish′ən *or* tranz mish′ən) *n.* **1** the act of transmitting or passing something along [the *transmission* of messages by telegraph]. **2** the part of a car that sends the power from the engine to the wheels

trans·par·ent (trans per′ənt) *adj.* so clear or so fine it can be seen through [*transparent* glass; a *transparent* veil]

trans·por·ta·tion (trans pər tā′shən) *n.* **1** the act of transporting **2** a system or business of transporting things

treas·ur·y (trezh′ər ē) *n.* **1** the money or funds of a country, company, club, etc. **2 Treasury,** the department of a government in charge of issuing money, collecting taxes, etc. **3** a place where money is kept —*pl.* **treas′ur·ies**

tri·an·gu·lar (trī aŋ′gyə lər) *adj.* of or shaped like a triangle; having three corners

tri·col·or (trī′kul′ər) *n.* a flag having three colors, especially the flag of France ◆*adj.* having three colors —**tri′col′ored**

tri·lin·gual (trī liŋ′gwəl) *adj.* **1** of or in three languages [a *trilingual* region] **2** using or able to use three languages, especially with equal or nearly equal ability [a *trilingual* child]

tril·o·gy (tril′ə jē) *n.* a set of three plays, novels, etc. which form a related group, although each is a complete work [Louisa May Alcott's *Little Women*, *Little Men*, and *Jo's Boys* make up a *trilogy*.] —*pl.* **tril′o·gies**

tri·ple (trip′əl) *adj.* **1** made up of three [A *triple* cone has three dips of ice cream.] **2** three times as much or as many ◆*n.* ☆a hit in baseball on which the batter gets to third base ◆*v.* to make or become three times as much or as many —**tri′pled, tri′pling**

trip·li·cate (trip′lə kət) *adj.* made in three copies exactly alike [a *triplicate* receipt]

tri·um·phant (trī um′fənt) *adj.* **1** having won victory or success; victorious [Our team was *triumphant*.] **2** happy or joyful over a victory [We could hear their *triumphant* laughter.] —**tri·um′phant·ly adv.**

☆**trol·ley** (trä′lē) *n.* **1** a device that sends electric current from a wire overhead to the motor of a streetcar, trolley bus, etc. **2** an electric streetcar: *also* **trolley car** —*pl.* **trol′leys**

trou·sers (trou′zərz) *pl. n.* an outer garment with two legs, especially for men and boys, reaching from the waist usually to the ankles; pants

Tru·man (trōō′mən) **Harry S.** 1884–1972; the 33d president of the United States, from 1945 to 1953

trust·wor·thy (trust′wʉr′thē) *adj.* deserving to be trusted; reliable —**trust′wor′thi·ness n.**

truth·ful (trōōth′fəl) *adj.* **1** telling the truth; honest [a *truthful* person] **2** that is the truth; accurate [to give a *truthful* report] —**truth′ful·ly adv.** —**truth′ful·ness n.**

tsp. *abbreviation for* **teaspoon** *or* **teaspoons**

tur·moil (tʉr′moil) *n.* a noisy or confused condition

☆**tux·e·do** (tuk sē′dō) *n.* **1** a man's jacket worn at formal dinners, dances, etc. It was often black, with satin lapels and no tails: now tuxedos have many patterns and colors **2** a suit with such a jacket, worn with a dark bow tie —*pl.* **tux·e′dos**

twitch (twich) *v.* to move or pull with a sudden jerk [A rabbit's nose *twitches* constantly.] ◆*n.* a sudden, quick motion or pull, often one that cannot be controlled [a *twitch* near one eye] —*pl.* **twitch′es**

ty·phoon (tī fōōn′) *n.* any violent tropical cyclone that starts in the western Pacific

typ·ist (tīp′ist) *n.* a person who uses a typewriter; especially, one whose work is typing

a	ask, fat
ā	ape, date
ä	car, lot
e	elf, ten
ē	even, meet
i	is, hit
ī	ice, fire
ō	open, go
ô	law, horn
oi	oil, point
ōō	look, pull
ōō	ooze, tool
ou	out, crowd
u	up, cut
ʉ	fur, fern
ə	a in ago
	e in agent
	e in father
	i in unity
	o in collect
	u in focus
ch	chin, arch
ŋ	ring, singer
sh	she, dash
th	thin, truth
th	then, father
zh	s in pleasure

ul·tra·son·ic (ul′trə sän′ik) *adj.* describing or having to do with sounds too high for human beings to hear

ul·tra·vi·o·let (ul′trə vī′ə lət) *adj.* lying just beyond the violet end of the spectrum [*Ultraviolet* rays are invisible rays of light that help to form vitamin D in plants and animals and can kill certain germs.]

un- **1** *a prefix meaning* not *or* the opposite of [An *un*happy person is one who is not happy, but sad.] **2** *a prefix* meaning to reverse or undo the action of [To *un*tie a shoelace is to reverse the action of tying it.]

un·a·void·a·ble (unə void′ə bəl) *adj.* that cannot be avoided; inevitable [an *unavoidable* accident]
—**un′a·void′a·bly** *adv.*

un·a·ware (un ə wer′) *adj.* not aware; not knowing or noticing [We were *unaware* of the danger in going there.]

un·be·liev·a·ble (unbə lēv′ə bəl) *adj.* that cannot be believed; astounding; incredible

un·con·di·tion·al (un′ kən dish′ən 'l) *adj.* not depending on any conditions; absolute [an *unconditional* guarantee]
—**un′con·di′tion·al·ly** *adv.*

un·due (un d<del>oo</del>′ *or* un dy<del>oo</del>′) *adj.* more than is proper or right; too much [Don't give *undue* attention to your appearance.]

un·fair (un fer′) *adj.* not fair, just, or honest
—**un·fair′ly** *adv.* —**un·fair′ness** *n.*

☆**u·ni·cy·cle** (y<del>oo</del>n′ə sī′kəl) *n.* a riding device that has only one wheel and pedals like a bicycle: it is used for trick riding, as in a circus

u·ni·form (y<del>oo</del>n′ə fôrm) *adj.* **1** always the same; never changing [Driving at a *uniform* speed saves gas.] **2** all alike; not different from one another [a row of *uniform* houses]
◆*n.* the special clothes worn by the members of a certain group [a nurse's *uniform*] —**u′ni·form·ly** *adv.*

un·i·lat·er·al (y<del>oo</del>n′ə lat′ər əl) *adj.* done by or involving only one of several nations, sides, or groups [a *unilateral* decision]

u·nique (y<del>oo</del> nēk′) *adj.* **1** that is the only one; having nothing like it [Mercury is a *unique* metal in that it is liquid at ordinary temperatures.] **2** unusual; remarkable [It is a *unique* motion picture.]

u·ni·son (y<del>oo</del>n′ə sən) *n.* sameness of musical pitch, as of two or more voices or tones

u·ni·ver·sal (y<del>oo</del>n′ə vur′səl) *adj.*
1 of, for, or by all people; concerning everyone [a *universal* human need]
2 present everywhere [*universal* pollution of the air we breathe] —**u·ni·ver·sal·i·ty** (y<del>oo</del>′nə vər sal′ə tē) *n.*

u·ni·ver·si·ty (y<del>oo</del>n′ə vur′sə tē) *n.* a school of higher education, made up of a college or colleges and, usually, professional schools, as of law and medicine
—*pl.* **u′ni·ver′si·ties**

un·matched (un machd′) *adj.* **1** not matching [These socks are *unmatched.*]
2 having no equal

un·paved (un pāvd′) *adj.* not paved; lacking a hard surface

u·su·al (y<del>oo</del>′zhoo əl) *adj.* such as is most often seen, heard, used, etc.; common; ordinary; normal —**u′su·al·ly** *adv.*

U·tah (y<del>oo</del>′tô *or* y<del>oo</del>′tä) a state in the southwestern part of the U.S.: abbreviated **Ut., UT**

veil (vāl) *n.* a piece of thin cloth, as net or gauze, worn especially by women over the face or head to hide the features, as a decoration, or as part of a uniform [a bride's *veil*; a nun's *veil*] ◆*v.* to cover, hide, etc. with or as if with a veil

ver·sion (vur′zhən) *n.* **1** something translated from the original language [an English *version* of the Bible] **2** a report or description from one person's point of view [Give us your *version* of the accident.] **3** a particular form of something [an abridged *version* of a novel; the movie *version* of a play]

ver·ti·cal (vurt′i kəl) *adj.* straight up and down; perpendicular to a horizontal line [The walls of a house are *vertical.*] ◆*n.* a vertical line, plane, etc. —**ver′ti·cal·ly** *adv.*

vi·bra·tion (vī brā′shən) *n.* rapid motion back and forth; quivering [The *vibration* of the motor shook the bolts loose.]
—**vi·bra·to·ry** (vī′brə tôr′ē) *adj.*

vid·e·o (vid′ē ō′) *adj.* **1** having to do with television **2** having to do with the picture portion of a television broadcast **3** having to do with the display of data or graphics on a computer screen ◆*n.*
1 *the same as* **television 2** *a short form of* **videocassette 3** *a short form of* **videotape**
4 a program recorded on film or videotape for viewing on television or with a videocassette recorder

vide·e·o·tape (vid′ē ō tāp′) *n.* a thin magnetic tape on which both the sound and picture signals of a TV program can be recorded by electronics

vir·tu·ous (vʉr′chσσ wəs *or* vʉr′chyōō əs) *adj.* having virtue; good, moral, chaste, etc. —**vir′tu·ous·ly** *adv.*

vi·sion (vizh′ən) *n.* **1** the act or power of seeing; sight [She wears glasses to improve her *vision*.] **2** something seen in the mind, or in a dream, trance, etc. ["while *visions* of sugarplums danced in their heads"]

vis·u·al (vizh′σσ wəl) *adj.* **1** having to do with sight or used in seeing [*visual* aids] **2** that can be seen; visible [*visual* proof] —**vis′u·al·ly** *adv.*

void (vσid) *adj.* **1** having nothing in it; empty; vacant [A vacuum is a *void* space.] **2** being without; lacking [a heart *void* of kindness] ◆*n.* **1** an empty space **2** a feeling of loss or emptiness [His death left a great *void* in our hearts.]

vol. *abbreviation for* **volume** —*pl.* **vols.**

voy·age (vσi′ij) *n.* **1** a journey by water [an ocean *voyage*] **2** a journey through the air or through outer space [a *voyage* by rocket] ◆*v.* to make a voyage —**voy′aged, voy′ag·ing** —**voy′ag·er** *n.*

vs. *abbreviation for* **versus**

wait (wāt) *v.* **1** to stay in a place or do nothing while expecting a certain thing to happen [*Wait* for the signal. I *waited* until six o'clock, but they never arrived.] **2** to remain undone for a time [Let it *wait* until next week.] **3** to serve food at a meal [He *waits* on tables. She *waits* on me.] ◆*n.* the act or time of waiting [We had an hour's *wait* for the train.]

wan·der (wän′dər) *v.* **1** to go from place to place in an aimless way; ramble; roam [to *wander* about a city] **2** to go astray; drift [The ship *wandered* off course. The speaker *wandered* from the subject.] —**wan′der·er** *n.*

wash·a·ble (wôsh′ə bəl *or* wäsh′ə bəl) *adj.* that can be washed without being damaged

Washington (wôsh′iŋ tən *or* wäsh′iŋ tən), **George** (jorj) 1732–1799; first president of the United States, from 1789 to 1797: he was commander in chief of the American army in the Revolutionary War

wa·ter·way (wôt′ər wā) *n.* **1** a channel through which water runs **2** any body of water on which boats or ships can travel, as a canal or river

weath·er (we*th*′ər) *n.* the conditions outside at any particular time with regard to temperature, sunshine, rainfall, etc. [We have good *weather* today for a picnic.]

weight (wāt) *v.* **1** heaviness; the quality a thing has because of the pull of gravity on it **2** amount of heaviness [What is your *weight*?] **3** a piece of metal used in weighing [Put a two-ounce *weight* on the balance.] **4** any solid mass used for its heaviness [to lift *weights* for exercise; a paper *weight*]

weird (wird) *adj.* **1** strange or mysterious in a ghostly way [*Weird* sounds came from the cave.] **2** very odd, strange, etc. [What a *weird* hat! What *weird* behavior!] —**weird′ly** *adv.* —**weird′ness** *n.*

wel·fare (wel′fer) *n.* **1** health, happiness, and so on; well-being **2** aid by government agencies for the poor or those out of work

wheth·er (hwe*th*′ər *or* we*th*′ər) *conj.* **1** if it is true or likely that [I don't know *whether* I can go.] **2** in either case that [It makes no difference *whether* he comes or not.]

whis·tle (hwis′l *or* wis′əl) *v.* **1** to make a high, shrill sound as by forcing breath through puckered lips or by sending steam through a small opening **2** to produce by whistling [to *whistle* a tune] —**whis′tled, whis′tling** ◆*n.* **1** a device for making whistling sounds **2** the act or sound of whistling —**whis′tler**

with·draw·al (wi*th* drô′əl *or* with drô′əl) *n.* the act or fact of withdrawing, as money from the bank

wit·ness (wit′nəs) *n.* **1** a person who saw, or can give a firsthand account of, something that happened [A *witness* told the police how the fire started.] **2** a person who gives evidence in a law court ◆*v.* to be present at; see [to *witness* a sports event]

woe·ful (wō′fəl) *adj.* full of woe; mournful; sad

wrath (rath) *n.* great anger; rage; fury

wreck·age (rek′ij) *n.* **1** the act of wrecking **2** the condition of being wrecked **3** the remains of something that has been wrecked

wrench (rench) *n.* **1** a sudden, sharp twist or pull [With one *wrench*, he loosened the lid.] **2** a tool for holding and turning nuts, bolts, or pipes ◆*v.* to twist or pull sharply [She *wrenched* the keys from my grasp.]

wres·tle (res′əl) *v.* to struggle with, trying to throw or force to the ground without striking blows with the fists —**wres′tled, wres′tling** ◆*n.* **1** the action or a bout of wrestling **2** a struggle or contest —**wres′tler**

wring (riŋ) *v.* **1** to squeeze and twist with force [to *wring* out the wet clothes] —**wrung, wring′ing**

wrist·watch (rist′wäch *or* rist′wôch) *n.* a watch worn on a strap or band that fits around the wrist

a	ask, fat
ā	ape, date
ä	car, lot
e	elf, ten
ē	even, meet
i	is, hit
ī	ice, fire
ō	open, go
ô	law, horn
σi	oil, point
σσ	look, pull
ōō	ooze, tool
σu	out, crowd
u	up, cut
ʉ	fur, fern
ə	a in ago
	e in agent
	e in father
	i in unity
	o in collect
	u in focus
ch	chin, arch
ŋ	ring, singer
sh	she, dash
th	thin, truth
th	then, father
zh	s in pleasure

185

xy·lo·phone (zī′lə fōn) **n.** a musical instrument made up of a row of wooden bars of different sizes, that are struck with wooden hammers

yearn (yurn) **v.** to be filled with longing or desire [to *yearn* for fame]
yel·low (yel′ō) **adj.** having the color of ripe lemons, or of an egg yolk —**yel′low·ish** ➤**n.** a yellow color ➤**v.** to make or become yellow [linens *yellowed* with age]

yield (yēld) **v.** **1** to give up; surrender [to *yield* to a demand; to *yield* a city] **2** to give or grant [to *yield* the right of way; to *yield* a point] **3** to give way [The gate would not *yield* to our pushing.] **4** to bring forth or bring about; produce; give [The orchard *yielded* a good crop. The business *yielded* high profits.] ➤**n.** the amount yielded or produced

zo·ol·o·gy (zō äl′ə jē) **n.** the science that studies animals and animal life

Spelling Notebook

_____

_____

_____

_____

_____

_____

_____

_____

_____

_____

_____

_____

_____

_____

_____

_____

_____

_____

_____

_____

_____

_____

_____

_____

_____

_____

_____

_____

_____

_____

_____

_____

_____

_____

_____

Spelling Notebook

Spelling Notebook

Spelling Notebook

Spelling Notebook

Spelling Notebook